The Battle for
FINANCIAL SECURITY

How to Invest in the Runaway 80's

RODGER W. BRIDWELL

A Truman Talley Book
𝕮imes BOOKS
New York

Published by *Truman Talley Books* · *Times Books,*
a division of Quadrangle/The New York Times Book Co., Inc.
Three Park Avenue, New York, N.Y. 10016

Published simultaneously in Canada by
Fitzhenry & Whiteside, Ltd., Toronto

Library of Congress Cataloging in Publication Data

Bridwell, Rodger.
   The battle for financial security.

   "A Truman Talley book."
   Includes index.
   1. Investments. 2. Finance, Personal.
3. Inflation (Finance) I. Title.
HG4521.B665 1980   332'.024   79-26444
ISBN 0-8129-0898-8

Manufactured in the United States of America

For
Val and Marg

CONTENTS

13   Low-priced, High-risk Hedges   205

PART III: TRADITIONAL INFLATION HEDGES

14   Precious Metals   225

15   Silver's Silver Lining   242

16   Diamonds   255

17   Art as an Investment   266

18   The Psychology of Speculation   278

      Acknowledgments   291

      Sources and Notes   293

      Index   295

NOTE TO THE READER

This book went to press in January 1980. Therefore statistics for the year 1979 were not yet available and these have been estimated by me. Prices for individual stocks and commodities are those prevailing during January 1980. While many of these will, no doubt, have changed appreciably by the time you read this book, the principles I strive to illustrate will not have changed. For example, whether gold sells for 15, 20, or 25 times the price of silver will not alter my estimation of their relative value, nor of their value relative to other goods and investments.

—R. W. B.

INTRODUCTION

Inflation is the response of governments to the threat of impending bankruptcy. If we agree that a bankrupt is anyone who spends more than he earns and can't pay his bills at the end of the month then most national governments have been bankrupt for many years. Of course, nations don't literally renege on their debts; they either postpone them indefinitely by borrowing from Peter to pay Paul, or else pay them off in depreciated currency.

Nor do governments admit to living beyond their means; i.e., to causing inflation. Any questions on that score are quickly blamed on those villains abroad who raise the price of oil. Or those villains at home who raise the price of everything else, in a vain attempt to keep up with inflation.

In the same vein, pledges by politicians to fight inflation by balancing the budget and shrinking the bureaucracy are nothing but empty rhetoric. The man in the street is beginning to realize this. He further realizes that the economic pie is not large enough to permit the government to grow unless his own personal standard of living contracts. And, finally, he recognizes that, while nations don't go bankrupt financially, their money does. And so do their citizens.

Nations do go bankrupt *politically* and this is what is happening throughout the world today. Citizens are losing faith in their leaders and refusing to cooperate with them any longer. In this sense, political bankruptcy is just as real for a government as financial bankruptcy is for an individual. The unfortunate difference is that individuals—rather than the bureaucracy—suffer from governmental mendacity.

For a decade now, most national governments have been expanding their activities and expenditures at a rate between two and three times faster than the growth of the economies that support them. This expansion has been paid for in part by inflation and in part by a constantly growing tax load on those least able to bear it. This tax load is disguised by inflation; thereby, recognition of it is often obscured. For example, wage earners who receive a raise expect to pay more income tax. But how many realize that the latest raise pushed them into a higher tax bracket; causing, say, 30% rather than 26% of their wages to be withheld?

The limits of taxation have long since been reached in most countries. Beleaguered citizens from Reno to Rome have resorted in desperation to a variety of strategies designed to promote the individual welfare, rather than the general welfare. The most telling of these methods is tax evasion. This inevitable development is openly acknowledged in European and Latin American countries, but officially ignored as if it did not exist in the United States.

The sentiment involved is not revolutionary in nature, but rather that of the loyal citizen who can take no more; who finally places the welfare of his family above that of the state. We have arrived at a point where the bureaucracy of one country has more in common with the bureaucracy of another country than either has with the citizens of its own country. This is the fundamental reason why civil disobedience, in the form of tax evasion, is increasing.

Whatever the motive, the end result is always more inflation. While governments never retrench, they still must pay somehow for their excesses and special privileges. If tax collections fall short because more and more citizens evade them, then the printing presses begin to roll. This is not only inflationary, it also leads directly to a lower standard of living. The evidence that this is actually happening surrounds us on every side and threatens to overwhelm us.

The citizens of every nation are beginning to realize that changing leadership has no effect whatsoever on the ever-expanding role of government in their affairs. Hence the steady decline in the number of citizens who take the trouble to vote.

What is to be done? This book offers one solution. It is not concerned with the theoretical aspects of political economy, but rather with the practical aspects of personal economic survival. In its simplest terms, this means: How can you most effectively cope with ever-expanding government and its handmaiden, inflation?

In the pages that follow, I first trace the history of inflation from ancient times. This ancient history may not seem relevant to our times. However, it really is because the two constants between yesterday and today are human nature and taxes. Both are always with us, and both play an important role in understanding and surviving inflation.

How have others coped with the problem? Look at Germany during the 1920's. I examine that dance of death in some detail because we are traveling down the same road, although we may not yet be willing to admit it. Americans traditionally think, "It can't happen here." Perhaps. However, the prudent person should at least consider the possibility and take appropriate action to prepare for such an eventuality. You can easily arrange your affairs, not only to survive such a calamity, but to turn it to your advantage.

Parts II and III are concerned with specific solutions to this looming problem. None of my solutions need upset your lifestyle in any way—just your way of thinking. In contrast, many professional pessimists agree that inflation will get worse before it gets better. But at that point we part company. They believe that the fabric of our society will disintegrate. The only way to survive is to take to the hills with plenty of dehydrated potatoes and ammunition.

I disagree. Stability is the outstanding characteristic of a social order that can survive Vietnam, Watergate, and riots in the cities. Additional inflation is not going to destroy it. Nor is growing political indifference on the part of its citizens.

I think that an annual inflation rate of 20%—and perhaps 30%—will become a way of life, as it has in several other countries where, nevertheless, life goes on as usual.

However, the division of the economic pie changes with inflation. Some people will prosper under the new conditions. Some will not. My aim is to help readers of this book adopt ideas and techniques that will enable them to welcome, rather than dread, the inflationary 80's.

PART I
2,000 Years of Inflation

1

The Survival Program

Do you want to beat inflation? Then you must switch from defense to offense before it is too late. Decide today to join the players who are winning rather than losing. Don't echo the common refrain: "How can I possibly make ends meet when prices are rising almost every day?" Ask instead: "How can I multiply my savings tenfold; yes, even a hundredfold?"

If you boldly risk your nest egg—no matter how small—what have you got to lose? If you don't, inflation will wipe it out anyway, sooner or later. Thus, with inflation surging at an annual rate of 12% to 14% (as of early 1980), you obviously are a certain loser if you are content with a return of 5½% on your savings which, ironically enough, is taxable! You are left with perhaps 4%—or a loss of 8% to 10% in purchasing power. How can you win with odds like these against you?

You can't. Not until you change the odds from a minus 10% to a plus 1,000% or even 10,000%. If multiplying your capital a hundred times seems like an impossible accomplishment, it's because you don't understand inflation and the limitless possibilities for gain it offers. But first you must understand how inflation works before you can make it work for you. And it helps to understand past inflations—including those of ancient times—because the psychology that produces inflation never changes; nor do its causes and effects, although these may differ superficially from age to age or country to country.

The runaway stage of our inflation has started, and it will get much worse. Yet we know it will produce millions of new millionaires, just as all past inflations have done. Why not resolve to be one of them? Two generations ago, millions of Germans became millionaires almost overnight. They were the ones who were able to adjust to a world turned upside-down by inflation. Of course, the measure was German marks not American dollars. Nor was the mark in those days the priceless jewel that it is today. Nevertheless, those Germans who owned assets worth millions of marks were noticeably better off than those who owned none.

The German millionaires were created by runaway inflation.[1] Heretofore, this form of monetary madness has been—at least in the public's imagination—confined mainly to the banana republics. However today, as everyone knows, inflation has gained a solid foothold in our own country. Moreover, it has become so well entrenched that the usual progression from inflation to runaway inflation seems assured.

While I do not anticipate that the runaway inflation now underway will ever assume the virulence of Weimar Germany, the history of every inflation proves conclusively that, once started, there is no turning back. Already we have sufficient momentum to ensure the creation of at least one million new American millionaires.

Who will graduate into the millionaire class? Any young couple in their thirties today should be millionaires before age fifty. If they aren't it will be because they knowingly ignore the lessons repeatedly taught by history. But they must learn how to take advantage of the inflation that is here to stay. This means throwing overboard traditional ideas about how to save and get ahead. Specifically, money should be switched from banks, savings, and insurance into tangible assets that will be in greatest demand as the flight from the dollar accelerates. Borrowing should be used to buy productive assets rather than consumer goods. But time may be short. Already cynical foreigners, as usual, are ahead of us. Hence the chronic weakness of the dollar abroad.

This book was written with the assumption that those who are ignorant of the past are bound to repeat the mistakes of the past. This is why I will examine in detail those who profited most from past inflations and exactly how they did it. By following these rules, our young couple will be firmly headed for wealth even if the more extreme forms of inflation never develop here because the aggressive approach to money management is timeless. It pays off under every condition, including deflation—if you really want to become a millionaire.

Does a million new millionaires sound like a lot? It isn't really. If a flight from the dollar develops (and it is already underway) similar to that experienced in all past inflations, then we will see a rise in the stock market that will make the legendary bull market of the 1920's look like a foothill in the Himalayas. Numerous stocks will soar 1,000%, 2,000%—perhaps 5,000% and more.

The Dow Jones Industrial Average, which has been struggling for a decade and longer to break through the 1,000 level will gradually rise to 2,000—then to 5,000 and beyond. A flood of dollars will flow from savings accounts, bonds, gold, Eurodollars, and other hiding places into American stocks, which are the last *undervalued, tangible, dividend-paying assets left in the world.*

Americans of modest means who buy the right stocks today (1980) and patiently hold them through the 1980's will become millionaires. How are we to recognize the right stocks? It will be difficult to miss them because a majority of stocks will rise. However, those companies holding natural resources and other productive assets that are currently priced at only a fraction of their replacement value should lead the way. I will cite examples later on.

Meanwhile, the important thing to bear in mind is that stocks are cheaper today than at any time since 1949—although this comforting fact will not be the driving force behind the great bull market that lies ahead. This is simply an added incentive to buy and hold stocks at a time when people with less vision are selling stocks and seeking the presumed safety of gold, real estate, bonds, savings accounts and even cash—the worst inflation hedge of all. At best such people will fail to participate in the boom. At worst, they will be wiped out as were those with similar misconceptions in Germany, Hungary, and other countries.

How realistic is it to say a couple of modest means can become millionaires within a few years? First, we must define the term "modest means." Obviously, people who are destitute cannot make something out of nothing. However, people who own their own homes or have some savings can participate.

Let us consider a couple who bought a home several years ago and paid $40,000 for it. They made a down payment of $10,000 and assumed a $30,000, 7% mortage. Today their home has a market value of $110,000, which reflects the impact of inflation on real estate values—an impact which has not yet spread to the stock market. They could readily refinance their mortgage (as many people are doing) and come up with $25,000 in cash. Judiciously invested in stocks, this nest egg could easily mushroom into $1 million in the coming stock market boom.

So if we assume a person of "modest means" has from $25,000 to $50,000 which can be parlayed into $1 million, it follows that people of more than modest means should become much more than mere millionaires. Millionaires will become billionaires. How can you open the door to this waiting wealth? By remembering twenty-four hours a day that we are entering a new era in which traditional economic thinking must be adjusted to the new realities of hyperinflation.

Shakespeare was only half-right when he advised:

"Neither a borrower nor a lender be."

One *must* be a borrower but never a lender. Does this mean that the unprecedented level of consumer debts is justified? Not at all. *Consumer* debts are counterproductive. Borrowed money should be used only to buy *productive* assets—assets that will appreciate rather than depreciate in value. Stocks, land, and other wealth-producing assets will appreciate. Cars, TV sets, and the like can only depreciate.

If my vision of the future proves correct, the heretofore exclusive millionaires' club is going to become much less exclusive, though it will still include far less than 1% of the population.

Just how many millionaires are there? According to the *Statistical Abstract of the United States,* there were the following number of millionaires in the years indicated:

1958	47,000
1962	71,000
1969	147,000
1972	218,000

How were these figures obtained? Mostly by guessing, I would guess, since they are based on taxes paid on estates and then extrapolated to include that larger portion of the population who were still alive. Moreover, these figures may be understated, since the rich make prodigious efforts to avoid paying estate taxes.

Consider the moderate increase in number between 1958 and 1962, which was a down year in the stock market. In contrast, from 1962 to 1969 and 1972, the number expanded sharply; probably because the latter years were up years in the stock market. Since 1972 stock prices have fallen, for the most part. However, real estate prices have soared and, in the aggregate, they affect more people. My estimate is that the current number of millionaires (on paper) would approach 500,000, or a little over 0.2% of the total population.

How accurate are these figures?

The same result can be obtained from income taxes paid on dividends and interest. Here, too, the projections are probably understated since wealthy taxpayers are adept at seeking out tax-exempt investments—that is one reason why they are wealthy. I won't go into a detailed analysis of the calculations because it isn't relevant to my argument. I just want to demonstrate that a million new millionaires is not an extravagant projection, even if inflation is restrained to moderate—rather than runaway—proportions.

All new millionaires share one characteristic: they avoid paying taxes on the large gains involved in getting there. Do they invest their money in savings accounts? No. Because *income* is taxed at the maximum rate. Instead, they invest in a capital asset, which is not taxed—no matter how much it increases in value—*until it is sold.* This all-important principle was summed up perfectly in *The New Millionaires and How They Made Their Fortunes,* a *Wall Street Journal* book published a few years ago. First the editors made the illuminating observation that contrary to what one might logically expect, high tax rates did not slow down the rate by which new millionaires were hatched.

During the postwar years, when large incomes were taxed at confiscatory rates of up to 91%, the number of millionaires increased steadily. Obviously, these canny individuals were actually aware of the essential fact that every dollar retained and not paid out in taxes would continue to multiply if properly invested. This means not only avoiding income taxes, but also capital gains taxes. The key paragraphs from this book are worth quoting:

Does that mean that today's new millionaires have made their piles by escaping the income tax and turning all their profits into capital gains which are taxed only 25%? Strange as it may seem, the answer to this question is "no" rather than "yes." Look over the lives of the fourteen millionaires whose lives are told in this book and you will see that they resemble each other in two respects. One is their willingness to work hard. The other is that they not only put all or most of their eggs in one basket and watched that basket, as Andrew Carnegie advised, but they also kept the same basket. In other words, they not only escaped in large part any income tax on the growth in value of their holdings, but they also escaped to a large extent the capital gains tax. Instead of selling from time to time and buying back again, they simply held on, and what they held was something that grew and grew.

Obviously, not everyone has the opportunity to create a business of his own which will grow and grow. Nor can everyone become a millionaire. But what a lot of people can very well do is copy the example of these fourteen people in one respect, and that is to invest in sound corporate enterprise with any surplus earnings and become, as it were, married to such investments by holding on to them while the companies they represent grow and grow.

Much of the literature about fortunes made—and lost—in common stocks stresses the speculative aspects. It tells about "bear raids" by men selling thousands of shares short and then buying them back cheaper. Or it tells about tricky methods of trading in the hope of catching stocks just before a quick rise. Too rarely does it tell about the rewards of careful patient investing in the outstanding securities of American industry and adding to them slowly over the years.[2]

To all of this I add my fervent "amen." But you may well ask: "So those fourteen millionaires got that way because they held onto a stock (their own) which happened to multiply many times in value. What about those investors who built up large positions in losers?" Fair enough. Not everyone can be a big winner—at least not in the old pre-inflation days. This, however, is not the point. The point is that if you attempt to outsmart the next fellow by selling at intermediate tops and then buying back on declines, you are certain to fail. Or, if you continually try to improve your position by succumbing to the allure of some new and seductive company, you are in trouble. It can't be done. But even if it could, you would only make your broker and Uncle Sam rich; you would remain poor.

Moreover, the foundation upon which all fortunes are made will be more important than ever in the years of accelerating inflation between now and the end of the century. Success will no longer depend on selecting the occasional big winner among many losers. The flight-from-the-dollar psychology will routinely cause hundreds of stocks to skyrocket. The secret to participating in the new stock-market boom will be found not in your head, but rather in the seat of your pants.

Never forget: Profits paid out in taxes are lost forever because only a tiny part of any subsequent losses can be recouped from taxes paid on previously realized profits.

But what if you want to use some of those paper profits to buy a yacht? Why sell your stocks? Why not borrow what you need using the stock as collateral? *The interest on your loan is deductible.* It *reduces* rather than increases your tax load.

Meanwhile, your paper profit remains intact. Of course, that profit may shrink because stocks fluctuate. Fortunately, stocks that decline in value usually recover. And, to repeat, money paid out in taxes is gone forever.

Perhaps I am overstating the case for holding stocks forever. If so, it's because when I was a stockbroker I could never consistently make money trading; nor can most stockbrokers I have known. Most of us are not psychologically geared to buy when things are going to hell and sell when the pathways of the future seem paved with gold. It was only when I got out of the business that the profits began to pile up.

Nonetheless, others are geared to the "get in and get out quick" gambit, which an early Rothschild advocated. Their theory is that if you can make large profits fast and consistently, then the taxes will take care of themselves. I don't agree, but then, as a trader, I'm a confessed failure. To those who have or hope to acquire this talent I dedicate Chapter 10, "The Six-Step Plan." Study it with loving care. It's the history of a client of mine who lived in Portugal and became a citizen of that country—possibly because there was no capital gains tax to slow down his fortune-building ambitions. In five years he parlayed less than $50,000 into more than $1 million. This is not a pie-in-the-sky story: I know because I entered his orders.

As the *Wall Street Journal* book of millionaires stresses, no one will ever become a millionaire by working for someone else. You must work for yourself or have others working for you indirectly through owning assets such as stocks and real estate that others will want to acquire from you because they are increasing in value.

However, as we will discuss at greater length later on, real estate, along with many commodities, tends to rise early in the inflation cycle. Therefore real estate today (and here I am referring to houses and commercial property, rather than undeveloped land) may already have realized a considerable part of its upside potential. In an absolute sense, appreciation possibilities seem limited compared with that of stocks, which are still cheap on a historical basis without allowing for future inflation.

Doubtless, real estate and new business ventures will account for many new fortunes—they always have. But, for reasons we will explore at considerable length, the stock market will produce the greatest proportion of the one million or more new millionaires waiting to be tapped by inflation. This is not to suggest that these new millionaires will have as much real wealth as those of the past. Inflation—which will create them—will also limit their real wealth. This new elite will eschew palatial mansions and yachts—the traditional emblems of the very rich. Instead, they will concentrate on beating inflation, which means making their money—even paper money—produce more money.

Finally, a word about the psychology that will dominate all of us in the years ahead. First: We must remember that fear and greed are the two powerful emotions that mold the economic future. Second: We must remember that these emotions exist in all of us. First one and then the other dominates, depending on the state of our collective thinking. In the financial realm, they result in alternating booms and panics, bear and bull markets. Third: We must remember that inflation is the name of the new national fear that has replaced nuclear war, depression, and communism.

Unlike the more traditional fears, fear of inflation is not antagonistic to greed, but rather is reinforced by it. The net result in the years to come, when moderate inflation turns into hyperinflation, will be a full-scale flight from the dollar in contrast to the mini-flight we have witnessed in the recent past. Talk of such an eventuality has been heard for years. Nonetheless, the American people have clung to a belief in a stable currency and income-oriented investments. Possibly this Victorian attitude has been reinforced by the almost unanimous prediction of economists that deflation and economic collapse are fast approaching. The fact is, inflation forces are so powerful that even the 1974–1975 recession slowed them down hardly at all.

The new millionaires will be those who recognize in time the powerful combination of greed and fear that will fuel the coming flight from the dollar. In recent years fear has prevailed—witness the flow of capital out of stocks, which most investors consider risky, and into savings accounts, gold, houses, and even cash, which are thought to be safer. Now an even more potent fear is about to take over: fear of holding money. To understand the psychological about-face that is now getting underway, we must first understand the age-old process of inflation and why—contrary to official doctrine and private hopes—it is an irreversible process.

2

Inflation, War, and Revolution

Can you name one country which, at some time during its history, has not experienced a period of hyperinflation? I can't. Even the American dollar lost 99% of its value during the revolutionary period. The phrase "not worth a continental" commemorates this event. Nor was the inflation during and following the Civil War negligible. In the North, prices rose at an annual rate of about 25%; in the South, the rate exceeded 100% *a month.*

Despite the evidence of their own past, Americans are especially prone to the "it can't happen here" psychology. Perhaps because such long intervals—generations, rather than

14

years—elapse between these periods of upheaval. Then, too, past inflations were caused, more often than not, by temporary phenonema such as wars or the discovery of new deposits of gold and silver. Today neither gold nor war is the villain. We have a new villain: credit, based on the discovery that money can be created out of credit or debt.

While the art of turning credit or debt into money is relatively new, the motives and procedures behind it are as old as the relationship between rulers and ruled. As far back as man can remember, rulers have existed for one reason only: to benefit the ruling class at the expense of everyone else. The techniques used have varied in detail from age to age, but have remained remarkably unchanged in principle. That principle is to levy the maximum possible taxes—using the threat of armed force, if necessary, to coerce reluctant taxpayers.

Power is the trait that sets rulers apart from other men, just as infallibility is the trait that distinguishes God from man. Since rulers usually consider themselves to be infallible, it is not surprising that they also consider themselves to be in the same class as the gods—not subject to human control. Many Roman emperors openly admitted—in fact advertised—their status as gods. Kings of a later age were divinities once removed. They merely claimed that their right to rule was divine.

Today the direct relationship between ruler and God has been deemphasized except on our paper money, which assures us that "In God We Trust." If we are to judge by the value of our money, then clearly our trust has been misplaced. While our rulers no longer openly claim to be gods, the evidence strongly suggests that their private convictions have not changed since Roman times. In any event, modern rulers, like their ancient predecessors, effectively control—through taxation and inflation—the lives and pocketbooks of those they rule. They have introduced some refinements of late, which are the direct descendants of the very earliest methods of debasing the coinage. These methods were introduced when rulers discovered that when taxes were boosted too much, the total take diminished. That point was reached when more and more citizens preferred to go to jail rather than pay. This posed a nasty problem for the ruler who, while unfailingly ruthless in such matters, was also unfailingly pragmatic.

When taxation reached the point of diminishing returns (which was most of the time), the custom among the more imaginative ancient rulers was to revamp the monetary system in such a way that the necessary revenues could be collected with less resistance on the part of the people. This meant inflating the currency. Gold and silver coins were adulterated with base metals while tax payments were calculated on the original precious metal content. Obviously, if you cut the gold content of a coin in half, you can issue twice as many coins for a fixed amount of gold.

The ruler then passed a law decreeing that the new coins had the same value as the old ones; this thereby effectively canceled half the government's debts. The defrauded citizens naturally tried to protect themselves by hoarding the old coins. In retaliation, the ruler would pass a law making it a crime for any citizen to own the old coins.

Today, of course, all governments—with the exception of such reactionary nations as Switzerland and Tonga—have progressed far beyond such crude measures. With today's fiat money it has become virtually impossible for the people to protect themselves against such fraudulent government action—except by exchanging paper money for tangible assets as rapidly as possible. Even the term "debasing the currency" has become an unmentionable. We now refer to it as "inflation."

Youthful readers should not conclude that time has tarnished the attractiveness of such crude measures. Only a few years ago, the silver content of American coins was reduced from 90% to 40%—and then eliminated entirely. This, then, is the time-hallowed, "legal" way that governments steal from their citizens. In modern times, of course, these picayune frauds play only a minor role in the vastly expanded scope of governmental financial manipulations. These modern inflationary methods were introduced in France by John Law—with whom we will get acquainted in the next chapter—and attained a peak of perfection (if the word can be used to label a catastrophe worse than war) in Weimar Germany.

There is ample evidence that coins have been clipped, sweated, adulterated, and devalued ever since they were first minted by the Greek city-state of Lydia around 700 B.C. However, the first well-documented case that we know about occurred some 500 years later. To finance the war against Carthage, whose armies were led by the inspired general Hannibal, Rome was forced to borrow heavily. (Today we refer to the process as "deficit financing.") More than once during these perilous years, Hannibal seemed on the verge of conquering Rome. Since war is always inflationary the outcome was predictable. To finance the endless war, the Roman senate gradually reduced the weight of the most widely circulated coin—the bronze *as*—from one pound to one ounce. (Perhaps the awkward size of the one-pound coin had something to do with the change.) Nevertheless, the end result was that Rome, in effect, repudiated more than 90% of her national debt. The savings of Roman citizens were virtually wiped out because taxes were paid in coin by number rather than weight. According to Adam Smith, this irresponsible fiscal policy contributed to the downfall of the Republic.

The next imaginative innovation in the esoteric business of money manipulation came in the twelfth and thirteenth centuries. By then rulers had stumbled on a more devious method of inflating the money supply known as seignorage: every so often, all coins were called in and reminted. This action may have been prompted because adulterated coins in circulation were a constant reminder of the government's duplicity. Whatever the reason, this gambit obviously cost money, so a tax of 10% or more was imposed—ostensibly to cover the cost of reminting. In practice, when a citizen surrendered ten old coins he received in return only eight or nine new coins. Naturally enough, heavy penalites were decreed for those canny citizens who preferred to hoard the old coins. While seignorage enriched the rulers, it also forced coins into circulation, thereby stimulating commerce and general prosperity.

Rulers and their wars inevitably produce inflation. So do discoveries of precious metals—when money consisted of gold or silver, rather than promises. Thus, when the vast flow of gold and silver from the New World hit Europe during the sixteenth century, prices in Spain rose about 400% and somewhat less in other European countries. The effect on even the primitive economies of that day proved that prices vary directly with the quantity of money in circulation. In the seventeenth century when the golden flood from Spanish America began to ebb, so did prices in Europe. The ensuing slow decline lasted until the time of Napoleon. The same sequence of inflation and subsequent deflation occurred in the nineteenth century following the discovery of gold and silver in California and Nevada.

At this point I should mention that banks and banking are among our most ancient institutions. Deposits, loans, foreign exchange, letters of credit, and other financial instruments were well developed in Phoenicia, Babylon, and Lydia shortly after coinage was introduced. Since the largest borrowers— then as now—were the city-states, it is not surprising that the

Cambridge Ancient History series (volume 8) informs us: "In early Hellenistic times the city-states had recourse for their own operations to private bankers. Later they endeavored to eliminate the private bankers or at least to make them her own concessionaires."

The same trend seems likely to prevail in the modern world. Thus, we already have the Federal Reserve System, which is the most profitable single enterprise in the world today. These profits—recently around $6 billion a year—go straight into the U.S. Treasury. In the 1930's the Reconstruction Finance Corporation functioned as a government superbank, which financed the ill-fated NRA and other ventures.

When, where, and how did paper money first appear? The answer depends on how paper money is defined. Are banknotes, Treasury bills, and letters of credit money? All are paper and, on occasion, serve as money. However, I will narrow the definition to include only notes issued by a national government as a substitute for coins or bullion and backed by a promise to redeem the notes for a specified amount of gold or silver on demand.

As far as I have been able to determine, the first such money in the West was issued in the seventeenth century by the Massachusetts Bay Colony. With this pregnant invention, the American colonies anticipated John Law by about thirty years. One naturally wonders to what extent Law copied the American experience when he introduced his scheme to rebuild the French economy and banking on a foundation of paper.

Not the least of the problems of the remote American colonies was an adverse trade balance. Local taxes were paid—when they were paid at all—mainly in local products, such as wampum, furs, and tobacco. As a result, colonial America suffered from a chronic shortage of gold and silver. In 1690 Massachusetts launched an expedition against French Quebec in an attempt to remedy this painful shortage. The objective was capture of the citadel, together with the hoard of gold and silver presumably sequestered within. Unfortunately for the colonists, the expedition failed. Nonetheless, the surviving soldiers clamored to be paid when they returned home, and they refused to accept wampum and such in lieu of gold or silver coins.

Sir William Phipps, the governor of the colony, solved this problem in a manner that was novel enough in his day, but one that we take for granted when mentioned today. He issued notes to the soldiers which guaranteed to pay the bearer the indicated amount of gold or silver at an unspecified date in future. He told his men the payoff would be when the treasury collected sufficient gold and silver from taxes to redeem the notes. Needless to say, the promised day was postponed from year to year—in fact, for fifty years. The subsequent governors of the colony had at least one thing in common with Sir William: none of them ever found it convenient to pay their gold to make good his promise. On the contrary, whenever they needed ready cash, they issued more of the notes.

At first the notes were accepted as readily as gold and silver coins—thereby demonstrating the touching faith of the people in their leaders. Later on, when it became increasingly clear that the notes would never be redeemed in coin—at least not for anything like their face value—the faith of the people began to weaken. Prices rose rapidly and coins became scarce, since people always hoard coins rather than paper when they have the chance. Eventually the notes were redeemed by the British government for a few cents on the dollar. Thus ended the first experiment with paper money: one that accurately anticipated the subsequent history of paper money wherever it was introduced.

Nor were the other colonies slow to adopt the imaginative

money-raising scheme introduced by Massachusetts. All of them issued paper currencies at one time or another and, to give credit where credit is due, I should point out that not all of this paper became worthless. From time to time some of the colonies—notably Maryland and Pennsylvania—redeemed their notes in much the same way that corporations and governments "roll over" their maturing debts today. Even the notorious Ponzi remained solvent for a while by borrowing from Peter to pay Paul.

The culmination of the colonial paper money saga, as noted, began shortly after the thirteen colonies declared their independence from England. When the Continental Congress assembled in June 1775, the most urgent business—as usual— was how to raise money. It was resolved in short order by the decision to print paper money. This is when the "continental" of the slang phrase came into existence. Despite an evil reputation, this fiat money financed the Revolutionary War at a time when the authority of the fledgling government was not strong enough to permit either taxing or borrowing.

So, in a sense, we are right back where we started. The continentals were backed by nothing more than the common need for a medium of exchange; which is precisely the status of our money today—with one important difference. Taxation in the earlier period accounted for perhaps 1% of government expenditures; today it represents about 90%. This difference explains the slower rate of inflation today. And it also explains why the hyperinflation that lies ahead will develop at a relatively slow rate—at least in comparison with our experience 200 years ago.

When the war ended, the new government wisely issued a new hard currency consisting of gold and silver coins and, eventually, banknotes backed by gold and silver payable on demand. (The U.S. government did not renege on its promise to exchange paper money for gold until 1933, for silver until

1965.) To his credit, the first Secretary of the Treasury, Alexander Hamilton, redeemed continentals in gold at the rate of one cent on the dollar. This rate was by no means as niggardly as it sounds; the notes were actually worth far less than one cent per dollar at that time. For example, a good suit of clothes cost several hundred thousand dollars, and it was said that a wheelbarrow full of continentals would hardly pay for a wheelbarrow full of groceries.

In the chronological history of inflation, the spectacular career of John Law in France and the South Sea Bubble in England come after that of Massachusetts, but before the Continental Congress. These extravagant examples of speculative madness will be examined in the next chapter. Meanwhile, I will touch on the paper-money inflation of the French Revolution, which was decisively influenced by the American Revolution.

Like the American colonists, the workers and peasants of France revolted against a system of taxation which they considered to be not only unfair but confiscatory. Therefore, when the Third Estate seized control, they could hardly continue the hated tax collections as though nothing had happened. Yet money was urgently needed to pay for the series of wars that the newly enlightened nation was about to undertake. The National Assembly, which was in no mood to take half-measures, solved the problem by abolishing all taxes. While this truly revolutionary measure met with the approval of the rabble, it did not eliminate the appetite of all governments—revolutionary as well as reactionary—for money, and lots of it.

The assembly's solution to the problem of raising revenues was quite as innovative as their abolition of taxes had been. The basic problem confronting them was essentially the same as that confronting the American colonists: there was not enough gold and silver in the land to serve as money. After all, the revolution had eliminated the wealthy classes who owned most of the gold and silver. To the rich, first things come first: They had long since removed themselves and their hard money from their native land; or, failing that, had hidden their treasure with all the ingenuity that matters of such importance inspire.

The temptation to take the easy way out and print paper money without anything to back it must have been great. However, the National Assembly successfully resisted that temptation. There were at least two obvious reasons for their rectitude. First, the recent and disastrous American experience with paper money had been widely publicized in France. Second, seventy years had not dimmed the memory of John Law and his Mississippi Bubble in the minds of Frenchmen. On the contrary, that moment of national insanity was as vivid in the national imagination as though it had happened yesterday.

The National Assembly considered a variety of substitutes for gold to serve as backing for the paper money (assignats) that they issued. Their final selection reached new imaginative heights. The new money would be secured by the fertile soil of France: assignats could be redeemed for actual land. After all, here was something that not even the cleverest owner could remove to some foreign sanctuary. Nor could the supply of it ever be expanded by even the most devious of politicians—or so they thought.

Whose land should be expropriated for this essential and praiseworthy cause? Not even the most fervent supporters of the revolution—if they happened to own a small plot of land— wanted to contribute *their* land to the glorious cause. Obviously, the land of those owners who wielded the least political power should be seized. In the eyes of these reasonable men (after all, the Age of Reason was at its zenith in 1789) the largest landowner with the least justification for owning it was the Church. Accordingly, the extensive lands owned by the Church were confiscated and held in reserve ready to be exchanged for any of the assignats that might be presented for this purpose. This backing seemed more than adequate since the land seized equaled about 20% of all the land of France, or some 25 million acres.

The initial issues of assignats totaled 400 million livres, which meant that a 400-livre note was backed by 25 acres of land. Holders of assignats could, if they chose, exchange them for a parcel of land of equal value; and, as it turned out, a disproportionate number of Frenchmen preferred land to assignats. This is hardly surprising, since the Church owned some of the choicest land in France. Perhaps the French were astutely anticipating the future value of an assignat by their own "bird in the hand is worth two in the bush" standards.

In any event, citizens who exchanged assignats for land were winners in 1789 and 1790 (providing they kept their heads), as those who prefer tangible assets to paper money have always been winners. And they did not have long to wait. Later in 1790, a second and larger issue of assignats was printed, with a claim against the same—though now diminishing—amount of land. As a result, prices rose moderately (about 50%) in terms of gold until April 1792, when France declared war against Austria and Prussia. The inflation gained momentum early in 1793, when the war was widened to include England, Spain, and Holland. These ambitious military campaigns consumed an even larger number of assignats, until finally assignats were being printed one day to pay bills coming due the next.

The final outcome was never in doubt—except, perhaps, in the heads and hearts of those loyal citizens who saw in the revolutionary slogan "Liberty, Equality, Fraternity" the promise of a secure financial future, as well as a more equitable social order. By 1795, the assignat, in terms of gold, was worth only a fraction of 1% of its face value. Little wonder, since the original 400 million livres had, by now, mushroomed to 40 billion. Thus, between 1790 and the emergence of Napoleon in 1795, France suffered unparalleled inflation. The only beneficiaries were those who exchanged their paper money for ecclesiastical land early in the game.

Napoleon emerged from amid the flood of paper money. Inflation does not invariably spawn dictators; however, as we shall see, Hitler also found the unrest associated with inflation provided fertile ground for the growth of his fascist state. Meanwhile, the next episode in our saga of inflation provides many other lessons for the connoisseur of irrationality, even though it blossomed and died more than 250 years ago.

3

Inflationary Bubbles

Before studying the great German inflation in detail, let's take a brief look at the famous "bubbles" which blossomed in all their glory 200 years earlier. The Mississippi Bubble represents the first modern example of runaway inflation; that is, inflation which had no theoretical limit because it was based on paper (fiat or printing-press) money. The potential for inflation before this time was limited by practical considerations (how much can be clipped off a coin), if not by governmental scruples.

It is true that paper banknotes (which represented deposits) had been circulating in Europe for some time before John

Law's "système" came into being. However, these banknotes were issued by private banks which guaranteed to redeem them in gold or silver on demand. In practice, they were as good as gold; a banker who failed to honor his notes faced unpleasant consequences.

The dubious honor of introducing Europe to hyperinflation goes to John Law, an imaginative, charismatic young man from Scotland, who was forced to flee his native land after killing a romantic rival. Law, who had a natural gift for figuring mathematical odds, supported himself on the Continent by gambling at cards and speculating in foreign currencies. He also studied the techniques of his Amsterdam bankers to good advantage.

These bankers had observed that the owners of the banknotes that they issued seldom presented them for redemption in gold at the same moment. It followed that they could safely [3] issue (i.e., lend at interest) notes having an aggregate value several times greater than the gold which they had received from depositors. Law's unique contribution to financial legerdemain extended this principle from private bankers to national states which, as it turned out, were considerably less concerned with ethics.

Most historians of the Mississippi and South Sea bubbles emphasize the spectacular rise in their stocks. Land, food, and all other commodities also skyrocketed. Does excessive speculation cause inflation, or does inflation cause excessive speculation? Actually the words can be used interchangeably. Both feed on psychological states of mind. What creates a bull market in stocks? Higher prices. And higher prices produce still higher prices.

The same is true with inflation. Of course, economists maintain that the fuel for inflation consists of an ever-expanding supply of money, easy credit, deficit financing, and so on. True enough. But psychology plays an equally important role.

Thus, in the 1930's, money and credit were made readily available and incredibly cheap by Roosevelt. We also had deficit financing on an unprecedented scale (up to then). Yet the problem of that day was deflation, rather than inflation. The difference between the 1930's and the 1980's is a difference in psychology as much as anything else.

Once established, a trend tends to perpetuate itself and endures far longer than appears logical. Whatever the reason for our present inflation, the plain fact is that it tends to feed on itself. For example, if you think that a Ford car will sell for $10,000 five years from now (I wouldn't want to bet against it), then the current price of $5,000 looks cheap. Aren't you more tempted to buy now than if you thought that the price next year would be only $2,500?

The first person to systematically explore the psychology of speculation—which is to say the psychology of greed and fear—was Charles Mackay, in his book, *Extraordinary Popular Delusions and the Madness of Crowds,* which was first published in 1841. Bernard Baruch considered this book to be the speculator's Bible. Mackay demonstrates again and again that speculative success depends on the ability to counter crowd psychology. After reading this book (which Baruch did once a year), speculators can get a better "feel" for how long trends might continue and when they are about to reverse. All inflations are essentially speculative, and a careful study of the examples given by Mackay (as well as studying more recent examples) leads me to conclude that our present inflation is still in its early stages. There are as yet only a few signs of the psychology that must prevail before it ends. This important question will be examined in greater detail in the chapters that follow. Meanwhile, I wish to acknowledge my debt to Mackay for much of the following information about the Mississippi and South Sea manias.

As Mackay indicates, John Law must be viewed as one of

the greatest creative geniuses of all time. After all, at the beginning of the eighteenth century, no ordinary mortal could even imagine the possibility of accepting a piece of paper as the equivalent of gold. At any rate, we know that Louis XIV couldn't—or wouldn't—because Law tried unsuccessfully to persuade him to issue paper money redeemable in gold. The otherwise boundless avarice of the Sun King could not rise to the heights of duplicity required by those who declare that paper is equal in value to gold. When he died in 1715, this was at least one folly to which Louis had not succumbed.

It would be a grave mistake to assume that the inventor of fiat money was cut from the bloodless, humorless pattern of his modern descendants: bankers and economists. He was colorful, to say the least; after all, he was a gambler by profession. However, it should be pointed out that the activities of a professional gambler in the early eighteenth century were viewed by society with the approval that we accord to stockbrokers and investment bankers today and, as a matter of fact, with much the same justification. Like every born gambler or speculator, Law patiently waited for the right moment to introduce his revolutionary ideas.

THE MISSISSIPPI BUBBLE

When Louis XIV passed out of this frustrating world and into a better one, he left France buried under a mountain of problems—mainly financial. Philippe d'Orléans, who was regent for the five-year-old Louis XV, was desperately looking for solutions, so he was finally persuaded to listen to Law, who claimed to have a solution for every conceivable problem. The most pressing problem was paying the interest on the national debt, which amounted to more than 3 billion livres (about $17.5 billion in today's money).

Law's solution was audacious. He proposed to form a private corporation—the Compagnie d'Occident (later popularly referred to as the Mississippi Company)—which would have the sole right to exploit and develop all of French North America, which we identify today as the Louisiana Territory. The new company would assume all of the French national debts in return for this monopoly. This was as if a newly formed American corporation was granted the exclusive right to develop the moon and in return for this privilege agreed to assume the national debt of the United States. The advantage of this deal to the Crown was obvious. At one stroke of a pen, the regent had transferred the French national debt to the Mississippi Company.

The problem of how to pay off the huge debt did not bother Law for a moment. First, he created—under government charter—the Bank of France, which issued paper money redeemable (theoretically, at least) in gold. By this inspired action, the now debt-free government was made still more solvent, since it could now pay its bills with paper money rather than gold.

Second, he offered to exchange Mississippi Company shares for outstanding government bonds. The bondholders snapped up the bait. After all, the Mississippi Company enjoyed the right to develop a large part of North America, which was rumored to be awash in gold and emeralds. Moreover, he guaranteed the success of the offering by giving the bondholders the right to exchange their bonds at face value although the bonds were selling in the market at less than half of this amount. Few owners could resist this apparent windfall and, as a result, the new issue was 100% subscribed and the public clamored for more.

Here was a venture with unknown potential, which always fires the imagination of speculators. It seemed that everyone in France wanted to own Mississippi shares, which could be purchased with a down payment of only 10%. The buying stampede that followed drove the original shares, with an initial value of 500 livres, to a final giddy peak of 28,000 livres.

The Mississippi Company had its offices in the narrow, squalid Rue Quincampoix, which became France's Wall Street. French citizens and foreigners of every description crowded the street, where it was not unusual for ladies and children to be trampled to death in the crush. Real estate values in the area soared. Soon tiny rooms near the street rented for more than whole villas had previously. Hopeful speculators were willing to pay almost anything to be where the action was taking place. No wonder! Rumor had it that an English merchant had parlayed 100 pounds into 20 million livres in less than a week. Nor was there any reason to doubt that the 10% margin (or binder) enabled fortunes to be made in short order—even in one day.

To finance this speculative madness (poorer people mortgaged homes, furniture, etc. to raise cash) the new Bank of France issued paper money as fast as it could be printed. The end result was the same as always, only quicker: instant inflation. Prices in Paris rose 600% within a few months. Just about everyone who speculated was suddenly rich—on paper. The sole topic of conversation in the evening was how much each person had made during the day just ended, and how much they would have made if they had only bought more. Finally even conservative citizens, who today would invest in savings banks, were forced to speculate in Mississippi shares in order to keep up with the rise in the cost of living.

Meanwhile, every effort was being made by the regent and other directors to develop and exploit the vast Louisiana Territory. The city of New Orleans (named after the regent) was founded with visions of it become the Paris of the New World. Prospective settlers were lured westward by offers of cash plus 450 acres of the new land on which they were expected to create coffee and tobacco plantations. The new colony did not prosper: Speculation at home held more allure than a life of pioneering in the wilderness of the New World. Moreover, the promise of untold wealth in the form of gold, silver, and precious gems, which had been extravagantly promoted in the company's prospectus, turned out to exist only in the heads of the promoters.

Toward the end of 1719, rumors began to circulate that all was not well in the new French utopia. The more astute (or lucky) speculators quickly exchanged their shares and paper money for gold—as long as gold was still available. This option was soon eliminated when the government passed a law forbidding private citizens to own gold. As a result, quite predictably, gold flowed out of France or into hiding. Still other speculators sold their shares and used the proceeds to buy land, houses, gems, and other valuables, which caused the price of these tangible assets to soar. In fact, the rush was now on to convert shares and paper money into just about anything—ranging from paintings and horses to silk stockings.

The year 1720 in the Rue Quincampoix was equivalent to 1929 in Wall Street. In another effort to stem the liquidation, Law had an emergency measure passed converting Mississippi shares into fixed-income bonds, with a sufficiently liberal return to encourage the owners to hold on to them. It did just the reverse, and the panic really got underway. Mississippi shares plunged froma high of 28,000 in January all the way down to 200 in December, when the regent dissolved the Bank of France and fired Law. Law, who had invested his own fortune in the company and believed in its future to the very end, was now destitute and was forced to flee France to escape from his vengeful stockholders. He stopped running in Venice, where he lived in poverty and obscurity until the end of the decade.

Law must have viewed the course of events in France following his departure with disbelief. Just about everyone who dealt in Mississippi shares lost, including those who made millions by selling at or near the top. In July 1721 the French government confiscated all profits realized from the sale of Mississippi Company shares. There was, however, one loophole: the new law exempted profits of the nobility. Thus, as usual, the rich became richer.

THE SOUTH SEA BUBBLE

Across the Channel, England in the early eighteenth century was on the threshold of the Industrial Revolution—a revolution made possible by cheap energy in the form of coal. The first large-scale textile mills and ironworks, which formed the backbone of England's foreign trade, were being built at this time. As a result the East India Company flourished and richly rewarded its shareholders, who were an exclusive group limited to a few hundred landowners, merchants, shipowners and clergy. Doubtless, this example of corporate success whetted the public's appetite for the more readily available and even more glamorous South Sea scheme that was soon to follow. Already, inherited wealth was in the process of being redistributed from the aristocracy, on whose land the iron ore and coal were mined that produced the underlying wealth of the industrial age, to the new middle class: merchants, entrepreneurs, lawyers, and doctors.

Although the South Sea Company was founded in 1711, when the pious and straitlaced "good" Queen Anne ruled England, it did not achieve its splendid zenith until George I had been on the throne for some six years. Incidentally, the parliamentary system, as it is practiced in England today, originated with this first George; not by any design on his part, but simply because he never learned to speak English. He therefore deferred matters of state to his cabinet, whose dominant member came to be known as the "prime minister."

Not only was George more lenient than Anne in matters of morality, but his attention (as well as a goodly number of English pounds) was devoted to his beloved homeland—Germany. As a result, gambling and other recreations flourished in England as never before or since. In most homes, gambling at cards was a popular as television is today. Public casinos resembling those in Las Vegas—if Hogarth's pictures are an accurate indication—were thronged with players of both sexes.

Drinking was, however, the principal vice of this loose-living generation. The most popular beverage was ale, which the average citizen consumed at the rate of about 100 gallons a year in addition to sizable quantities of rum (from the West Indies sugar plantations), gin and whiskey. Little wonder, since in those days you could drink all you wanted for a penny. This, then, was the background which encouraged the South Sea madness that was soon to sweep over England.

As we have seen, European bankers had only recently learned how to create money by issuing banknotes worth several times as much as the gold they held in reserve to redeem them. Bankers loaned money that previously did not exist, and this new money stimulated investment in new business enterprises. For this purpose, joint stock companies were formed with shares which could be transferred from one person to another. To facilitate such exchange, a stock exchange was established in the City of London in 1698, and within a few years speculators were actively trading these shares. Thus was the stage set for the debut of the South Sea Company.

Despite the frugal government budget under Queen Anne, by 1711 the national debt exceeded 50 million pounds, and the question of how to meet the interest payments on it preoccupied the nation. The problem was eventually solved by eliminating the debt, and the method used was inspired, no doubt, by the example of John Law and his "système," which had only recently accomplished a similar coup in France with spectacular success.

The English solution came in the form of the South Sea Company, which was granted a monopoly to trade with the Spanish colonies in America and also with the virtually unknown—but presumably rich—islands that adorned the Pacific beyond. The owners of government securities were then presented with an offer to exchange them for South Sea shares on terms which appeared most advantageous. As a result, about two-thirds of the outstanding government debt was exchanged for stock in the new company. Encouraged by the response, the government proceeded to offer more shares to the general public, and a flood of new buyers came forward to participate in this once-in-a-lifetime opportunity. After all, hadn't the hated Spanish been reaping a bonanza of gold and silver from their American colonies for the past 200 years?

Moreover, the public's appetite for such imagined riches had been recently stimulated by several newly issued travel books. First, William Dampier's *New Voyage Around the World*, which was followed by Woodes Roger's *A Cruising Voyage Around the World*. (Dampier sailed with him on this famous voyage.) Defoe's immensely popular tale, *Robinson Crusoe*, was based on the true experience of a seaman who was rescued by the two circumnavigators. Dampier, who dreamed of wresting America from Spain or, less ambitiously, of developing an extensive British trade in the area, inspired Defoe to draw up plans for such a project. He presented these to Lord Harley, Earl of Oxford, who quickly adopted them and took full credit for founding the South Sea Company. As Mackay tells us, "The minister took great credit to himself for his share in this transaction, and the scheme was always called by his flatterers, 'The Earl of Oxford's masterpiece.' " Thus, the legend that Defoe was responsible for the South Sea Bubble is true in the sense that he very likely originated the idea with an assist from Dampier.

The public was well conditioned to the possibilities inherent in turning distant wealth into immediate reality. Their government had at least as great an interest in securing this distant wealth; but, like all governments, their more immediate concern was how to transfer local wealth from the citizen's pocketbook into the state's. One way to accomplish this was to sell more South Sea shares, and at the highest possible price. This required some manipulation, but that posed no problem. As Defoe assures us, by 1720 stock jobbers were adept at rigging pools. As South Sea shares began to climb, the public scrambled to get aboard before it was too late. Then, as now, rumors were manufactured at least as rapidly as the public's desire for them. The most persuasive story claimed that Philip V of Spain had granted the company the exclusive right to unlimited trade with the Spanish colonies on the west coast of South America.

Of course, Philip never considered permitting unrestricted trade between England and Spanish America; nor, in fact, any trade at all unless it was absolutely certain to result in a net transfer of English money into his treasury. The South Sea Company was granted permission only to supply black slaves to the Spanish colonies and, in addition, could send one ship a year to exchange English goods for Spanish gold and silver. The details of this latter arrangement were not publicized, since Philip was to get 25% of the profits plus a 5% tax on the total value of the goods traded. Nonetheless, the one and only trading voyage (made in 1717) provided proof that there was some substance behind the South Sea venture. More important, it provided a potent source for the circulation of increasingly extravagant rumors which, in the end, persuaded virtually the entire nation to buy a share in the Earl of Oxford's "masterpiece."

During 1719 and early 1720, as the enterprise increasingly captured the imagination of the public, South Sea shares gradually rose from £50 to £150. Large gifts of stock to members of the royal family, as well as to influential members of parliament, helped pave the way for increasingly favorable government cooperation. Even dire warnings by a few killjoys backfired. When Robert Walpole dismissed the entire operation as a "pernicious stockjobbing" scheme that would ruin the country and suggested that a ceiling should be placed on how high the stock should be allowed to rise, reverse psychology made buyers only more eager to get in before any such ceiling was imposed.

On April 12, 1720, the company took advantage of the universal state of euphoria to issue new stock at £300 a share. The offer was oversubscribed immediately. New buyers ranging all the way from fashionable courtesans to clergymen were catching the South Sea fever and jostling one another in Exchange Alley. A week later, the company declared a special (and unexpected) dividend of 10%. On April 23, the company—responsive as ever to the public welfare—floated still another new issue of stock at £400 a share, which was sold in minutes.

At this point, let us pause and consider what was involved. One South Sea share cost £400. How much was this equivalent to in 1980 dollars? An accurate comparison is difficult to make because the value of goods relative to money constantly changes. However, we will not be far off if we assume that one pound in 1720 would buy about as much as $60 will today. Therefore, one share cost $24,000. To make the new issue more readily available to those of moderate means (presumably, wealthy people got in earlier), a down payment of only

20% was required, with the remainder to be paid in four equal installments. Nevertheless, a new buyer still had to come up with the equivalent of $4,800 in cash now to buy only one share and another $19,200 later on.

This is why ordinary people all over England found it necessary to mortgage their jewels and other possessions (to those who had sold shares bought earlier and lower?), so that they could participate in the expected bonanza. This was not as difficult as it sounds. In England, as in France, the inflated value of South Sea shares spread throughout the economy, where prices in general were rising rapidly, although not quite as rapidly as the price of South Sea shares.

Day after day the stock climbed until by August it finally reached the unbelievable and final peak of £1,000 per share. By then Exchange Alley was a madhouse, where people risked physical as well as financial ruin. As a result, secondary (or curb) markets sprang up—especially in taverns and coffeehouses for men and millinery shops for ladies. By now, the more canny speculators (including the Prince of Wales and the Duke of Bridgewater) and stock jobbers realized that the South Sea money tree itself could not keep growing forever—so they planted some new ones. Over 100 new enterprises were floated and sold to the greedy and gullible public.

These new bubbles which, once the subscribers' money was pocketed, seldom developed beyond the idea stage, ranged from visionary dreams to outright swindles. Nothing that seemed likely to separate the public from its money was too preposterous—not even the cloak-and-dagger enterprise, described in somewhat guarded language as "A company for carrying on an undertaking of great advantage, but nobody is to know what it is." Unfortunately, the "nobodies" referred to the new stockholders themselves, rather than potential competitors that might have been lurking in the wings. I personally wonder if the story itself is not a hoax—it's too good to be true. However, I can no more doubt Mackay than the bubble buyers could doubt their promoters, especially since Mackay goes on to tell how this rogue guaranteed an annual income of £100 on shares which cost £100 but required a down payment of only £2. This makes it believable. On the first day of the offering, the promoter sold 3,000 shares, then closed his books and departed for the Continent where, let us hope, he succumbed, in turn, to the Mississippi madness.

The ideas behind many of the bubbles were logical enough. Among these were new whaling ventures, textile and steel mills, consumer finance companies, and fire insurance companies. Less convincing were projects which proposed to:

- ☐ Manufacture a wheel for perpetual motion.
  Capital: one million pounds.

- ☐ Insure, and increase children's fortunes.

- ☐ Import walnut trees from Virginia.
  Capital: two million pounds

- ☐ Dry malt by hot air.

- ☐ Extract silver from lead.

- ☐ Manufacture square bullets and cannon balls, thereby revolutionizing the art of war.

When the bubble frenzy was at its height, all new enterprises, whether in the former or latter categories, were banned by His Majesty's government, which did not relish any competition at all to the officially sponsored South Sea Company. The ban simply drove the promoters underground; it did not prevent thousands of investors from losing millions of pounds.

We should not conclude that all of the buyers of these bubbles were credulous hicks who believed in the unbelievable.

On the contrary, Mackay says, a significant proportion were "sophisticated and worldly." They bought with their eyes open on the same "greater fool" theory which causes hard-nosed businessmen to buy gold today with the expectation of selling it to a greater fool at a higher price tomorrow. They hoped to sell their newly acquired shares at a higher price. When? As soon as possible, but definitely before the first installment payment fell due. Few managed to do so because the boom was destroyed by the very same psychology that created and sustained it.

Soon after reaching £1,000, the bubble burst and the stock started to slide. The fear and panic on the way down surpassed—if possible—the hope and greed on the way up. Goldsmiths (bankers) who had lent huge sums with South Sea stock as collateral were bankrupt and were forced to flee to save their lives. By the end of September the stock had plunged to £135; thousands of families were ruined, and hundreds of people committed suicide. However, those who owned fully paid for shares were relatively well off since the Bank of England, together with the still-prosperous East India Company, eventually bailed out the South Sea Company, which continued to operate for another 130 years in the marginally profitable slave trade. When the slave trade ended, so did the once-glamorous South Sea Company.

4

Runaway Inflation
in Germany

The post–World War I inflation in Germany is the most sensational example of modern inflation and one that has profound
implications for America in the 1980's. We want to learn how
many Germans not only managed to survive it, but grew rich
in the process. If you deplore the present rise in the cost of
living, consider the plight of the average German citizen in
1922. During the final six months of that otherwise forgettable
year, the cost of living rose at the rate of more than 100% a
month. And this seemed like stability in comparison with
what occurred in 1923. What was happening in Germany?
The figures in Table 1 tell part of the story.

TABLE 1

CURRENCY IN CIRCULATION

Year	Millions of Marks
1913	6,000
1914	8,700
1915	10,050
1916	12,300
1917	18,500
1918	33,100
1919	50,100
1920	81,600
1921	123,000
1922	1,295,000
October 1923	2,500,000,000,000
November 1923	92,000,000,000,000
December 1923	500,000,000,000,000

As the figures in Table 1 reveal, the money supply grew significantly between the end of the war in 1918 and the end of 1922. However, inflation increased even faster. To understand why, we must distinguish between monetary and price inflation.

Monetary inflation occurs when the supply of money increases faster than the rate of growth of goods and services. This is a condition that obviously prevailed during 1922 and 1923. It can also occur when the supplies of money and goods are growing (or holding level, for that matter) at the same rate, if the existing supply of money turns over more and more rapidly.

Price inflation occurs when the demand for goods exceeds the supply; it can occur without the help of monetary inflation. Price inflation can also occur when a real shortage of goods does not exist, but when the fear of such a shortage creates it—if only temporarily. Currently, we have a combination of these two factors to contend with in America. Not long ago, people would pay any price for sugar or for gasoline. (I will examine this subject later, at greater length, because Americans find it hard to view their great nation among the "have-nots.")

What triggered the German inflation? The causes are complex and not especially relevant to us today. Traditionally, the blame is attributed to the heavy burden of postwar reparation payments imposed by the victorious and vengeful Allies. However, apart from these factors, the expenditures of the German government climbed to unprecedented heights. Tax receipts lagged far behind. The difference was made up by borrowing; i.e., deficit financing or, to use a less polite term, printing-press money. Does this sound familiar?

The years before the war represented a period of extraordinary price stability for all Europe which, according to the gold bugs (who may well be right) can be credited to the gold standard. In any event, this desirable condition was upset by the armament race in which Germany was a front-runner. The inflationary forces were put into motion as early as the summer of 1914. As war fever mounted, did the German people patriotically line up to buy government bonds, which were being energetically promoted around the country? No. Instead, they lined up at the Reichsbank to convert their marks into gold. Such unpatriotic behavior was not acceptable, so Kaiser Wilhelm passed a decree on August 4, 1914 making it unlawful for citizens to own gold or gold coins, which, until then, were circulating as freely as our base-metal coins do today. This was the essential first step toward inflation that every government has followed since the beginning of history.

The final nail in the money coffin was driven by the French

when, in January 1923, they marched into the Ruhr and attempted to collect overdue reparation payments. The Germans reacted with a massive display of passive resistance. The unparalleled prosperity of the year before was replaced overnight by a demoralizing depression, which caused unemployment to soar from virtually zero to almost 25%. Did the depression or the unemployment slow inflation? Not at all. In fact, it signaled the beginning of the most virulent stage of the inflation. This experience should be an object lesson to those government economists who feel that recessions and resulting unemployment are the only certain way to stop inflation.

Despite the steady erosion in the purchasing power of the mark during and immediately following the war, average citizens failed to comprehend what was happening (and what was about to happen) for a long time. In fact, when they realized it, it was too late to take the measures necessary to survive financially. During the first years of the inflation, the response of the German people was similar to that of the American people today. People economized and saved their money either because they were in the habit of doing so, or because they anticipated lower prices when the unreal situation returned to normal. As a result, the mark retained more of its value (difficult as that may be to imagine) in Germany than it did abroad. As a newspaper reported in July 1922: "Because of the hoarding of great quantities of notes the internal depreciation of our currency was not fully shown in internal prices as compared with foreign depreciation." In short, the folly of hoarding a depreciating currency was not apparent to millions of Germans.

In due course, people began to realize that such frugal behavior spelled disaster. In general, the very rich and the very poor adjusted most easily and quickly to inflation. The slowest to adjust was the middle class, which considered the stock market too hazardous and other types of trading as being beneath their dignity. They preferred to put their money in life insurance, government bonds, savings banks, and urban real estate. They lost everything and were often reduced to begging or accepting the hopelessly inadequate public dole.

One such example is described by a lady in her memoirs: "My father had taken out endowment insurance for his three children. The insurance was calculated to cover my brothers' university education and I was to have a similar amount. When my eldest brother got his money it was just sufficient to buy a bicycle. When the second got his, he could just buy a pair of boots. When my turn came I got nothing." [4]

Another rather surprising group of losers were small businessmen, who failed to realize to what an extent old values were becoming obsolete. They were often lured into selling their businesses for a price which, by past standards, seemed high but was actually much less than its current value and only a small fraction of its future value as measured by the eroding mark.

Price controls and excess profits taxes were imposed and, as any rational person would predict, both proved to be totally ineffective and were eventually abandoned. In the interim, those who abided by them were ruined. Those who ignored them had a better chance of surviving. Rent controls provide an example of how this worked—or didn't work—in practice. Investors who bought real estate as an inflation hedge were crucified when the politically popular rent controls were introduced. Such rents turned out to be negligible in comparison with maintenance expenses and taxes, which kept pace with inflation. Moreover, since subletting was not controlled, a tenant could rent a single room at whatever the market would bear—possibly 100 times more than he was paying the owner for the entire house or apartment.

However, in time, even the petty bourgeoisie, with their frozen ideas began to catch on. The news story quoted above was followed a year later by another one describing how workers, as soon as they were paid, would rush out to buy something—anything—of concrete value. "At noon every day the new value on the mark was announced and if by that time you hadn't converted your money into some '*sachwerte*' [real values] you stood to lose a large part of your salary."

How did people manage to beat runaway inflation?

Some were well situated through no fault of their own. Farmers were relatively well off since the real value of farm products—which were an ideal form of *sachwerte*—kept pace with inflation. Furthermore, the German farmer whose lands were heavily mortgaged was able to pay off his loan with increasingly worthless money. As a result, many farmers had a steady surplus of money to invest; their farms became the nucleus for land-based conglomerates, almost by accident. Herbert Hochfeld, a widely read reporter of the current scene, describes in one sentence how one farmer accomplished this feat: "There was no point in putting any of his profits into a bank, or any other form of saving, so all he could do was expand, expand, expand and the whole thing became an empire."

Huge industrial empires were also founded on a foundation of inflation. The best known was that of Hugo Stinnes, which would put ITT to shame. He, as well as many others, prove conclusively that the conglomerate phenomenon of the 1960's was no American invention. Stinnes acquired more than 4,000 companies, ranging from shipping lines, coal mines, steel mills, and oil refineries, to paper mills, tobacco companies, newspapers, banks, and electric utilities. Inflation made all this possible, since he realized that stocks were undervalued in terms of paper money (as they are today), and that accumulating a large cash position would be courting disaster. Like the farmer mentioned, he used his available cash to expand; unlike the farmer, he also borrowed heavily to buy new companies and then was able to pay back these debts in depreciated currency. He had another advantage over his less farsighted competitors: he made sure that his companies raised their prices faster than the rate of inflation. By these methods, Hugo Stinnes became a billionaire—as measured by real values, rather than paper marks.

As inflation gained momentum, more and more ordinary people lost faith in their money and made every effort to convert marks into dollars or pounds. This turned Germany into a mecca of cheap living and cheap goods for foreigners, but it also precipitated a whole series of government countermeasures. Endless laws were passed forbidding German citizens to purchase foreign currencies and compelling those who acquired foreign currencies in the natural course of their business operations to sell them to the Reichsbank. These measures merely aggravated the situation by advertising its seriousness.

The dollar was the standard of value by which the depreciation of the mark was measured. Each day the newspapers published the exchange rate, and this became the best measure of the inflation rate. In 1914 the exchange rate was 4.2 marks to the dollar. By 1919 it had risen to 8.5, which reflected the wartime inflation. (Bear in mind that the dollar was also depreciating, although at a much slower rate.) The slide picked up momentum in 1920, when the rate jumped to an average of 50 marks to the dollar, and by November 1921 it reached 270 marks to the dollar. This accelerating rate of depreciation was caused, in part, by worldwide speculation against the mark, by speculators who correctly gauged the adverse impact on the mark because of the enormous reparation payments demanded by the Allied powers.

The German bank rate, which hovered around 5% until mid-1922, gradually rose to 30% a year later and reached 90% in the fall of 1923. From a practical standpoint, the discount rate of 90% was equivalent to zero, since call money (shortest-term loans, usually made to brokers) was being loaned at 10,000%. Did higher interest rates boost costs, and thereby promote inflation? Certainly they did not prevent it, nor even slow it down.

Why did business continue to boom right up until the final phase of the inflation? First, wages failed to keep pace with the inflation rate to such an extent that by the fall of 1922 the real purchasing power of workers was only half as much as it was in 1918. This is one reason why German industry prospered while the rest of the world stagnated in the postwar slump. However, wage earners were well off compared to the plight of people who depended on pensions and similar fixed incomes.

As we shall see, the stock market reflected the prosperity of industry and, perhaps, for this reason proved to be one of the best hedges against inflation.

The more carefully we study the German experience, the more we question the widely accepted theory that an increase in the money supply *causes* inflation. Did the flood of paper money cause the mark to depreciate? Or did the depreciating mark result in the flood of paper money?

There are persuasive arguments in support of the latter theory. The prosperity of German industry was due in large part to the favorable balance of trade. As the mark became cheaper in terms of foreign currencies, exports increased while imports decreased; the favorable balance boosted profit margins. Needless to say, industry leaders stressed the importance of maintaining these favorable relationships and repeatedly warned against efforts to strengthen the mark.

Until 1919 stock-market investors were drawn almost exclusively from the wealthy and managerial classes. This picture changed rapidly when the dangers of inflation became apparent to an increasing number of ordinary citizens who realized that they must expand their horizons if they were to survive financially—indeed, all too often, if they were merely to avoid starving. Soon—as in America, a few years later—everyone was taking a flier in the market.

We can get some idea of what was going on by quoting from a letter written by Harold Fraser, an Englishman, who worked as a bank clerk in Hamburg, to his head office in London on June 30, 1923:

> The majority of people, finding it quite useless to save money, either use their surplus (at present not much) for purchasing clothes, or else in speculating on the Bourse. They buy shares of industrial companies and in many cases with quite small capital, are able to realize good profits upon selling them. As a rule, however, if a profit is taken, the money is at once put into something else. I can say without exaggeration, 90% of the men employed at the Deutsche bank keep their money (such as it is) in this manner.[5]

Volume surged on the Berlin Stock Exchange to such an extent that it had to be closed every other day so that the clerical staff could keep up with the paper work. Moreover, the extraordinary activity had repercussions far beyond the exchange—e.g., at the telephone companies. Farmers and others who lived in remote areas of the country seldom had telephones, until they found that they needed instant communication with their banker who, in Germany, at the time, provided the services of a stockbroker. If they were really big operators they had private lines installed directly to the floor of the stock exchange. Installation of all these new telephones caused phone-company profits to soar, as did their stocks on the exchange.

The end result of this ultimate inflation was huge unemployment and economic chaos. After all, if the price of a cup of coffee jumped from 5,000 to 8,000 marks while you were drinking it—as was reported at the time—it must have seemed futile to attempt to carry on business as usual. Instead of trying to cope with the frustrating situation, more and more people tried to turn it to their personal advantage. Speculation looked more attractive and often turned out to be more remunerative than hard work.

At any rate, during the summer and fall of 1923, when business was at a virtual standstill, the stock market boomed as never before. One financial columnist summed up the situation: "There have been extraordinary rises in the quotations of all shares, the chief cause being the catastrophic change in the economic scene."

Probably a majority of these new investors—who certainly numbered in the millions—were traders who needed quick profits in order to buy the daily necessities of life. Although most succeeded because of the generally rising market, the big winners were those who bought during the early stages of inflation (i.e., in 1920 and 1921), when stock prices were depressed and then added to their positions during the periodic—though brief—bear markets. This presupposes, of course, that they bought the shares of well-established, well-managed companies; many other companies, unable to adjust rapidly enough to the unprecedented conditions, went bankrupt.

In addition to the unprecedented, frenzied boom in stock prices there was a mania among the German people to own anything but money. This preoccupation with owning *sachwerte* might include almost anything, since almost anything will appeal to someone. For example, the paintings of starving second- and third-rate artists were, to their surprise, suddenly in demand. In fact, just about everything that wasn't nailed down was in demand—or, more accurately, was in danger of being stolen. Thus, clothing, brass doorknobs, and the like were more valuable than money because the supply of them was limited. After all, a brass doorknob had as much intrinsic value as a handful of coins; whereas, a 10,000 paper mark note was worth less than the same piece of paper without the engraving on it.

When stock prices reached their final giddy peak in November 1923, investors were slightly ahead of the inflation rate, as measured back to prewar days. At that point, inflation ended literally overnight, when the old and now worthless mark was replaced by the new rentenmark (the exchange rate was one billion to one), which was backed—at least psychologically—by the land and industrial assets of the nation. How did this affect shareholders? Theoretically, they were not affected, since the owner of, say, Daimler Motors stock retained his proportionate ownership regardless of the value of the money he used to purchase it with. In the long run, the value of such shares rose far above the inflation-inspired gyrations of the hectic period. The inflation-beleaguered investor of today might profitably retire to his inflation-proofed shelter and ponder upon this fact.

The outcome over the near term, however, was less rewarding. Stocks surrendered a considerable part of their relative gain in purchasing power once the mark was revalued. This loss was not due to the revaluation, but rather to the mass exodus out of the stock market, when the currency stabilized and the need for a hedge against inflation no longer existed. The frenzied activity diminished, and the stock exchange returned to normal. The aftermath was somewhat similar to what followed the big bull market on Wall Street.

Speaking of coins, did Gresham's law prevail in Germany? Did worthless paper money drive intrinsically valuable coins out of circulation? Of course it did. Yet as late as May 1923, the Reichsbank was still busily—and foolishly—churning out coins. These 200- and 500-mark aluminum coins naturally went straight to scrap-metal merchants, since their face value was much less than the metal value of the aluminum they contained. One marvels at the universal stupidity of governments.

Does anyone doubt that our base-metal coins now in circulation will suffer the same fate? Already proposals are heard from time to time to discontinue the penny. The reason given is that inflation has reduced the need for it. After all, it's pointless to sell gasoline for 99.9 cents a gallon when one dollar would be essentially the same. More to the point, nothing for sale today costs only one cent. The real reason? The same as when the silver content of our silver coins became worth more than their face value. They were withdrawn from circulation and the resulting shortage—as most of us can remember—created all sorts of economic problems. Banks were paying a premium (in paper money) for those rapidly disappearing coins.

It is only a matter of time until our present base-metal coins suffer the same fate. The copper content of the penny will be worth more than its face value when copper sells for $1.75 a pound. Doubtless, millions or billions are now being hoarded by citizens in an attempt to protect themselves against the ravages of inflation. This makes sense in theory, but not in practice; the storage problem is too great. There are many better ways of hedging against inflation, as the Germans discovered. However, if for sentimental reasons you still like traditional coins, then your best bet is a bag of silver coins, which are traded in volume at only a small premium over the value of their silver bullion content.

Finally, let us bear in mind that as their money became worth less and less, the German people invented a variety of substitutes. In fact, they reverted to methods—such as barter—that were practiced before money was invented. Many merchants would not accept the official paper money and insisted upon receiving goods in kind for their merchandise. These might include buckets of coal, food, clothing, and other items, depending on the value of the transaction.

Then again, the manager of a manufacturing company would go out in the country, from farm to farm, exchanging its products for food, which was then used in place of paper money, to pay its employees. In addition to such makeshift tactics, the company might issue "emergency money" redeemable in company products. Thus, a grain dealer would issue a note promising the bearer five pounds of flour upon presentation. This "money" would then circulate and be readily accepted because the recipient knew that five pounds of flour would retain its value.

INFLATION EXPORTED

The inflationary forces triggered by World War I were not restricted to Germany. Germany was just the most widely publicized because Germany was the largest and most conspicuous example. All of the Central European countries were affected. Unlike the Germans, their Austrian cousins of the post–World War II generation did not profit from the experience of their fathers. In 1946 they repeated the follies of their fathers following World War I.

Stefan Zweig, who lived through the earlier period, left us a vivid description of what happened in Austria. The following excerpts are from his autobiography,° *The World of Yesterday:*

In the beginning the peasants gloated over the shower of money for which they had sold their butter and eggs, and which made them profiteers. However, when they brought their bursting wallets to town to make purchases, they discovered to their exasperation that while they had merely quadrupled normal prices, the scythe, the hammer, the kettle, which they had come to buy had meantime risen twenty or fifty times in price. . . . The whole country was seized with a grotesque traffic. The city dwellers hauled out to the farm whatever they could get along without—Chinese vases and rugs, sabers and rifles, cameras and books—thus, entering a Salzburg's peasant home, one might be surprised by a staring Indian Buddha, or a rococo bookcase with French leather-bound books of which the new owners were particularly proud. Substance, anything but money, became the watchword. There were those who had to take the wedding ring from their finger or the leather belt from around their body in order to keep that body alive.

The chaos grew from week to week, the population became more excited. The progressive devaluation of money became more manifest. The first sign of distrust was the disappearance of hard money, for people tended to value a bit of copper or nickel more highly than mere printed paper . . . soon nobody knew what any article was worth. Even a goldfish or an old telescope was "goods" and what people wanted was goods rather than paper. In consequence of this mad disorder the situation became more paradoxical and immoral from week to week. A man who had worked hard for forty years and who, furthermore, has patriotically invested his all in war bonds, became a beggar. A man who had debts became free of them.[6]

Zweig's description of Austria during 1919, 1920, and 1921 reminds one of our present American culture and moral standards (or lack of them):

Homosexuality and lesbianism became the fashion. The general impulse to radical and revolutionary excess manifested itself in art too. The new painting declared that all that Rembrandt, Holbein and Velasquez had created as finished and done for and set off on the most fantastic cubistic and surrealistic experiments. The comprehensible element in everything was proscribed, melody in music, resemblance in portraits, intelligibility in language. Every extravagant idea reaped a golden harvest: theosophy, occultism, spiritualism, palm-reading, yoga, etc. Anything that gave hope of newer and greater thrills, anything in the way of narcotics, morphine, cocaine, heroin found a tremendous market.[7]

Zweig managed to be where the action was. He was in Germany when his friend Walter Rathenau, the foreign minister, was assassinated. As a result:

A panic broke out and the tremor spread through the whole Reich. Abruptly the mark plunged down, never to stop until it had reached the fantastic figures of madness, the millions, the billions, the trillions. Now the real witches' Sabbath of inflation started, against which our Austrian inflation with its absurd enough ratio of 15,000 old to one new currency had been shabby child's play. To describe it in detail with its indescribable incredibilities, would take a whole book and to readers of today it would seem like a fairy tale. I have known days when I had to pay 50,000 marks for a newspaper in the morning and 100,000 marks in the evening; whoever had foreign currency to exchange did so from hour to hour, because at four o'clock he would get a better rate than at three, and at five o'clock he would get a better rate than he had got an hour earlier.

Paradoxically, in terms of hard money (not gold, which was nonexistent, but rather American dollars or British pounds) fixed assets in the early stages of the inflation were dirt cheap. First, because they could not readily serve as a substitute for money when it came to buying the daily necessities of life; and second, people were slow to adjust their appraisal measurements: they tended to think in terms of the old values (just as Americans tend to appraise stock values today). To quote Zweig once again:

For a hundred dollars one could buy rows of six-story houses on Kurfurstendamm and factories were to be had for the equivalent of a wheelbarrow. In contrast, some adolescent boys who had found a case of soap forgotten in the harbor, lived like kings by selling a cake a day, while their parents who were formerly well-to-do slunk around like beggars.[8]

Zweig's analysis of how the superfinancier, Hugo Stinnes, built up his empire should be underlined:

Expanding his credit and in thus exploiting the mark he bought whatever was for sale, coal mines, castles, ships, factories, stocks, country estates, actually for nothing because every payment, every promise became equal to naught. Soon a quarter of Germany was in his hands and, perversely, the masses who in Germany who always become intoxicated with a success that they can see with their eyes, cheered him as a genius.

The unemployed stood around by the thousands and shook their fists at the profiteers and foreigners in their luxurious cars who bought whole rows of houses like a box of matches. Everyone who could read and write traded, speculated and profited and had a secret sense that they were being deceived by a secret force that brought about this chaos deliberately in order to liberate the state from its debts and obligations.

To summarize, stocks were an excellent hedge during the early stages of the inflation, a poor hedge during the middle stages, and a fair hedge during the final stages. When it was all over and the mark was revalued, stocks retained their value better than almost anything else.[9]

5

The Inflationary 80's

All I have said about inflation as the method whereby the government legally steals from its citizens is painfully true. However, this does not mean that a great many of those citizens don't gain more than they lose in the process. Basically, this is why we have inflation and why a majority of the people support rather than oppose the duplicity of their elected representatives.

While I cannot prove it, I suspect that there are more people right here in America today who benefit from inflation than are hurt by it. Among the former are homeowners—millions of them. Do you know of anyone who hates inflation and wants (someone else) to fight it, will voluntarily reduce the price at which he is willing to sell his home? And thereby do all he can to combat this evil in order to promote the general welfare? I don't. That is why inflation is not about to go away.

Inflation *has* to continue to speed up—it's not in the nature of the beast to remain stable. How else can the millions of debtors, who now stand to benefit from more and more inflation, avoid disaster? Thus, a majority of those people who rail against inflation are secretly and silently in favor of it. Like everyone else, they favor lower prices for what they buy, higher prices for what they sell—usually their labor.

During the two decades up to 1969, the inflation rate averaged 2% a year. During the 1969–1979 decade, it averaged about 7% a year. Stated differently, in twenty years the cost of living increased 50%. Then, in only ten years, it increased 100%. Clearly inflation is accelerating at a dangerous rate—which is not exactly news to anyone who buys anything these days.

More important, this rate of inflation is understated by a very substantial margin. Not only do the necessities of life always seem to rise faster than the index itself, so do other essentials (services especially), which are not included in the cost-of-living index.

Anyone can tick off numerous examples of goods and services that have soared not from 50% to 100%, but rather from 500% to 1,000%. To mention a few: New York subway fares, car repairs, U.S. postage stamps, gold, real estate. Runaway inflation à la Germany, Hungary, and Latin America has not yet arrived, but can anyone doubt that it is knocking very urgently at your door?

Certainly those people who ought to know don't doubt it. International bankers as well as Arab oil ministers, who were educated in this country and England, are betting that runaway inflation is inevitable during the 1980's and probably during the 1990's, if it has not collapsed beneath its own weight before then.

Nicholas Deak lived through the German inflation of the 1920's. His firm, Deak, Perera & Co., conducts the largest foreign-exchange business in the world, so his views concerning the outlook for inflation carry weight. He declared in an August 1978 interview in *Time* magazine:

World inflation has reached crisis proportions, only we do not realize it. Various measures taken by the government can affect inflation and the dollar, but only very little. I'm afraid that inflation will increase, and eventually our monetary system will collapse and our social structure will change. I went through all this before—in Hungary, Austria and Germany in the 1920's—and the trend is inevitable.

Why is the trend inevitable? Why is runaway inflation unavoidable in the 1980's? There are hundreds of reasons. Here are three or four of them. First, there is ample precedent to prove that when the inflation cycle reaches a certain stage, a flight from the currency ensues, regardless of traditional measures taken to prevent it. We have reached and probably gone beyond that critical stage. Now the choice has narrowed to more inflation or a depression and soaring unemployment. The only medicine that will prevent the sick patient from dying is the same medicine, only more of it: more credit, more money, more inflation.

Is there a politician living (or dead) who would hesitate for even a moment between these choices? I think not. In fact, at this point, the choices may be purely academic. Consider the tables below.

These trends cannot and will not be reversed suddenly—at least, not until they have reached a point of no return, such as occurred in Germany in the early 1920's. Happily, this point may not be reached for several more years, which gives you plenty of time to profit from the runaway phase and to prepare for the aftermath. After all, the U.S. inflation rate could double and double again, yet still remain below the rates considered normal in many other countries with economies that are inherently less stable and complex than ours.

What exactly are we talking about when I refer to "inflation"? I have already distinguished between monetary and price inflation. The usual measure of price inflation is the Consumer Price Index. During the 20 years ending in 1967, prices increased at an annual rate of less than 2%. The trend since 1967 is shown by the following figures:

1967	100.0
1968	104.2
1969	109.8
1970	116.3
1971	121.3
1972	125.3
1973	133.1
1974	155.4
1975	166.3
1976	174.3
1977	186.1
1978	202.9
1979	225.0E

E—Estimated by author.
Source: Survey of Current Business, U.S. Department of Commerce.

Monetary inflation is what I am referring to when I use the word "inflation" in this book. The money supply, traditionally, consists of Time and Demand Deposits (M2). As the following figures show, the rise in the price index has almost duplicated the rise in the money supply.

	Billions
1967	$450
1968	489
1969	513
1970	585
1971	614
1972	677
1973	688
1974	754
1975	793
1976	845
1977	947
1978	1003
1979	1100E

E—Estimated by author.
Source: U.S. Federal Deposit Insurance Corp.

To understand inflation, we must first understand how money is created.

Where does money come from? In the past, it was created by mining gold or silver and then turning them into coins. Today—when gold and silver are no longer money—it is created either by the government or by private individuals or corporations through the banking system.

First let's look at the government role. The Treasury borrows money every day, even when the budget is balanced. Typically, the Treasury sells debt obligations (Treasury bills, bonds, etc.) mainly to the Federal Reserve System and its member banks. How do the banks pay for these debt obligations? Simply by writing checks for sums (now totaling more than $100 billion) that previously did not exist. This is the source of new money.

Let us assume that the Treasury sells $1 million in bonds to a bank. The bank credits the Treasury with a $1 million deposit, which the Treasury then draws against to pay its obligations, which may range all the way from a new sub chaser to Social Security checks. At the bank, the newly acquired bonds now represent a legal reserve, which can be used to create still more new money via the lending route. (This is why bankers like to make loans—they make money by lending money which previously did not exist.)

Of course, they are not allowed to loan 100% of the previously nonexistent money—only about 85% of it. The actual percentage that can be legally loaned varies depending on the size and location of the bank. Small country banks can lend more than large metropolitan banks. An average reserve requirement of 15% might be in the ball park. Assuming this figure, then the bank "buying" the original bonds must keep $150 out of each $1,000 deposit in reserve. (This is to protect its depositors in case there is a run against the bank.)

Now the bank—let us call it Bank A—can loan or invest an additional $850, which it did not previously have in any form. Let us assume further that it loans this amount to an individual customer, who plans to use the money for an excursion to Las Vegas. This person deposits the money in Bank B pending his arrival in Vegas. Bank B can now loan 85% of $850—or $725—to one of its customers who, in turn deposits it in Bank C. Bank C can now loan 85% of $725, and so on. In recent years, about $800 billion of new money has been created in this fashion. This is what feeds the fires of inflation.

The U.S. Treasury is not unique in being able to originate such a credit cycle; it is unique only in never being turned down when it wants to borrow. Actually, the private sector originates more new money than does the government. A typical business transaction illustrates how this works. Assume you devise a better mouse trap and decide to manufacture and market it. You need $100,000 to build a plant. Your credit rating is good (or perhaps your connections are); in either event, your bank agrees to lend you the money and deposits $100,000 in your checking account. Only $15,000 of this represents already existing money (reserves) in the form of other deposits, savings, or paid-in capital of the bank.

You now have $100,000 to spend and may not realize that $85,000 of it represents money that you and your bank have just created. In any event, you are not concerned about that aspect of the transaction; you go on about your business of spending the money. The money you spend is deposited by your suppliers and employees in their banks, where it, in turn, acts as backing for similar new loans. Until your loan and all the other loans generated by your loan are repaid, your transaction contributes to inflation. When you and the others finally do repay them, this particular inflation cycle is canceled out and we are back where we started. But suppose, in the meantime, two other businessmen have embarked on similar expansions; their activities more than counterbalance yours, and inflationary pressures have doubled.

Very often, in practice, the mouse-trap maker may be able to finance his new traps using only half the loan he gets. He uses the other half for speculative purposes, such as buying stocks or soybean futures. This is one source of the new money required to make the stock and commodity markets rise. They decline when the process is reversed.

I hope I have made it clear why all borrowing is inflationary. If I have, then Table 2 should reveal equally clearly why we have inflation and why it is getting worse.

I cite these figures to support my contention that an ample

TABLE 2
U.S. GOVERNMENT BALANCE SHEET

Year	Budget Deficits (Surplus) (billions)	Federal Debt (billions)	Private Debt (billions)	Inflation Rate %
1947	(3.9)	257	–	14.4
1948	(12.0)	253	–	7.8
1949	(0.6)	257	–	(1.0)
1950	3.1	257	77	1.0
1951	6.1	259	88	7.9
1952	1.5	267	101	2.2
1953	6.5	275	114	0.8
1954	1.2	279	125	0.5
1955	3.0	281	138	(0.4)
1956	(4.1)	277	154	1.5
1957	(3.3)	275	169	3.6
1958	3.0	283	185	2.7
1959	12.9	291	201	0.8
1960	(0.3)	290	217	1.6
1961	3.4	296	236	1.0
1962	7.1	304	267	1.1
1963	4.7	309	297	1.2
1964	5.9	318	327	1.3
1965	1.6	321	344	1.7
1966	3.8	329	370	2.7
1967	8.7	345	392	2.9
1968	25.1	358	428	4.2
1969	(3.2)	368	451	5.4
1970	2.9	389	472	5.9
1971	23.0	424	528	4.3
1972	23.3	449	606	3.3
1973	14.3	470	689	6.2
1974	3.5	493	750	11.0
1975	43.6	577	810	9.1
1976	66.6	654	902	4.9
1977	71.5	720	1,026	6.7
1978	39.6	790	1,160	9.0
1979	40.0E	850E	1,300E	13.0E

E—Estimated by author.
Sources: Economic Report of the President, Handbook of Basic Economic Statistics

base exists for still more inflation. Every government loan and every private loan represents a potential source of new money.

So the base on which an inflation pyramid can (and is) being built is the total of columns 2 and 3. That is, more than $2,000,000,000,000—or $2 trillion. Is this dangerously high? I don't know. But I do know that these figures represent only a small part of the nation's total debts. These are only the *officially recorded debts on which interest is being paid.*

We all know that most of our personal borrowing and lending is never recorded. Nor is a great deal of the government's debts, which might be more of a surprise to most of us. The official national debt of about $800 billion includes only those bonds, Treasury bills, etc., on which interest must be paid to outsiders. Other debts and potential obligations total perhaps another $2 trillion, ranging from student loans and FHA loans, to loans to finance foreign military sales and a host of others.

If a private firm headed, most likely, by a retired U.S. Air Force general sells a couple of jet fighters to Zambia or Upper Volta, he borrows the money to buy the planes from a bank or an agency of the government: Zambia does the same. In either event, Uncle Sam guarantees the loans. How much would *you* loan to Zambia? These loans which, as I see it, have about as much chance of being repaid as I have of winning an Olympic gold medal in gymnastics, are nonetheless the stuff from which still more loans and still more inflation are made.

Inflation feeds on itself because borrowing encourages more borrowing as prices rise. (This is an observation—not a critical judgment. The basic strategy of those who hope to survive runaway inflation is to be a borrower rather than a lender—so long as you borrow to buy productive—rather than consumer—assets.) In addition to the basic types of borrowing cited above, there are others, which would not exist at all without inflation—the currently popular second mortgages, for example.

INFLATION AROUND THE WORLD

Currently (1980) worldwide inflation has surpassed its 1974 peak, after subsiding somewhat in 1976 and 1977. The 1974 inflation was blamed on a series of presumably nonrecurring factors—namely, the quadrupling of crude oil prices (except for some U.S. domestic producers), disappearance of anchovies off the coast of South America, crop failures, and so on. Since then crude oil prices have risen less than the inflation rate, the anchovies have returned, and bumper crops have been harvested in most parts of the world. Yet inflation persists and grows worse. Why?

Inflation in one country or part of the world promotes inflation in another country or another part of the world. We no longer live in a vacuum. As Table 3 reveals, the United States is only beginning to catch up with the rest of the world in the fine art of inflation.

TABLE 3
RECENT AVERAGE INFLATION RATES
(Percent)

Argentina	150	Germany	5
Australia	15	India	28
Brazil	40	Indonesia	40
Bolivia	35	Israel	80
Canada	11	Japan	16
Chile	25	Mexico	25
England	15	Spain	18
France	12	United States	13

The first nation on the list starts us off with a flying start because Argentina hardly qualifies as a LDN (less developed nation) in the usual sense of the word; yet it has the highest inflation rate in the world! The situation in Argentina is worth examining because inflation there has become institutionalized with a vengeance—a fact that those who advocate a similar solution to the inflation problem in this country might well ponder. Wages, pensions, and just about everything else is indexed. In addition, the graduated feature of the income tax has been eliminated to prevent forcing taxpayers into ever-higher tax brackets.

Then, too, in order to promote thrift, income received from savings accounts is not taxed. Even so, few Argentine savers even consider the passbook savings accounts that are so popular in this country (despite the fact that they yield a negative return even before the interest is taxed).

Instead, Argentinians favor CDs (certificates of deposit), which pay a higher rate of interest (85%) and can be cashed in in 30 days if a more attractive investment opportunity presents itself. Of late, that more attractive opportunity for an increasing number of people has been the stock market, where it is not unusual for a stock to double and triple in a week—and sometimes in a day.

Another instructive feature of Argentina's inflation is that periodic recessions have not slowed it down, but have actually speeded it up. The reasons for this may seem perverse, but they illustrate the change in psychology which permeates a society when inflation becomes a way of life for everyone. Thus, when business slows down, retailers and manufacturers don't reduce prices in order to stimulate sales. Instead, they raise them because they know from experience that their inventories increase more than the profit they would have realized by selling at lower prices. Don't be surprised if a similar psychology begins to undermine our competitive economy as Americans become more knowledgeable about beating inflation.

It is also instructive to know that since the military junta took over four years ago, it has significantly reduced the budget deficits; an action which has not yet slowed down inflation at all.

High inflation rates in the LDNs can be attributed, in large part, to rapid population growth. Also, debtor nations have a powerful incentive to inflate their countries' currencies in terms of those of other nations, which means that the LDNs must inflate faster than the nations they borrow from, if they are to have any chance at all of avoiding bankruptcy.

PRODUCTIVITY

In America, until recently, one powerful long-range anti-inflation force has been the steady growth in worker productivity. All this has changed, until productivity growth has become negligible. This has ominous implications for the future because it certainly seems logical to conclude that decreasing productivity adds to the cost of production—and therefore higher prices. Usually the blame is laid on shrinking capital expenditures per worker. However, in my opinion, population growth and changes in worker composition are far more important causes.

Population growth in the United States with its declining birthrate? How is it possible? One reason is the worldwide migration from the LDNs, most of which is illegal. This flow appears to be irreversible; constant and strenuous efforts to stop it have failed. I am not concerned with the legal or moral aspects of such movements, only with their impact on inflation.

Why are such mass movements inflationary? Consider an

unskilled, penniless Mexican who crosses the U.S. border. If he is fortunate and finds a job, he will probably replace an older and more experienced worker, who may be retiring. His impact, in general, will be to lower productivity. If he is less fortunate, he may be forced to rely on welfare or other state aid. This, of course, contributes to higher government deficits, and therefore to inflation.

The United Nations estimates that world population by 1990 will increase by more than one billion souls. Almost all of this growth will take place in the LDN. Whether legally or illegally, a sizable percentage of these people will migrate to Western nations, including the United States. This migration will lessen, but not solve the problem of a subsistence-level standard of living for the people at home. It can't be done—at least not by all those nations all of the time. Famines will occur in the future, as in the past, and may even become worse. The LDN will pose a threat (perhaps real, perhaps imaginary) in the minds of the developed nations, which will encourage the growth of military expenditures and this will add to all the other inflationary forces.

Another form of population growth contributes to inflation. This is the growth in the number of older people eligible for Social Security, as well as those covered by numerous other public and private pension plans. I am not passing judgment on such plans; after all, those people who are unable to support themselves must be taken care of whatever the reasons may be for their inability to do so. My main purpose is to understand why these plans are inflationary. My secondary purpose is to reveal that they represent a concealed tax that, like other taxes, contributes significantly to inflation.

Social Security and income taxes are modern forms of taxation without representation. Our forefathers rebelled against their mother country because of a paltry 2% excise tax on tea. Do you have any more say when inflation automatically promotes you from the 25% to the 30% tax bracket? How many citizens realize that their tax load is substantially greater than they ar told? The Social Security payments that are withheld from payrolls are not a form of savings that will be invested and returned to you beginning when you retire. On the contrary, they are a disguised form of income tax because these payments are treated exactly the same as payments received from income tax collections; they go into the general fund used to pay current government expenses.

Moreover, for wage earners in the lowest tax brackets, Social Security payments are more burdensome than income taxes. For instance, if you earn $8,000 a year and have normal deductions, you will pay little or no income tax. However, FICA payments will amount to about $500, and even more in future years. $500! Any wage earner age thirty or thereabout, who invests these payments in accordance with the principles blueprinted in the next chapter and Part II of this book, will not only survive inflation with flying colors, but, at the end of thirty-five years, when he is eligible for Social Security, will have far more than he can ever expect to receive from Social Security. It is my personal conviction that he has about as much chance of collecting any meaningful benefits at all from it in his old age as a snowball has in Hell.

This conclusion is confirmed by studies carried out by the Social Security Administration itself (although this was not the purpose of the study). They project that by the middle of the next century (when children born today can expect to start collecting benefits), the average worker will be earning $656,000 a year and the averaged retired worker will receive $259,000 a year in retirement benefits! Anyone who believes that will believe anything. Moreover, these projections are based on an inflation rate of only 5.75%, or about half the current rate. At the current rate, these projections would come to pass in a little over thirty years. (More on why this won't happen later.) The Social Security Administration is really saying that the only way that these projections could materialize would be for them to pay future benefits in worthless dollars, which is exactly what will happen.

In addition to the army of Social Security recipients that will grow steadily during the inflationary 80's, consider the impact of those who receive military and industrial pensions. To introduce this subject, I should explain that when I recently returned from living in Europe I chose to live in the Monterey Bay area, because it is a beautiful, smog-free area with marvelous sailing. The history of one of my neighbors seems especially relevant at this point. When the Korean War started in 1950 he entered the army and decided to make a career out of it. When he retired three years ago, he had risen to the rank of Major. After 26 years of service his pension amounts to 75% of his base pay of $23,064 a year, or $17,300.

He retired when he was only 45 years old and had no trouble finding a good civilian job at the nearby Naval Post-Graduate School. I don't know what this job pays—probably about the same as he was getting in the army. So he has an extra $17,300 a year coming in for as long as he lives and the pensions are often indexed, and increase automatically at the same rate that the cost of living increases. Multiply such pensions by a million recipients, and you come up with another powerful reason why inflation will not go away.

Another example: One of my oldest friends recently retired after working 30 years for a major corporation. He received a provident fund, which paid him $90,000 in a lump sum, and in addition a pension of $20,000 for life. He was only 55 when he retired and a recognized expert in his field. He is now a consultant and makes more money than he ever did while an employee. His impact on inflation was immediately apparent, because he used the $90,000 for a down payment on an expensive horse farm and uses his pension to meet the mortgage payments.

INDEXING INFLATION

A more descriptive phrase might be "institutionalizing." In other words, what can be done to guarantee that we have inflation permanently? We can "index" wages, pensions, interest rates, and so on—to guarantee that they will go up at the same rate that the cost of living does. Once this principle is put into practice, you begin to wonder which is causing which. If the inflation rate rises 3% without any assist from a rise in wages, interest rates, etc., then the latter are boosted 3% because of the former, does not this add further to upward pressure on prices?

If nothing worse, politicians are hardheaded realists. They well know that the only way to reverse the glacial advance of inflation is to drastically reduce the flow of new money—which would produce an immediate depression and soaring unemployment. They also remember, all too well, what happened to the party in power when this last occurred. The Republicans were the party out of power for twenty consecutive years.

So it is not surprising that indexing, which appears to protect the interest of nearly everyone—from labor unions and the elderly to large leaders—is becoming increasingly popular with politicians. Yet indexing seems certain to promote rather than prevent runaway inflation. For one thing, as the practice spreads, the Federal Reserve's control over the money supply will become progressively less effective. Obviously, high interest rates will not deter, nor low rates encourage, a borrower, if the borrower knows that he will pay the going rate, whether high or low, during the life of the loan.

The somewhat limited history of indexing seems to bear out these conclusions. When indexing was introduced in Brazil, the inflation rate dropped appreciably, but now seems to have stabilized on a relatively high plateau. This, as well as other evidence, suggest that indexing does calm—at least temporarily—the type of fear-inspired action in which future events are caused by efforts to circumvent them. Yet indexing can cover only well-organized activities. It certainly cannot cover the huge ($200 billion a year?) underground markets, which operate on the cash or barter system in a largely successful effort to avoid taxes.

Then, too, indexing more or less legitimizes, rather than combats inflation. Another long-range drawback is that indexing bypasses unorganized workers, and this has ominous implications for future political stability. Thus, in Brazil during the 1960's, real wages fell by 30%. The rich grew richer, while the poor grew poorer, since inflation doesn't destroy wealth, it merely hastens the redistribution of it. The same trend is unfolding in this country. The real income of organized workers—especally government bureaucrats—has kept pace with inflation, whereas the income of unorganized labor has fallen drastically.

There is still another powerful force promoting worldwide inflation. Every nation strives for a favorable balance of trade, which it can achieve either by producing goods more efficiently than other nations or, failing that, by selling them at a lower price. Internal inflation automatically accomplishes the latter objective by devaluing a domestic currency in terms of foreign currencies. This is why almost every nation (Japan has been the exception) has a vested interest in promoting inflation.

It follows that inflation at home should reduce our trade deficit. Instead it has risen because many foreign countries have inflation rates even higher than ours. In addition, each year we import more and more crude oil at higher and higher prices. The obvious solution to the problem is to import less crude oil. This solution is politically out of the question because we are so dependent on oil.

Let's face it: We would much prefer to pay the Arabs in dollars that will buy less from one day to the next than to reduce our consumption of their oil. Unfortunately, this sets in motion a vicious circle of price increases to which our only answer is more inflation. The position of the OPEC nations is understandable enough, and the wonder is that they did not arrive at it long before 1973. After all, they are exchanging their oil, of which there is a finite supply, for American dollars, of which there is an infinite supply.

This payment problem could have been solved by paying the OPEC nations with constant-value dollars. However, since quantities such as $50 billion a year for the United States and a similar amount for Europe are involved, this would have meant raising taxes and reducing our standard of living. Such a solution was clearly less acceptable than the always-attractive alternative of paying bills with borrowed money, which will never have to be paid back. Remember also, that before the OPEC oil-price increase, the inflation rate had shot up to a new postwar high; the Arabs only added fuel to a fire that was already burning brightly.

WHEN THE BUBBLE BURSTS

How long can inflation continue to undermine the economic virtues which every person knows are morally—as well as practically—right in the eyes of God and man? Because the only question involved is one of time, not of the ultimate consequences of our folly. As Emerson warned us more than a century ago:

The Dice of God are always loaded. The world looks like a multiplication table or a mathematical equation which, turn it as you will, balances itself. . . . Every secret is told, every crime punished, every virtue rewarded, every wrong redressed, in silence and certainty.

A wise man will extend this lesson to all parts of life, and know that it is the part of prudence to face every claimant and pay every just demand on your time, your talents, or your heart. Always pay; for the first or last you must pay your entire debt. Persons and events may stand for a time between you and justice, but it is only a postponement. You must pay at last your own debt. If you are wise you will dread a prosperity which only loads you with more.

Sooner or later we must pay the price. Will it be sooner or later? After thirty years of studying inflation, I believe that the final reckoning will be put off until we have witnessed an inflation rate several times that of today, which will produce an unprecedented rise in the stock market. Such a sequence will take several years.

Governments have repeatedly demonstrated one of Adam Smith's favorite observations: that they always defraud their creditors by manipulating the currency which they alone control. He called the borrowing-inflation cycle "a disguised form of bankruptcy." And certainly the bankruptcy of the U.S. government is not exactly disguised, if we consider bankrupt anyone who owes far more than he can ever hope to repay in anything but worthless money. Our government, like all governments, has painted itself—and us—into a corner.

I would like to mention one reason for this irreversible trend, which is not usually pointed out or even discussed: the decline in moral values. Morality is perhaps the most serious casualty of inflation. As the rewards of thrift are eroded, so is the foundation upon which the other and more important virtues are built.

First, thrift gives way to gambling. Then, more and more

people devote less time to productive work and more time to speculative and middleman activities, as well as illegal activities of every kind. This causes productivity to fall, which promotes inflation. The decline in moral values spreads throughout society, finally reaching the highest corporate and government levels. It is no coincidence that a new high in the inflation rate and the Watergate scandal occurred simultaneously. A general atmosphere of cynicism, distrust, and corruption prevails.

This manifests itself in a variety of ways. Honest citizens who, only a short while before, would not even think of avoiding taxes, now make every effort to do so. This is one very important—though unstated—reason for the gigantic federal deficits. There is a whole new generation of potential taxpayers who are not even filing tax returns and, from a practical standpoint, there is virtually nothing that the IRS can do about it—other than try to collect more from those who do file, which exacerbates rather than solves the problem. As a result, cash transactions increase in volume since they leave no record and therefore cannot be traced. This—obviously—is only one of many reasons for ever-mounting deficits.

Whatever the reasons, the situation has finally reached the point of no return. As the deficits grow, it becomes progressively more difficult for the Treasury to finance them in the traditional way, by borrowing from lenders in the open market, in competition with corporate and individual borrowers. The existing supply of money is simply not large enough. When the nonproductive public sector can borrow at the expense of the productive private sector, inflation results.

The time finally arrives when the government can no longer borrow all the money it needs, without forcing most—if not all—borrowers out of the market. If other borrowers don't have a reasonably good chance of making a profit on the money borrowed, they cancel their plans. In my opinion, we are dangerously close to this point right now, but it can never be permitted to come to such a head; if it did, the economy would go into a catastrophic tailspin.

Such a crisis is referred to in money circles as a "credit crunch," and these crunches have become a way of life in recent years. The significant omen is that each new one tends to be worse than the last one. Interest rates chalk up new highs, bond prices new lows, as faith in the government and its fixed interest obligations (including the currency) erodes away at an alarming rate.

The choices open to the government become increasingly unpleasant. It can reduce spending to the level of tax receipts. However, this cannot be done quickly if, indeed, it can be done at all, in view of the built-in price escalators and irreversible nature of most government commitments.

The only other alternative is to stop competing with other borrowers for the existing supply of money and start rolling the printing presses. As we have seen, this process is thinly disguised via the charade of the Treasury's selling bonds and bills directly to the Federal Reserve banks, who in "paying" for them create new money. This is the route every past government has taken when faced with bankruptcy, and there is no reason to hope that America in the 1980's will prove to be an exception. The inevitable outcome is runaway inflation.

Nor is the government the only disguised bankrupt. More and more individuals and corporations live beyond their means or expand their operations faster than they can pay for the expansion. Paradoxically, most of these champions of the new monetary morality are going to win because they understand the magical aspect of inflation, which enables them to repay only part (in real terms) of what they borrow. They are betting—correctly—that they have little to lose and much to gain by what appears to be excessive borrowing. In this way, wealth flows from those who save to those who spend. The latter group includes the government, corporations and farmers, who are becoming more articulate and organized than ever before.

The farm bloc alone just about ensures future inflation. The deflation of the 1930's hit the farmer harder than anyone else because he got less money for his crops while paying off the mortgage with increasingly expensive money. Lately farm debt has risen faster than just about any other kind. Politicians are much more responsive to this situation than the size of the farm vote would suggest.

And for a very good reason. Famine stalks many parts of the world, and the American farmer is the food supplier of last resort. Farm exports partially offset our unfavorable trade balance, and from that standpoint, the higher they are priced, the better. Every effort will be made by all concerned to boost the price of grain we export—at least as fast as the price of oil we import rises.

These, then, are some of the forces that ensure future inflation.

How much longer can it continue before reversing? In *The Coming Credit Collapse* Alexander Paris states the case for his title in convincing fashion and concludes:

Finally, the growing deflationary pressures will be too much to handle: the entire debt structure will collapse and liquidity will be restored after a painful interval. The timing of this event will, as always, be difficult to predict *because the government has the power to delay it almost indefinitely by supplying money to continue the trends.* (emphasis added) [10]

Exactly. And bear in mind that this was written five years ago. This is why I think that the runaway phase of inflation still lies ahead, as does the coming flight from the dollar into stocks.

This is not based on my personal hunch or opinion; study of past inflations show that there are three well-defined phases. The important lesson to be learned is that, contrary to orthodox theory, prices do not rise in direct proportion to the increase in the money supply. During the early stages, prices rise more slowly than the supply of money; during the middle stages, at about the same rate; and during the final stages, much faster.

In the first stage, when the money supply is increasing faster than prices, the average person is not aware of what is happening. He realizes, of course, that prices are rising, but his response is to save, rather than spend his money. He still has faith in the stability of money and expects prices to return to their old level, as they have always done in the past.

During the second stage, prices rise at about the same rate as the supply of money. More and more people become aware of what is going on and begin to lose faith in the integrity of their money. The traditional wisdom summed up in the aphorism "a penny saved is a penny earned" is replaced by the new shibboleth: "Borrow and buy before prices rise still further."

When this new psychology takes over, it produces the third phase. People now cynically assume (correctly) that the inflation is a plot designed by the minority to swindle the majority. They lose all faith in the currency and, as the desire to exchange money for tangible goods becomes more urgent, prices rise much faster than the money supply.

We are now entering phase 2, which usually lasts a much shorter time than phases 1 and 3. Does anyone doubt that phase 3 will follow, in due course, as surely as night follows day?

How will it end? Just as all inflations end. As phase 3 develops, prices start to rise much faster than the money supply because a majority of people holding the money (and the goods available for it to buy) agree tacitly that its value will decline even faster than it has in the past. And, contrary to popular belief, there is absolutly nothing the Federal Reserve can do to counter it, any more than the Reichsbank could do in Germany.

People who own money want to get rid of it regardless of how much it will buy by past standards. If they own goods—including stocks—they can be persuaded to part with them only at higher and higher prices—until, finally, they refuse to sell at any price. Economic activity then comes to a halt—and the inflation destroys itself, or the government steps in and replaces the old money with the new.

Will we then revert to the gold standard as the gold bugs loudly proclaim we should? No. For one thing, we no longer own enough gold. After all, when you are on the gold standard, the fellow who owns the most gold is king of the hill. Today this means Russia and South Africa, neither of whom we are wildly enthusiastic about enriching. In addition, the gold standard succeeds only if everyone is willing to play the game. If the gold have-nots won't play—i.e., exchange their valuable raw materials and other goods for worthless gold—then there is no game.

They, too, remember that those crying the loudest for a return to the gold standard admit that a much higher price for gold would be necessary. On the one hand, they proclaim the discipline enforced by the gold standard while, on the other hand, they advocate inflation for one commodity—gold—of which they presumably have a good hoard at home under the mattress. If gold is money, how can you fight inflation by increasing its price? The whole point of the gold-standard system is to *not* increase the price. Increasing the price of gold under the gold standard is the same as printing money under the paper-money standard.

When the end does arrive, what form will it take? What

should we watch for? I would expect the Consumer Price Index, which only recently crossed 200 (1967 equals 100), to approach 500 toward the end of the 1980's; at that point, we can expect the demoralizing phase of runaway inflation—the phase when our complex economy begins to break down. As barter increasingly replaces money as the medium of exchange, supplies of all kinds will be hard to get and to transport.

Drastic action will be required and demanded by the increasingly panic-stricken population. Such action will take the form of an overnight revaluation of the currency. An executive order will be issued by the President, ordering all citizens to turn in all old dollars (the present ones) for new dollars at the rate of, perhaps, 100 (or 1,000?) old for one new. The same ratio will apply to bank and savings accounts. If you have 5,000 dollars in the bank one day, the following day you will have only 50 new dollars. This is why you should own anything but money when this fateful day arrives. That goes for any form of assets valued in money terms: bonds, savings deposits, mortgages, insurance, and so on.

6

Saving Is Suicide

As we have seen, 32 million people receive Social Security payments that rise with the inflation tide. Similarly, the wages of another 20 million are boosted at least as fast as (and usually more than) the cost of living rises. How many of these 50 or so million people—who with dependents constitute the majority of the American people—realize that *they* are the cause of inflation? Probably 99.9% of these people are opposed to inflation. But how many of them would agree to have the size of *their* checks reduced, even if they were certain that such action would check inflation? Very few, because they have come to view such automatic increases as a right which they will not surrender collectively under any circumstances.

Basically, this is why inflation is not going to go away and why those of us who do not have indexed incomes must immediately reinvest all of our savings into productive assets which will increase in value faster than the inflation rate. Furthermore, we should also convert our nonproductive assets, such as gems, coins, gold, paintings, etc., into more liquid and productive assets. (See Part III of this book for the logic behind this apparently heretical advice.)

The problem is that indexing seems on the way to becoming a way of life. Already a majority of long-term business contracts—to supply raw materials, in particular (and please take note of this)—are indexed. The contractual price will be increased at the same rate as inflation. This concept is rapidly being extended to long-term business loans—currently about 65% carry an indexed or floating interest rate—and it is being advocated by many spokesmen for the savings and loan industry. They correctly foresee the coming flight out of fixed-income savings and are desperately searching for alternatives. Table 4 reveals why, and what would be involved. The right-hand column reveals that savers have suffered a net loss in all but three of the last ten years.

Here we have the extraordinary phenomenon of a home buyer borrowing money at a cost of 10% or 11% while, at the same time, lending his own surplus funds to the same savings company and receiving only 5½% interest. Only the first half of this equation makes any sense during an inflationary period—except to the savings company. True, you may feel that the unequal transaction is justified because the homeowner must borrow $50,000, while having only $2,000 a year to invest or save. My point is that there are several thousand better ways to invest $2,000 than in a savings bank.

TABLE 4
RETURN ON SAVINGS—1970–1979

Year	Interest Rate	Total Savings S&L Associations (billions)	Inflation Rate (%)	Loss (Gain) to Saver (%)
1970	5%	146.4	5.9	.90
1971	5	181.6	4.3	(.70)
1972	5	206.8	3.3	(1.7)
1973	5¼	227.0	6.2	1.0
1974	5¼	243.0	11.0	5.75
1975	5¼	285.7	9.1	3.9
1976	5¼	335.9	4.9	(.30)
1977	5¼	386.9	6.7	1.5
1978	5¼	410.0E	9.0	3.75
1979	5½	400.0E	13.0	7.50

E—Estimated by author
Source: *Savings Bank Fact Book*, published by U.S. League of Savings Associations, 111 East Wacker Drive, Chicago, Illinois.

Unless, of course, you put the welfare of the savings-bank executives above your own. Let us assume that the savings-and-loan industry pays an average of 7% (large depositors are better paid than small ones) at a time when the inflation rate is running at 11%. No matter how you may rationalize the matter, their depositors are losing 4% a year in real terms. In effect, depositors are paying their friendly local association 4% to use their money. In reality, the loss is greater than 4% by the amount of income tax they pay on interest received. Nor do these figures take into consideration how much more they might have realized by investing their savings in inflation hedges.

Stated differently, the $400 billion loaned to savings associations suffered a net decline in purchasing power of nearly $30 billion last year alone. This must surely represent one of the greatest legal thefts in history, equaled only by the annual theft by the government, which we refer to as "deficit financing."

Moreover, these losses are understated by the amount of income taxes each individual depositor pays on the interest earned. When will the owners of this huge concentration of money wake up to this reality? Soon, I'm sure. Already indexing has been introduced for large depositors, who receive ¼% above the Treasury bill rate on deposits of $10,000 or more that are not withdrawn for eight years. This practice obviously discriminates against the small saver, who can least afford to be discriminated against.

So the next step must inevitably be to extend indexing to all depositors, small as well as large. This means, in turn, that principal repayments on loans must also be adjusted upward by the same amount that interest payments are raised, or the lender will operate at a loss and thereby run the risk of eventually going bankrupt, with disastrous consequences for depositors and borrowers alike.

Already the limited indexing that has been introduced has attracted affluent new depositors at the expense of those of modest means. Clearly, when and if indexing is made available to everyone, it will attract huge amounts of new money. Would it not, however, discourage the mortgage buyers, who would be undertaking a long-term obligation of unknown dimensions? In the event of runaway inflation, those home-owners least able to beat inflation would have their mortgages foreclosed; the savings-and-loan association would wind up with surplus funds on which they could not meet the upward spiraling interest payments.

The end result would be the same for depositors, but for different reasons. Without indexing, the savings-and-loan depositor is a sure loser. In my opinion, with indexing he would also be a certain loser. However, with this alternative, the final reckoning might be delayed longer—then occur with less warning.

In the short run, indexing savings accounts can have only an adverse affect on the stock market. After all, I think it can be safely assumed that a great many stockholders would be satisfied if they could be certain that their stock investments appreciated at the same rate as inflation. I doubt that the owners of stocks will ever be given such a guarantee (nor should they), and they all know it. Those stock-market investors who are now switching into high-yielding savings accounts will be the first to switch back again, when the profit margins of savings associations are squeezed by the very policy of indexing that they now see as their salvation.

If indexing is not extended to small savers, the question arises: Why would anyone put money into a savings account if they are going to suffer a net real loss? Part of the answer is that if you save $100 a month, what else can you do with it? At least you are reducing the size of the loss you would suffer if, instead, you put it in a safety-deposit box or under your mattress. Another apparent advantage is that the return increases in proportion to the length of time the deposit is left undisturbed. Thus, you must leave it 90 days to be assured of receiving even the minimum 5½%. Or you can earn 8% if you are prepared to tie up your capital a minimum of 8 years.

In the context of runaway inflation, the difference between a yield of 5¼% and 8% is not only meaningless, it is positively dangerous because it will encourage the depositor to hang on (the return is sharply lower in case of early withdrawal) even when the handwriting on the wall plainly tells him to get out. This is as it should be, because anyone who ties up capital for 8 years, during a time when inflation clearly is out of control and for a paltry return of 8% deserves to lose not part, but all of it.

Increasingly higher interest rates forecast increasing inflation: they should serve as a warning sign that repels rather than attracts you. Annual interest rates that are 8% and 10% today will be 14% and 16% tomorrow and eventually even higher.

The fact that this seems improbable now merely confirms the fact that our inflation has, as yet, advanced no further than phase 2. Remember that in Germany, call money (roughly equivalent to our money-market funds) went to a preposterous 30% *a day*. People did not want to lend money no matter what the return—they wanted to get rid of it.

INSURANCE

Insurance salesmen like to talk about the investment merits of the product they sell. The fact that they can and do sell this nonsense to the gullible public every day is hardly less surprising than the fact than an enterprising salesman can sell refrigerators to Eskimos.

I carry automobile liability insurance, but I certainly don't consider it to be an investment. Unless I have an accident, I don't expect to get anything back from it. This is—or should be—the sole function of insurance.

It is understandable if a young man responsible for two small children and a pregnant wife, signs up for some life insurance. After all, he is concerned for their economic security in case he should die. He should, however, buy only the cheapest available term insurance and avoid the paid-up varieties which are heavily promoted by insurance salesmen because they get a much larger commission on these policies.

I know because I have been victimized along with most of

my peers. For instance, in a weak moment, when I was much younger and less knowledgeable (I trust), a fast-talking insurance agent sold me an endowment policy on each of my three children, the youngest of whom was a year old. The idea that sold me was that these policies would give the children a start in life when they needed it most. When they were twenty-one they would each receive $2,500—or so I thought. The payments were only $115 a year, so I signed up without really knowing what I was doing.

When my children turned twenty-one, we discovered that the $2,500 face value was good only in case of death, and that the cash surrender value was only $2,162.50. Fair enough—it was my fault for not fully understanding what I was buying. What really hurt was that the real value of the $2,162.50 my children received was—due to inflation—less than $1,000, compared to the $2,000 I had paid in. And this was during a period when the inflation rate was much less than it is today.

The real problem was that my healthy babies needed insurance about as much as a wandering Bedouin in Arabia needs a heat lamp. Life insurance should be viewed strictly as insurance, never as an investment. As an investment, the money I paid in on these insurance policies would have returned much more if it had been invested in a savings account yielding only 5%.

To add to my misery I figured that if I had invested these insurance payments in IBM stock, $2,000 would have grown to $13,350. Admittedly, I rubbed salt into my wounds by imagining I had invested in IBM. There were a few stocks which would have returned less than the insurance, but I would have had to search diligently to find them.

It might be inferred from the above that the shares of publicly held life insurance companies must be a good investment precisely because the insurance that they sell is not. Not necessarily. As we have seen, investors who buy bonds and mortgages during an inflationary period are certain losers. Unfortunately, this is where, by law, the bulk of an insurance company's money must be invested. Even investors who buy insurance company stocks on the theory that if you can't beat them, join them, run the risk of suffering heavy losses in the long run, when bonds and mortgages are paid off in near-worthless dollars. It makes much more sense to invest in corporations that are *selling* these bonds to the insurance companies.

Despite the disastrous consequences that past inflations have had for most ordinary people, there is no reason why people who are aware of what is taking place should suffer. With a bit of foresight, they can succeed. Parts II and III of this book describe investment strategies in detail.

Meanwhile, the first and most important steps in any inflation survival program are:

☐ Switch money out of savings accounts and into productive assets that will appreciate (or, at least, have a good chance of appreciating) in value faster than the dollar depreciates.

☐ Switch paid-up life insurance or annuities into term insurance, or else borrow the maximum amount of money possible on your policies. After all, where else can you borrow money at one-half of the interest rate charged elsewhere?

☐ Switch money out of bonds and similar fixed-income investments into common stocks, following the program outlined in the following chapters.

PART II

The Stock Market 1980–1990

7

Fifty Years Later

As the 1970's began, I felt increasingly pessimistic about the stock market, the war in Vietnam, the California smog and traffic, as well as about most other aspects of American life. Accordingly, I moved to Majorca, and later to England. I was fortunate because by then I could, unlike most people, make such a change. I had sold various business interests and earned my living by speculating in the stock market. (I almost wrote "investing." However, in an inflationary age, there are no investments; everything is a speculation.) As it turned out this was an especially good time to be away from the market since

I am not temperamentally attuned to short selling, which was about the only way to survive in the 1970–1975 period.

And was I out of touch! When the final leg of the 1973–1974 bear market was spreading doom, I was preoccupied with a different kind of survival—sailing alone across the Atlantic. After weathering five gales in the English Channel and the Bay of Biscay, I ran out of food and water 500 miles from Barbados. During a stretch of 65 days I didn't think even once about the stock market. However, when I finally made it to Barbados the second thing I bought (the first was a bottle of Mount Gay rum) was a copy of *The New York Times* to make up for lost time. After another year of wandering among the islands of the West Indies and the Bahamas, America's drawbacks looked less and less distasteful compared to those of Europe, not to mention the cultural vacuum that smothers the Caribbean Islands.

When I finally returned home I could understand why political defectors and bail jumpers chose to return and face the music rather than live out their lives on alien soil. I was prepared to admit—at the risk of sounding maudlin—that America remained the best place in the world to live. Of course, things had changed. For example, it seemed as though a new financial era had dawned. I was aware, of course, that inflation was an increasingly serious problem. Besides I was used to it since the inflation rates in Spain and England were running at an annual rate of about 20% or about twice the rate in the U.S. What came as a shock was the difference in absolute prices. Even with inflation raging out of control—judging from the compaints of Spaniards and Englishmen— the cost of living in Spain averaged, perhaps, half that in the U.S. (We rented a luxurious three bedroom, two bath, furnished apartment, with a private beach looking out over the Bay of Palma for $150 a month) and in England 20 to 30 percent less. Wages were even lower.

I came to the conclusion that the official inflation rate published by our government was drastically understated. When I left this country a salary of $20,000 a year was considered generous for college presidents, corporate executives, engineers, and the like. When I returned garbage collectors, postal clerks, and truck drivers were making as much. Or again, our local hospital cost $28 a square foot to build in 1962. A currently planned addition to it will cost $200 a square foot, which represents a jump in cost that is ten times greater than the official inflation rate during those years. What had happened while I was abroad?

A great deal had happened. I recalled a series of essays I had written in 1962 (the same year the hospital was built) discussing the impact of a $100-million Federal budget on the economy and the stock market. When I returned in 1976 the Federal budget had grown to more than $400 billion, or about three times faster than the inflation rate.

Another development that intrigued me was the similarity between the current scene and that during the 1920's. Not in every respect to be sure. For one thing, the role of the government in those long gone days was, happily, minor. Nor was "inflation" a household word, although people complained loudly about the high cost of living as people are wont to do in every age. In short, there was little price inflation as distinguished from monetary inflation. There was quite a bit of the latter although it was not due to government borrowing and deficit financing as it is, in large part, today. The source of monetary inflation in the 20's was credit created by soaring real estate and stock prices, as well as another and relatively new source—consumer financing debt.

Most other prices moved in a narrow range or, like farm prices, declined during that decade. In contrast, in recent years the price of virtually everything has risen steeply with the single exception of stock prices. I will examine the reasons for this laggard performance in the next chapter, because it is important to understand them if we are to understand why the stage is now being prepared for a great new bull market in the 80's.

The lesson to be learned from the 20's is that huge government debt and deficit financing is not an essential component of inflation—private debt will serve nicely, and did in the 20's. Today we have *both* in abundance. This is why financial restraint on the part of the Federal Reserve Board will have no bearing, whatsoever, on the outcome of the battle against inflation. The necessary inflation base has already been created and the battle has already been lost.

The real estate boom alone has created sufficient debt to fuel inflation for many years to come. The equity of home owners has skyrocketed in recent years. Those who refinance their mortgages or take on a second mortgage create, as we have seen, in addition to the money borrowed, several times as much new money which contributes to inflation without producing any offsetting goods or services. Inflation, in this way, creates more inflation.

Inflation also creates the psychological atmosphere in which still more inflation flourishes. Here we find striking parallels, indeed, between the current situation and that prevailing half a century ago.

Without any question, the second decade of this century was the most spectacular peacetime decade in our history. Anyone who bothers to leaf through the yellowing newspapers and magazines of the period cannot fail to be fascinated by the extravagant behavior that distinguished that decade. We tend to view our own time as being unexciting, yet the similarities between now and then are uncanny. It is my belief that history repeats and that the psychological attitudes that produced the "roaring 20's" will also dominate the inflationary 80's.

Let's look at some of these similarities.

SPORTS

The two greatest heavyweight boxers of all time—Jack Dempsey and Mohammed Ali—were drawing unparalleled box office gates and publicity.

The two greatest golfers—Bobby Jones and Jack Nicklaus—dominated this sport and set records which may never be broken.

AVIATION

As the earlier decade began all attention was focused on Alcock and Brown—the first men to fly across the Atlantic (with a stop in the Azores). Even more sensational was the mind-boggling feat of Lindbergh, the first to fly across the Atlantic alone and non-stop.

Comparable feats in our time: The first men (American, of course) set foot on the moon and flew in a balloon across the Atlantic to a reception in Paris reminiscent of the one showered on Lindbergh.

FASHIONS

The woman's lib movement of today was paralleled by the woman's suffrage movement of the early 1900's, which in 1920 finally gave women the right to vote, although the political reforms widely anticipated by women failed to materialize.

The first females who bobbed their long (often knee-length) hair in the 20's were the object of outraged indignation—which was not repeated until the process was reversed by men only a few years ago—and with similar results. By 1930 every woman under the age of 50 wore her hair short and shingled. Similarly, by the end of the 70's even the most virile professional male atheletes displayed shoulder-length hair. Thus, do fashions come to full circle.

ECONOMICS

The burning subject as the 1920's opened was the high cost of living, especially for food and rent (the latter being caused by an acute housing shortage). Even worse, in just a few years steak had jumped from 27 to 42 cents a pound, butter from 30 to 60 cents a pound, and eggs from 35 to 62 cents a dozen. Not that prices, in general, rose all that much during the 20's, they were just higher than before the war. By our present-day advanced standards there was hardly any price inflation other than in real estate and Wall Street.

THE GENERATION GAP

The "generation gap" of our day is mild compared to the problem that the "younger generation" of the 20's imposed on its elders. When the decade began skirts modestly covered a ladies' ankles and the thought of any nice girl drinking, smoking, or petting in the back seat of a closed sedan was enough to make any mother swoon. Yet by 1926 hemlines barely reached the knee, while the liberated sex openly smoked cigarettes, read *True Confessions,* downed their bootleg gin from flasks (somewhat less openly), and displayed their charms in one-piece bathing suits. All this led to constant family quarrels between rebellious children and anxious parents. While sons and daughters were out until three in the morning joy riding or dancing to jazz bands led by the saxophone—that invention of the devil—mothers and fathers lay sleepless in their beds lamenting the fate of their lost generation of children.

POLITICS

While the younger generation was preoccupied with the pursuits of the young of every age and place, their elders were equally preoccupied with the Big Red Scare, formulas for making bathtub gin, and, as always, get rich schemes. An uncle of mine must have been typical. I well remember when he lost his shirt in wheat, recovered, lost again in a Florida real estate venture, and was finally wiped out in the stock market at the very time we all thought he was wealthy at last and set for life.

When the Big Red Scare subsided somewhat (just as it has today) the public's attention was centered on the Teapot Dome and other scandals of the Harding administration. The only conclusion is that history does repeat—with one difference. Today we managed to combine the chief anti-Communist inquisitor with the architect of the Watergate scandal. Come to think of it, there is another difference: Harding died in office while our man resigned.

The prohibition experiment which spawned gangsters and rum-runners is paralleled by our present prohibition of marijuana and the law breakers and smugglers it produces.

REAL ESTATE

The decade of the 1920's witnessed one real estate boom after another. To begin with, the price of farm land soared following the war. This was hardly surprising, since wartime demand had pushed the price of wheat, corn, and cattle to record levels. Farmers were not immune to the universal desire to become rich and about the only way they could see to accomplish this laudible objective was to buy more land on which to raise more wheat, corn, and cattle.

Unfortunately, the average farmer could only acquire additional land by borrowing heavily and when the additional deluge of wheat, corn, and cattle hit the market, prices collapsed both for farm products and farm land. Thousands, in fact, hundreds of thousands of farmers were unable to meet their mortgage payments and property taxes, which had risen along with the inflated land values. When their mortgages were foreclosed, these suddenly landless farmers were forced to migrate to the cities. So were many country merchants and bankers, whose personal fortunes were closely tied to that of their rural customers.

As a result of this migration, as well as an even greater influx of immigrants from abroad (more than four million during the 1920's), American cities mushroomed as never before. Mushroomed literally, since across the land new buildings called "skyscrapers" could be seen growing daily out of the barren prairies and along the seashores. Real estate values grew along with the skyscrapers until enough new subdivisions had been staked out to accommodate the future growth of the cities for 10 years, 20 years, or, as some said, for 100 years. For every buyer of a lot who actually planned to build a house, or of a builder who actually planned to live in it, there were several who confidently expected to sell them to a greater fool at a higher price. Such confident expectations are not unjustified during an inflationary period and it worked for awhile during the 20's. However, before long most cities were surrounded by row upon row of unoccupied, deteriorating houses and weeds were growing in the subdivision streets. The speculators who, after all, could abandon their speculations with the loss of only a small down payment, looked around for greener pastures which, they discovered, were to be found in a canyon called Wall Street.

FLORIDA

First let's look at the biggest real estate bubble of them all, which grew like the proverbial beanstalk along Florida's gold coast. This phenomenon would, no doubt, have earned a special place in the heart of Charles Mackay, had he lived to witness it. Certainly it would have ranked high among the follies described in his book.

In 1920 the population of Miami was 30,000. By 1925, when the land boom had reached its dizzy peak, it had jumped to 75,000. This did not include tourists and other transient speculators who would probably have swelled the population at any one time to more than 100,000. Even counting those transients, Miami was then a town about the same size as Peoria, Illinois, or Topeka, Kansas, today.

Yet in 1925 the *Miami Herald* was the world's largest newspaper; at least if one measured advertising lineage rather than editorial content. A single issue might run to 500 pages—most of it devoted to real estate ads. People from Boston to Seattle subscribed to the *Herald* to keep up with the constantly rising value of the land they had bought or were planning to buy, just as people today subscribe to *The Wall Street Journal* to keep up with business opportunities and the stock market.

In the Miami of 1925 real estate offices were more numerous than saloons had been in Virginia City and every office employed 10 or 20 agents who were selling, it seemed, instant passports to wealth. Anyone who could afford the trip to Florida could afford to take a flyer in land because the usual terms were 10% down. In return the buyer received a piece of paper or "binder" which gave him immediate title to the land he had bought (more often than not without seeing it)—at least until the next payment came due in 30 days. The problem of how to pay these deferred installments did not worry the eager new buyer half as much as the problem of where he was to spend the night when all of the hotels were full.

As for the second payment, the new buyer confidently expected to sell his binders to still newer buyers long before the payment came due—and most of them did—for awhile. Binders were bought and then resold at higher and higher prices despite the fact that land for sale was about as scarce as the ever present mosquitoes. Just about all of the land from Miami to Palm Beach, plus miles of inland swamplands, where not even a model T could penetrate, had been subdivided into 50-foot lots. Even submerged lots that no one had ever seen sold for at least $5,000 and were promptly resold for $10,000, $15,000, and even $20,000.

Obviously, such madness could not last for long. By the spring of 1926 the bubble began to deflate. New buyers became scarcer and/or were put off by the ever-mounting prices. Binder buyers, who had neither the money required nor the intention of paying any second installment, began to default in increasing numbers. In fact, it was not unusual for a whole series of binder buyers to default and when this occurred the original sellers would find themselves once again the owners of land which was now encumbered with back taxes and other assessments, which were now much higher due to the inflated assessed valuations.

The final knockout blow was delivered by a particularly severe hurricane, which leveled most of Miami plus many of the surrounding housing developments which, it was discovered with the aid of hindsight, had not been built to withstand hurricanes. Many a newly created nabob also discovered that if paper fortunes could be created with unbelievable speed in Florida real estate they could be wiped out even faster. The bustling real estate offices that had decorated every street corner were suddenly abandoned, as were half-completed housing developments and skyscrapers. Overnight

Miami became, comparatively speaking, a ghost town that did not fully recover until after World War II.

Enthusiasm for real estate speculations went into a nation-wide tailspin following the Florida debacle. Nor did it revive for some time. Not, in fact, for nearly half a century and then in California rather than Florida. However, the speculative appetite of the country had only been whetted by stories of quick fortunes emanating from Florida. Needless to say, the fortunes made received far more publicity than the fortunes lost and, no doubt, lingered longer in the public's imagination. After a year or two of recuperation, even those who had been badly burned in Florida were ready to try their luck in the new gambling arena which had shifted northward. The small talk at parties across the land was about to shift from binders, tropical lagoons, and Coral Gables to margin accounts, Radio, and General Motors.

THE BIG BULL MARKET

I believe that history will repeat, and that the 1980's will repeat the 1920's. On a time scale, 1980 can be equated to 1926, bearing in mind that the time required for the cycle to unfold is two or three times longer, reflecting an economy that is two or three times larger.

Early in 1928 the Dow Jones Industrial Average chalked up an all-time high when it broke through the magical barrier of 200. Veteran observers of the market felt, almost unanimously, that the bull market that had started seven years earlier at the DJIA level of 65 had finally reached the dangerous stage. Therefore, many prudent traders were holding cash, bonds, or had sold the high-fliers short. They concluded—correctly—that the public was finally entering the market in a big way; in the twelve months just ended, margin debt had risen by almost $1 billion; an unprecedented rise, which indicated that speculative activity was reaching the dangerous stage. Volume of trading had also jumped to previously unimagined levels, and when that happened it was time for them to get out. But they were premature.

What was happening? First, a general feeling of euphoria pervaded the country (except among farmers); anyone willing to take a little risk could get rich—and during the Roaring Twenties, it seemed just about everyone was willing to risk more than a little. In fact, millions were not only willing but eager to stake their all on a piece of Florida landscape they had never seen. Or, when that went sour, how about buying 50 shares of Radio on a conservative 20% margin? After all, only $1,000 was needed to handle that transaction, and the arithmetic was simple enough. If you put $1,000 in a savings account at 5%, a year later you were richer by $50. In contrast, Radio might go from 100 to 500 (which it did), and at that point you would have multiplied your original not by a multiple of five, but by a multiple of twenty! Such were the lures of margin trading. Moreover, if you were lucky enough to latch on to two or three real movers like Radio, Stutz Motors, or National Bellas Hess, you could become wealthy.

In addition, the general atmosphere of euphoria proved contagious. It even infected the usually immune Federal Reserve Board members, who had just encouraged the easy-money environment needed by lowering the discount rate and buying government securities in the open market. Not that these steps were taken to encourage speculation—perish the thought. According to offical explanations, they were intended to help England weather an ill-conceived return to the gold standard.

Most economists and investment services issued pessimistic statements concerning the outlook for the market and for business activity. One notable exception was the usually silent Calvin Coolidge, who publicly announced that, in his opinion, brokers' loans were not too high. So with professional opinion almost unanimously bearish (contrary opinion doesn't always work), or at least cautious, the stage was set for the totally unexpected: the most spectacular phase of the bull market. Nothing like it had ever been experienced before—or since. In the spring of 1928, as noted, most stocks were considered to be overvalued and much too high by those most knowledgeable in the ways of Wall Street. The Jesse Livermores and Roger Babsons were about to learn that credit inflation in the form of low margins, plus a get-rich-quick psychology, could completely overthrow their cherished concepts of what constituted normal price-earnings ratios, dividend yields, and the like.

Admittedly, in the spring of 1928, stocks were already ridiculously overpriced by all past standards. Yet, in the subsequent eighteen months the Dow Jones Industrial Average almost doubled, while speculative favorites soared twice and then three times as much. Nor were these spectacular gains confined to offbeat secondary stocks and groups. The speculative favorites of that day were not at all comparable to the speculative favorites of our day, such as the gambling stocks of recent memory. Instead, blue chips led the parade.

Radio soared from 100 to 500 (without ever paying a dividend), American Can went from 80 to 180, Union Carbide from 145 to 415, Westinghouse from 90 to 310, and General Electric from 130 to 400. Of course, many low-priced stocks chalked up much wider percentage gains. And remember these gains came *after* the bull market was already seven years old!

Who was paying these preposterously high prices? Mr. Average Man was. Dreams of unimagined wealth to be realized in common stocks captured the imagination of the whole country, just as tulips had mesmerized the Dutch, the South Seas the English, and the Mississippi Company the French.

Moreover, the panjandrums of the big bull market occasionally took time off from masterminding their notorious pools to further inflame the mass hysteria. For example, John J. Raskob, who was a top executive of both General Motors and du Pont, published an article in the *Ladies' Home Journal* with the enticing title, "Everybody Ought to Be Rich." How was this universally desired objective to be achieved? By investing only $15 a month in common stocks; at the end of twenty years you would have at least $80,000, plus an income of $400 a month (equivalent, perhaps, to $1,500 a month today).

Like most prophecies (including mine?), this one fell somewhat short of the mark. However, in fairness to Mr. Raskob, I estimate that anyone who managed to follow his advice wound up with about $20,000 and an income of $100 a month—which wasn't such a bad achievement, considering the war, depression, and other unpleasant events that intervened.

There were also some more down-to-earth forces behind the big bull market: namely, big money. Men who had made fortunes elsewhere converged on Wall Street simultaneously— whether by coincidence or design, no one knew for sure. They included men like W. C. Durant, who had recently sold his interest in General Motors and had millions to throw into the market; Arthur Cutten, who had amassed a fortune in wheat; George F. Baker, who had made several fortunes in real estate; the Fisher Brothers, who had recently sold their chassis company to General Motors; and others, all of whom brought money into Wall Street.

A comparable force today would be for Arab oil money to flow out of real estate, gold and money-market funds into American stocks (which may conceivably happen). Or, for a massive shift of money to occur from savings accounts to the stock market—which is not only a possibility, but a certainty if inflation assumes runaway proportions.

Did this new breed of speculator, with so much new money to invest, realize that the market was already too high by past standards? Perhaps this is exactly what attracted them to Wall Street at this particular time. After all, when all of the smug individuals, who watched in amazement as General Motors, Radio, or Montgomery Ward jumped three or four points one day and nine or ten the next sold out, who would be left to sell? The same potentially explosive situation could develop when present-day stockholders appreciate the implications of the runaway inflation that lies ahead of us.

In addition, these new bulls knew that thousands of presumably sophisticated (in their own eyes, at least) operators had been selling stocks short on the time-tested theory that stocks were too high and therefore could only go down. But they were wrong. Raskob, Durant, and the others knew that if, instead, prices were pushed still higher, the shorts would be squeezed and forced to cover at the higher level, just as buyers were forced to sell when the market declined and they could not meet their margin calls. This, of course, is exactly what happened. Even wily old-timers like Jesse Livermore got caught in this bear trap. However, Jesse—unlike many others— realized what was happening before it was too late and switched from bear to bull in time to avoid catastrophe.

Week after week the market climbed higher although the advance was interrupted from time to time by terrifying reactions—terrifying, at least, to the thousands who received margin calls they were unable or unwilling to meet. All too often they were sold out at the bottom and left penniless, only to watch helplessly as the stocks they had sold rebounded to new highs within a few days or weeks.

Many economists and professors now proclaimed the arrival of a new era in which stock prices would remain on a new and permanently higher plateau. Who could—or wanted to—argue with them? However, there were forces at work that would eventually break the back of the big bull market. For one thing, the Federal Reserve Board raised the discount rate three times (to 5%) and sold the government securities they had previously bought, plus a lot more. Theoretically, these moves should soak up surplus funds and act as a brake on rising prices. They did no such thing—at least, not immediately. The bull market was generating its own momentum, fueled by funds supplied by corporations, as well as by the banking system. In fact, money was flowing into Wall Street from all over the world—attracted by call-money rates, which eventually reached 20%.

As 1928 turned into 1929, the predictions of Professor Fisher and others about permanently high stock prices seemed justified; after all, hadn't the demand for stocks permanently outstripped the supply? As it turned out, not for long. Since no one wanted to own bonds anymore (and with good reason, when stocks were soaring), corporations stopped issuing them. Instead, attracted by the unprecedented levels at which their stocks were selling, they obligingly stepped in and filled the demand with a deluge of new common-stock financing.

This addition to the supply side of the equation contributed to the crash of October 1929. However, it was only one of many factors. A sustained rise in the stock market can continue only so long as two fundamental conditions are fulfilled. First, it must attract a steady flow of new money; either newly created money or money released from the sale of other assets. In this connection, it should be remembered that there was no general inflation during the 20's. The big bull market was, in effect, a vampire feeding on the remainder of the economy. Had inflation prevailed at the current double-digit rate, the "higher plateau" witnessed in 1928 and 1929 would probably have been maintained and surpassed. More important, the subsequent stock-market crash and prolonged depression might have been avoided—or at least postponed for many years beyond 1929.

Second, the psychological atmosphere must also favor buyers rather than sellers. Bullish psychology can maintain control only so long as *forced* selling does not grow to unmanageable proportions. The point to remember here is that nobody *has* to buy stocks, whereas every day some people are *forced* to sell due to their personal circumstances. In the fall of 1929, the psychological balance favoring the bulls was overwhelmed by an avalanche of forced selling: the "personal circumstances" behind it were one million active margin accounts.

Even today, with margin requirements set by the Federal Reserve at 50%, a steep market decline produces margin calls, which can trigger additional selling, as occurred in 1974 and again in October 1978. In 1929 the only margin requirements were those set by the member firms themselves. These varied from one firm to the next, and no one knows for sure what the average was. However, it is certain that hundreds of thousands of accounts were financed on a margin of no more than 20% of the value of the stocks held and, in some cases, even less. When overnight margin calls were not met, the stocks held in the account were sold at the opening the following morning— regardless of the price they would bring.

Each such spasm of forced liquidation was followed by a vigorous rebound as bargain hunters rushed in to buy stocks that now seemed dirt cheap. During the early stages of the bear market, these buyers were confident that the bull market would resume as soon as the "normal" reaction ran its course. However, once the tide had turned, rallies failed to last more than a few days before the decline resumed. If these new buyers bought on margin and could not meet the calls for additional money, they, too, were forced out almost immediately. Needless to say, this Niagara of forced selling was swelled by those investors who owned their stocks outright (the majority, by far), but were now infected by the contagious atmosphere of fear and rushed to sell while they could still "get out even" or, barring that relatively painless outcome, sold to "cut their losses."

Unlike those investors who failed to meet margin calls, these sellers had some capital left, so they were able to keep the dismal cycle going until they finally gave up in disgust or ran out of money. In this way the bear market fed on itself, just as the bull market had a short time before. However, there was one conspicuous difference: the astonishing gains achieved during the final two years of the big bull market were canceled out in only two months of the new bear market.

Where in the cycle of psychology do we stand today if current trends continue to parallel those of the 20's? First, we must bear in mind that inflation plus a larger economy will stretch out the time sequence by a factor of two or three. Allowing for this, I think that 1980 overlaps 1926; i.e., when the Florida real estate boom began to run out of steam. If so, then an inflationary, flight-from-the-dollar-fueled bull market will dominate the decade of the 1980's, which will make the big bull market of the 1920's seem like a pre-game dry run before the real game begins.

8

1980-1990:
The Bull Market Decade

For a quarter of a century after the first atomic bomb was dropped, the stock market boomed. Investors discovered that if they held common stocks patiently, they could realize a far greater return in terms of income plus price appreciation than if they invested solely for income. In fact, they realized, well over twice as much. After all, top-quality bonds were yielding between 2% and 3% so there was not much incentive to hold them in preference to stocks, which were yielding more than that and, in addition, regularly chalked up new all-time highs—at least for those who patiently held them through the inevitable intermediate declines and periods of consolidation.

111

Toward the end of this period, interest rates started to climb, while stocks stopped climbing and began to decline. Like programmed robots, investors turned in unison to bonds, Treasury bills, and savings accounts and away from common stocks, which then declined in a positively alarming manner. But the investors failed to consider that, owing to inflation, these alluringly liberal yields were not as liberal as they appeared to be by past standards.

In fact, this urge to switch turned into a stampede when interest rates (and commodities) went through the ceiling and stocks sought the basement during the early 1970's. As a result, the most severe bear market since the 1930's coincided with the most severe inflation since the days of the Continental Congress. This was contrary to all orthodox theory and led to the now-popular belief that stocks are not a good hedge against inflation.

What had happened? The laws of money and human nature had not been repealed. Far from it. When inflation fears mount, money always seeks out those assets which promise to yield the greatest gains. High interest rates were not the only attraction. A whole host of exotic commodities, ranging from gold and silver to grains, cotton, cocoa, coffee, and sugar were soaring into the stratosphere, and a monumental rush to buy them got underway. The very nature of these markets—especially as it affected newcomers to them—led to still more selling of stocks. To trade in commodities, investors need to put up only 5% to 10% of the value of the contract they are buying or selling. This means that a relatively small decline in price may result in a call for more margin. When the markets are moving fast, as they were in 1973 and 1974, traders who take a position on Monday may get a call for more margin on Wednesday or Thursday. This is exactly what happened to many traders who were forced to liquidate stocks in order to meet such calls. The end result was a flow of capital out of the

stock market which, in turn, tended to feed itself as the resulting declines of 80% and 90% in many stocks will testify.

When the commodity bubble finally burst (perhaps only
temporarily?) speculators turned to farmland and suburban
real estate as the ideal inflation hedge. This demand, combined with the normal demand by people seeking roofs over
their heads, produced the greatest real estate boom in half a
century. How much of this demand was artificial and how
much was real is debatable. However, there are some clues. In
California, for example, an estimated 30% of new houses were
sold but not lived in. They were built or bought by speculators, who expected to resell them at a quick profit and often
did so.

How inflated have real estate values grown? They have outpaced the inflation rate by a margin of at least two or three to
one. I know from first-hand experience. In 1965 I sold a house
in Los Altos, California for $40,000. The same house was re-
sold last year for $166,000. This particular piece of real estate
appreciated three times faster than the rate of inflation. I also
happen to know that the latest owner is a salesman earning a
modest salary. What if he gets laid off?

Already there are numerous signs suggesting that the real
estate bubble may be approaching the bursting point for urban and suburban properties. Rural property may still be a
good inflation hedge—the pros and cons are weighed in Chapter 11. While inflation benefits borrowers, there are exceptions
which every reader of this book should guard against. Be a
borrower, but don't become so overextended that you are unable to meet the interest payments when some unforeseen
difficulty arises. Forced liquidation usually happens at the
worst possible time. If homeowners are unable to sell in a
falling market, they will simply walk away (if their equity in
the property is small) and let the lenders repossess it. This is
already happening in many areas. However, this does not

mean that the defaulters are destitute. Most of these speculators have other assets and, as happened in the 1920's, when
the real estate party is over, they will make an effort to recoup
in the only remaining game with a real chance: the stock
market.

Even those stock-market investors who maintained the faith
changed their operating philosophy; at least this is true of
those professionals whose performance is a matter of record.
In a nutshell, their "hold stocks forever" philosophy was replaced by a "buy-today, sell-tomorrow" philosophy. These
new prophets (the old crop faded along with their super-
growth stocks) preached that the key to successful investing
was to trade from stocks to gold, to commodities, to bonds, to
Treasury bills, to foreign currencies (though not necessarily in
that order) depending on the position of the inflation cycle. In
short, trading in stocks alone, à la Jesse Livermore and company, was not enough. Stocks were not the only things that
responded to the pressures of inflation. In addition, investors
must also master the intricacies of money-market instruments,
gold, commodities, and foreign currencies.

What exactly is this new "inflation cycle" school of investing? The premise is that the money-credit policy set by the
Federal Reserve causes *predictable* cycles. If you hope to consistently transfer money from other and less knowledgeable
pockets into your own, you must anticipate and take advantage of these future cycles. You will then know when and
what to buy and sell.

It's really quite simple—or so they say! When the inflation
rate accelerates—i.e., interest rates turn up—you sell stocks
and bonds and buy Treasury bills, gold, and commodities.
When it begins to slow down—i.e., interest rates turn down—
you sell your Treasury bills, gold, and commodities, and buy
stocks and bonds. If this sounds complicated and difficult, wait

a minute. It's only the beginning. You must also know exactly where you are in the cycle in order to determine which of these offers the greatest potential and therefore should be bought or sold at any given moment.

There is one thing wrong with this strategy: It can't be done. Not even if we are to experience the same more-or-less regular heating up and cooling off of inflation experienced during the past decade. (And by now you know that I, for one, don't think that this orderly progression of inflation will continue in the future.) Even if it does, mastering the art of trading in stocks alone—as distinguished from buying and then holding them indefinitely—is an impossibility in itself, without trying to anticipate the swings in commodities, gold, foreign currencies, Treasury bills, real estate, and bonds as well.

The fact that this strategy worked—on paper, and with the aid of hindsight—during the 1970's does not mean that it will work during the 1980's and 1990's. Any hindsight series of events can be made to predict future market trends—such as the winners of the Rose Bowl. Even if the more-or-less orderly uptrend in the inflation rates should continue, with the now-familiar speed-ups and slowdowns, the idea that investors can move in and out of each vehicle based on its potential gain during each stage of the cycle will assure nothing but losses. The ability to effect such timing is a figment of the money manager's imaginations. This is why their records of performance are not as good as that of an unmanaged broad-market index.

This sweeping statement is not based on mere theory, nor on a revelation received during a session in my prayer chamber. It is based on bitter personal experience, plus many years of observing the bitter personal experiences of others who tried it—usually at the urging of their friendly stockbroker. During the years I was a stockbroker with one of the largest

member firms, I studied the records of traders in both stocks
and commodities, and never encountered a single successful
one—not over the long term.

If 99% of in-and-out traders lose money, who makes money?
The winners are long-term investors, brokers, and the tax collector. This means that traders support the brokers and Uncle
Sam, whereas the long-term investor does not—or at least not
to the same degree. I cannot repeat too often that short-term
profits are taxed as straight income, and that part of the profit
is gone forever because only a tiny part of subsequent short-
term losses can be offset and recovered from taxes already
paid.

As for the broker's cut, commission rates have risen at least
as fast as inflation. Because of this, and higher taxes, the pe-
rennial question: "Where are the customer's yachts?" is even
more pertinent today than it was in the time of J. P. Morgan.
Which reminds me of the old-timer who managed the brokerage office where I was a new recruit. His advice when
dealing with customers was summed up in one sentence; "We
don't care what they do as long as they do something." Perhaps, he was thinking of one of his occasional customers—Jesse
Livermore—who once gave him an order to sell 30,000 Steel
"at the market." Jesse was the greatest trader of them all, yet
he died broke and a suicide as well.

WHY STOCKS ARE CHEAP

Stocks are cheap because current fashion regards them as the
worst possible hedge against inflation. How did this belief gain
such a wide following, when it contradicts rational reasoning
as well as common sense?

First, other types of inflation hedges have dominated the
headlines for several years. One after another they soared to
record levels, and some of them are still doing so. Remember

the headlines? Gold, Swiss francs, silver, coffee, cocoa, sugar, houses, farmland—not to mention oil? In contrast, stocks throughout these inflationary years have failed to exceed their best levels achieved nearly fifteen years ago. Then, too, a debacle like that of 1973–1974 is not quickly forgotten—and once burned, investors tend to avoid the fire. How cheap are stocks compared to just about everything else?

In 1967 the Value Line composite index of more than 900 industrial stocks [11] earned $1.43 a share; by 1979 this figure had risen to an estimated $4.40 a share. Dividends paid on each share had risen from $.80 to $1.65, tangible book values shot up from $13.05 to $29.80, yet are substantially understated since, for the most part, they reflect the low cost of fixed assets rather than their current value. Despite these gains, the market price of the index has remained unchanged since 1967.

The better-known Dow Jones Industrial Average tells the same story. It confirms the conclusion that, even ignoring the probability of more inflation, stocks today represent better value than at any time since the 1930's. When the Dow Jones Industrial Average first touched the 1,000 level early in 1966, the 30 stocks included in this index earned $55.00. At a similar peak in 1972, they earned $68.00, despite price controls, which the demagogues who rule us figured would get votes and maybe even slow down inflation. It did neither. By 1979 the earning power of the Dow Jones stocks had doubled, which means that it has risen about the same rate as inflation; yet the price of the index has remained well below the 1,000 level.

Critics may argue with justification that stocks were overvalued in 1966 and again in 1972. However, by 1976, when the Dow average touched the magic 1,000 mark once again (but only for a few days), the picture was changing decisively. Since then corporate executives who, after all, usually own a sizable amount of their own stock, have awakened to the potential of their own company's stock as an inflation hedge. Dividend payments expanded sharply and are now being increased at a faster pace than inflation. This alone could trigger a massive flow of funds back into stocks, when investors who keep their funds in bank and savings accounts wake up to what is happening.

Since World War I, stocks have yielded an annual return of 9%, divided about equally between price appreciation and dividend income. There is every reason to assume that this relationship will continue to prevail during the remainder of this century. If it does, then on the basis of current dividend rates, a combined return of at least 15% annually can be anticipated *without any future inflation.* If inflation merely continues at the present rate or reaches runaway proportions, which seems likely, then this conservative projection of a 15% return will jump to 30%, 45%, or even higher. As a result, a flight from sterile assets, such as insurance, savings accounts, gold and money into the stock market will itself assume runaway dimensions.

So a convincing argument can be made to prove that stocks are more undervalued than they have been at any time in the past thirty or forty years. While stocks sell for less and earn far more than they did over a decade ago, everything else has skyrocketed. Gold is up more than 1,000% (an equivalent rise would take the Dow Jones average to over 10,000), old houses are up half as much, while most commodities have at least doubled.

What is the yield on houses? To the owner, there is none. Instead, you pay taxes and maintenance expenses. What is the yield on gold or silver? Again, nothing. You must pay to insure and store your hoard—plus worry about it. What is the yield on pork bellies or sugar? Again, nothing—unless you are in the business of manufacturing bacon or candy. In contrast, most corporations own tangible assets worth far more than the market price of their stocks and pay dividends that are rising at least as fast as the inflation rate. In fact, there is no limit to how high, in dollar terms, the yields on stocks can go.

Nor is there any limit on how high the value of their underlying assets can go. Steel plants, oil refineries, forest lands, coal, and other mineral deposits all will rise in value—at least as fast as inflation. This is why the next great speculative boom will be concentrated in the stock market and will push the Dow average—which has fluctuated between 700 and 1,000 for the past fifteen years—to 2,000, 3,000, and 5,000 or more.

Second, corporate profits are said to be overstated due to inflation. Of course they are. By past standards, everything is overstated and overpriced! These Cassandras of doom cite two reasons why higher profits are illusory. First, they say, the value of inventories is rising; therefore, when they are sold, the "windfall" profits realized are nonrecurring. This would be a valid argument only if deflation—rather than inflation—lies ahead. Meanwhile, the only reason for being in business is to sell your products at a higher price than you paid for them. If you can accomplish this end by adding value to your product—for example, by converting crude oil into more valuable gasoline—fine. If, in addition, the crude oil you own is increasing in value, due to inflation, better still. As long as prices continue to rise, the profit realized from inventory gains is just as real as the profits realized from processing them.

The second and more serious criticism of inventory profits is that inflation makes depreciation charges, which provide the cash flow needed to replace and expand plant capacity, grossly inadequate. This means that income taxes are reduced by the amount of depreciation that companies can write off. Therefore, during an inflationary period, corporations are paying more income taxes than are justified. As a result, this money is not available to replace plants and equipment, which are now more costly in dollar terms. The corporation must borrow to make up the difference. This argument is valid and, as a matter of fact, this borrowing is actually taking place.

However, like depreciation charges, the interest on the new debt is tax deductible. Moreover, the gain to be realized from paying back the debt in depreciated dollars, while retaining the new plant and equipment, will probably at least equal the taxes paid as a result of inadequate depreciation charges. This line of reasoning obviously breaks down when and if inflation slows down permanently or reverses. After all, taxes paid—at least, by a consistently profitable company—are gone forever. So when stocks decline in the face of rising profits and underlying assets, investors are betting that inflation is not here to stay and will not get worse in the years ahead. I have great faith in the Theory of Contrary Opinion, which holds that majority opinion is always wrong. I think the theory will be vindicated in spectacular fashion during the 1980's.

Let's look at the arithmetic involved. We all know from practical experience that a properly maintained capital asset (a manufacturing plant, office furniture, or automobile) will continue to provide useful service long after it has been fully depreciated. In fact, mechanics tell me that a well-maintained five-year-old car may well be a more valuable asset than the latest model costing twice as much. In short, this argument implies that at the end of the depreciation period the value of a capital asset will be zero. On the contrary, we know that during an inflationary period the value may, in reality, be two or three times *higher than its original cost.*

Assume that a plant cost $1 million fifteen years ago. Today the replacement value is $3 million. Yet the company has been able to write off only $1 million. Admittedly, if it had been able to write off the entire replacement value of $3 million, its taxes would have been reduced by one-half or more.

The stock market realizes this and values the stock accordingly. But does it take into account the fact that the company's property and plant may have appreciated in value even more than the depreciation that was not charged off?

Inadequate depreciation charges are more than canceled out by the inflation that causes them. Corporate managements are well aware of these facts of life. To illustrate, Robert H. Allen, chairman of the board of Gulf Resources and Chemical, in 1978 appraised the underlying value of his company's common shares (which had fluctuated in price between $10 and $15 for many years) in his annual report to the stockholders:

Products such as salt, fertilizer, lead and silver have been produced in this country since the arrival of the earliest settlers. They will continue to be produced and their consumption will continue to grow. The ownership of facilities in place, which produce them, gives Gulf Resources a franchise made unique by the enormous difficulty and cost of duplicating capital assets today.

There are many ways of looking at this "facilities in place" analysis. Each share of Gulf Resources stock represents about $17 of book value. My best estimate would indicate that if the cost of new facilities were substituted for property, plant and equipment included in the balance sheet, the resulting value would be about $100. Even this amount does not include the value of reserves in the ground. Gulf Resources has more than 70 million tons of coal reserves in Pennsylvania and substantial additional tonnage at the Cardiff project in Tennessee. Gulf Resources holds the equivalent of 28 billion cubic feet of proven and probable natural gas reserves. The lithium ore reserves equate to almost 50 years of production at current rates. It is more difficult to quantify accurately the lead, zinc and silver reserves held by Bunker Hill. It is perhaps significant that these veins have been mined for almost 100 years with never more than a few years' reserves established with a high degree of certainty.

My own calculations indicate that these reserves in the ground are worth more than $100 for each share of Gulf Re-

sources common stock. This, together with Mr. Allen's estimate of the replacement value of fixed assets, totals $200 a
share. By the time this book is published, these assets will be
worth much more than that. Yet, as I write, Gulf Resources
stock is valued by the market at around $20 a share. This
means investors currently value 2½ ounces of gold as equivalent to 100 shares of Gulf Resources stock. Such are the irrationalities of the marketplace.

To sum up: When we complain that depreciation schedules
do not adequately reflect inflation, we are saying that it would
be nice to lower the corporate income-tax rate via more liberal depreciation schedules. Since corporations and retailers
pass on higher taxes to the consumer, it is not the corporation
that pays; as usual, it is the hapless individual consumer.

STOCKS TO BUY

Inflation has turned the everyday world topsy-turvy and it has
shaken up the financial world even more. Thus, in the pre-
inflation world—other things being equal—being debt-free was
the ultimate corporate status symbol. Today, the management
of any company that is free of debt is obviously lacking in
initiative and imagination. After all, if you can borrow one
dollar today and pay back only 50 cents tomorrow, you owe it
to your stockholders to do so; especially in view of the tax
laws that make it impossible to adequately depreciate capital
assets.

It follows that if two companies are equally well managed,
the one with the largest ratio of debt to equity will benefit
most from inflation. How can you lose if you use 50- or 25-
cent dollars to replace aging plants or to add to your natural-
resource base?

Equally obvious—but not to the market, these days—those
companies with large reserves of natural resources and/or low
labor costs (less than 25% of sales) are especially well placed

to ride out the inflationary years ahead. Another yardstick to watch for: Can the price of a company's products be raised without advance notice and without noticeably reducing demand? These yardsticks immediately rule out all regulated industries, such as utilities, banks, most railroads and airlines—all of which are plagued not only by regulation, but also by high labor costs.

The lesson taught by OPEC has been learned by many smaller natural-resource-rich companies. When supply exceeds demand, they hold back production until demand catches up with supply and the price rises accordingly. To quote Mr. Allen of Gulf Resources once again: "During 1978 production of zinc was intentionally held back because of oversupply in the world's zinc markets." This strategy evidently worked because by early 1979 the price of zinc had risen from 29½ cents a pound a year earlier to an all-time high of 39½ cents a pound—an increase of 33.9%. A famous pre-OPEC example of this practice is DeBeers Consolidated Mines which, as long as anyone can remember, has controlled diamond prices by withholding production. Such companies are in a position to raise prices "without noticeably reducing demand."

In a nutshell, any nonregulated company with a high debt-to-equity ratio and low labor costs (in the range of 10% to 20% of sales) should be in an ideal position to prosper during the inflationary 1980's. Another type of company that is certain to prosper is one that has engineered, or is about to make a "unique profit breakthrough." I will go into this approach in more detail in Chapter 10.

More conservative investors should consider the merits of closed-end investment trusts. Every bull market is selective—even one that is fueled by an inflation-inspired flight from the dollar. One of the features of the 1921–1929 bull market was its great selectivity. Numerous stocks topped out as early as 1925, 1926, and 1927. No doubt, the bull market of the 1980's will prove to be equally selective. To correctly select the super-winners that will lead the parade will require more astuteness (or luck) than most of us possess. One way to ensure participation is to own shares in mutual funds or closed-end trusts.

There are three choices available: (1) mutual funds that sell at net asset value plus a sales "load" or commission that averages 8%; (2) mutual funds that sell at net asset value without a sales commission charge; and (3) closed-end investment trusts which do not issue new shares at net asset value and which therefore may sell either above or below net asset value.

Since the long-term performance of all three will be about the same, choice #1 can be eliminated. There is no reason (except the gullibility of uninformed investors) to pay an 8% commission for one fund when an equally good one which charges no sales commission is available. Thus the choice narrows down to either a no-load mutual fund or an investment trust. The fund issues new shares and redeems outstanding shares at net asset value. It does not take a financial genius to see that a no-load fund represents a better buy than a similar fund that gives a salesman 8% to sell it to you. It also represents a better buy than a closed-end trust that is selling at a premium over net asset value. However, the closed-end trust represents a better buy when it is selling for a substantial discount from net asset value.

Closed-end trusts sell at a premium when speculative sentiment views the future with a high degree of optimism; and at a discount when pessimism dominates the market. In recent years, pessimism has prevailed to such an extent that closed-end trusts are now selling at discounts of between 20% and 30% below net asset value, which presents built-in upside potential. Even assuming justification for a small discount representing management expenses—which is never available when you buy mutual funds—these trusts are still drastically undervalued.

If you conclude that this situation is irrational, you are right; the market is made by people and people are irrational—or, possibly, to use a more charitable word—uninformed. Of course, there are also more tangible reasons for such opportunities. Thousands of salesmen are actively out ringing doorbells and telephones selling mutual funds; whereas, once the original issue is sold, no one is actively selling investment trusts: Not even stockbrokers, because a customer buys a closed-end trust for the long pull and therefore no longer represents a good source of commission business for a broker.

As of late 1979, the following trusts were selling at a substantial discount below net asset value. Their prices are carried daily in most newspapers and every Monday their net asset value as of the previous Friday's close is listed in *The Wall Street Journal.*

TABLE 5
CLOSED-END TRUSTS

Trust	Traded	Discount
American General Convertible	NYSE	22%
Baker, Fentress & Company	OTC	34
Bancroft Convertible	ASE	24
Central Securities	ASE	30
General American Investors	NYSE	22
Lehman Corporation	NYSE	24
Madison Fund	NYSE	21
New American Fund	OTC	24
Tri-Continental Corp.	NYSE	22
U.S. & Foreign Securities	NYSE	26

Traded: OTC—Over the counter
ASE—American Stock Exchange
NYSE—New York Stock Exchange

STOCKS TO AVOID

By now it must be clear why I think that the people who lend money will be among the unavoidable victims of inflation. This includes banks, savings-and-loan associations, and finance companies. All have prospered from moderate inflation for the same reason that most other companies have prospered: volume of business plus interest rates have grown faster than costs. However, in an environment of runaway inflation, those who borrow short and lend long are in trouble.

The finance companies will be the most vulnerable because their profit is determined solely by the spread between the cost of borrowing and lending. Unlike banks, they do not create new money directly, but rather profit from the spread. Banks do not have quite the same problem of replacing their inventory of money at higher prices because a good part of the money they lend did not exist previously. However, they have other problems—especially with credit-card debt. As inflation worsens, personal credit ratings become less and less meaningful.

In ordinary times, bank customers make every effort to maintain unblemished personal credit ratings. This laudable resolution weakens as inflation strengthens. While delinquent individual accounts are small, considered individually, collectively, they represent a serious threat to bank liquidity. After all, credit-card debt is not like a mortgage that is backed by land and a house—both of which are most likely rapidly increasing in value. There is very little a bank can do to collect these debts other than use threats and whatever other forms of intimidation they can think of.

What will be the fate of all those trusting individuals who have been taught that their neighborhood savings bank is the safest possible haven for their money, when their less-trusting neighbors finally recognize the dangers spelled out in this book and rush to withdraw their money?

The usual answer is that you have nothing to worry about because each deposit of up to $40,000 is guaranteed by the Federal Deposit Insurance Corporation. This is only a semi-truth, like all other government propaganda. It may be of some help to you—if you are standing somewhere near the head of the line of depositors waiting to withdraw their money. But you had better be pretty far up front—because the total assets of the FDIC represent only about 5% of total bank deposits.

Furthermore, if you read the fine print in a savings-and-loan association or commercial bank charter of incorporation, you will discover that, under certain circumstances, they are not required to pay back depositors upon demand. Not, in fact, without 30 or 60 days' written notice of their intention to withdraw funds. Furthermore, in a "national emergency," which translates to mean in case of a run on the banks, the President can freeze all withdrawals for the duration of the emergency.

However, my concern here is not with the fate of depositors—hopefully, by now, depositors who read this book will have withdrawn their money and are preparing to invest it in the type of inflation hedges discussed in the next few chapters. My concern here is to stress the danger of investing in the *stocks* of banks and savings-and-loan associations. Again I repeat: they are all borrowing short and lending long, the most dangerous possible combination during a period of runaway inflation. No matter what happens, the banks are in trouble. In a period of deflation, rather than runaway inflation, a large percentage of these loans, with their inflated carrying charges will never be repaid. In a runaway inflation period, they will be repaid in dollars worth only a fraction of their original value. Nor does this dismal outlook allow for the towering structure of doubtful debts made to the developing countries. ("Doubtful" is an overly charitable word to use, in view of a record that comes pretty close to 100% failure to repay.)

Or what about the billions of dollars of Middle East oil money, which is held by the New York banks and their European branches, in the form of demand deposits and negotiable instruments? What happens when these funds are withdrawn? It is often said that this gigantic reservoir of dollars has nowhere else to go; although there is evidence that some of it is going into foreign currencies, such as the yen, pound, and mark, as well as into real estate.

My contention is that the only haven for this hot money sufficiently large and liquid is Wall Street. Inevitably, this Arab oil money will join the flight from paper money into the only available undervalued, tangible assets left: American stocks.

In addition to the above-mentioned drawbacks, it is almost impossible to determine what the true financial position of a bank is at any given time. More than 50% of the loans of major banks are made to foreign customers; similarly, more than 50% of earnings are generated abroad. These "earnings" are not only, in large part, an invention of bank accountants; the foreign earnings are in foreign currencies. Also, a bank's reserve position may be distorted because a government bond carried on the books at par (100) may be selling in the market for half of its par value. If forced to liquidate these assets in order to meet an unusually large demand by depositors to withdraw funds, or should a few customers fail to renew CDs, many banks might turn out to actually be bankrupt.

LIFE INSURANCE STOCKS

These darlings of Wall Street (from time to time—and right now is one of those times) should also be avoided. You may wonder why, if life insurance is such a bad investment for the insured, is it not a good business for the insurer? Under normal conditions, it is. However, this is not true during a period of runaway inflation. As people wake up, they may well reason: "Of what benefit is the $10,000 policy I have been paying all these years, if it finally pays off in dollars that are worth only $1,000 in purchasing power?"

Then they will either cash in their paid-up policies or borrow against them. You should do this right now. In the future, you may have difficulty getting the insurance companies to honor their legal obligation to make policy loans because this is a money-losing proposition for them—even today. Where else can you borrow money at 5%? This is one sure way to offset your shrunken insurance investment without surrendering the protection you were seeking when you took it out in the first place.

Assume that you bought a $20,000 paid-up life policy several years ago, which today has a cash surrender value of $5,000. You can borrow the $5,000 at 5% interest and still retain $15,000 insurance protection. As more and more policy holders take advantage of this feature insurance company profits will be reduced.

Then, too, the investments held by insurance companies, which are there to ensure that they will be able to pay off death claims, are heavily concentrated in bonds and mortgages which, during runaway inflation, are the worse investment of all. Thus, insurance stocks should be avoided for the reasons discussed in Chapter 6.

THE BLUE CHIPS

Most manufacturing companies such as Ford, General Motors, General Electric, du Pont and similar industrial giants, should be avoided for two reasons. First: their labor costs are high;

and due to the strength of organized labor, are certain to rise at least as fast as the inflation rate. Second: they are able to exert increasingly less control over the prices they must pay for raw materials.

Then, too, the outlook for the auto industry hardly appears bright in view of runaway gasoline prices and the huge capital investment required to turn out more fuel-efficient cars. Remember: failure to meet these government standards and deadlines will result in costly fines and litigation. A possible exception to this line of reasoning would be provided by any company which achieves a breakthrough in a car driven by some entirely new power system, which is more efficient and less polluting, such as fuel cells, more efficient batteries, hydrogen, or some entirely new method. But the very nature of such developments is that they will come—if ever—too late to help those of us whose immediate concern is to survive the inflationary 1980's.

The chemical industry has relatively low labor costs, but is caught in the squeeze of fast-rising raw-material costs. For example, synthetic fibers, such as nylon and dacron, plastics, fertilizers, and other products, are all made from petroleum derivatives. The old-line chemical companies are going to have more and more trouble competing with those oil companies which have chemical divisions that produce the same end products. As oil becomes too valuable to waste as fuel, the oil companies will be in a relatively favorable position since they already own large reserves of low-cost oil and the margin of profit on chemicals and fibers is much higher than on fuel.

A final word: The shares of real estate investment trusts (REITs) should be avoided, because they, like insurance companies, invest in mortgages and construction loans, which means that they, too, borrow short and lend long. This is why most REITs have been in trouble ever since they made their initial and unfortunate appearance a decade ago, and why, as inflation accelerates, their problems will increase rather than diminish. Many REITs have gone bankrupt in recent years, and more can be expected to follow suit during the inflationary 1980's. In fact, the REITs provide a perfect example of how *not* to invest your money during an era of ever-growing inflation.

9

Stocks That Make Millionaires

Not a day passes without the Cassandras along the Potomac assuring those lesser mortals who pay their wages that the nation's number-one problem—inflation—will soon be solved. Well, even a stopped clock tells us the right time twice a day, and, no doubt, inflation will slow down from time to time in the future as it has in the past. It even happened in Germany—but if people so much as nodded off, they missed the slowdowns. By the time they had awakened, the inflation rate had doubled or tripled.

Suppose a major miracle does occur: First, the budget is balanced and then substantially reduced; our lawmakers and

132

labor unions voluntarily reduce their salaries and wages. The government sets an example for price cuts by reducing postal rates and Social Security payments. Farmers and businessmen follow suit by cutting prices all along the line. The Pentagon announces that the Russians are no longer a threat and slashes defense spending. Landlords voluntarily reduce rents. In short, inflation ends overnight. No doubt even more startling miracles have occurred, although I can't immediately think of any.

Nonetheless, something of the sort *could* happen; if not overnight and due to the self-sacrifices of all concerned, then after several more years, when runaway inflation destroys the currency and forces such revaluations. In either event, the program blueprinted in this book is designed to cope just as effectively with normal conditions (or even deflation and depression) as with runaway inflation.

The success of this program depends on allocating your available funds about equally among three categories of assets. The first two include natural resources and other tangible assets which will be discussed in subsequent chapters. The third category will be discussed here. Regardless of whether inflation or deflation, prosperity or depression prevails, some companies will always prosper spectacularly. You can share in their growth and prosperity if you learn how to recognize them when they are still in the early stages of achieving a Unique Profit Breakthrough (UPB). Such a company is on the threshold or very early stages of raising its earning power to a permanently higher plateau.

This is certainly not an original concept. All of the glamour stocks of the past have made Unique Profit Breakthroughs. However, at early stages, few investors are aware of the magnitude of the breakthrough or its unique quality and significance. New standards are needed to identify those companies that qualify.

What causes a common run-of-the-mill company to turn into a UPB winner? It may be a unique and superior new . product. Almost any product you use represented a UPB for some company at one time. For example, Xerox and its dry electrostatic copying machine. It may be a new approach to marketing—McDonald's and franchising, or Avon and door-to-door selling. It may be due to a shift in consumer trends, such as Black & Decker tools, for the do-it-yourself trade. Or a company may exploit a new opportunity ahead of its competitors, as Resorts International did at Atlantic City. A new management might revive a staid old company—for instance, Crown Cork & Seal. I could go on and on because there are many more such UPB opportunities than we realize.

How are we, who are not on the inside, to know the true significance of such developments, as distinguished from the optimistic news continually being pumped out by the public relation departments of just about every corporation? The best way is to know what the insiders are *doing* as contrasted to what they are *saying*. Those who are on the verge of bankruptcy tell us that things never looked better. In contrast, a discovery of a gold deposit is a bonanza to be concealed as long as possible. In short, are the insiders buying or selling their own stock? Fortunately, they are required by law to divulge this information. The complete record is available on the reference shelves of most libraries, or it can be obtained directly from the U.S. Government Printing Office, which publishes once a month the basic information that is filed with the SEC and the stock exchanges.

This information is especially valuable in a potential turnaround situation, when a new management enters the picture. Ordinarily, the new team will not own any of the stock of their new employer. Watch to see if they start buying it and continue to buy it. If they do, you, too, can buy with a great degree of confidence, even if you buy a couple of months later than they did and at a higher price, because the full flowering of the developments they anticipate may lie many years in the future. Patience now becomes all-important.

Sometimes you may watch a stock decline after a new management team has been buying heavily. You may ask, "What good does it do to know the insiders are buying if the stock declines after they buy?" The answer is this: the insiders are measuring the current price of their stock against the earning power they anticipate a year, two years, or even five years ahead. Suppose several insiders have been buying XYZ shares, which have been selling at 15 and earning $1 per share. In recent years, profits have been flat or even declining; in either case, the stock looks like anything but a bargain. More than likely, several brokers and investment services are advising clients who own XYZ to sell and switch the funds into whatever issue their firm is currently pushing. Selling from these sources is swelled by a severe general market decline, which encourages some XYZ holders to give up entirely on the treacherous stock market and switch their money into a savings account, where they won't have to worry about it. As a result of all this selling, XYZ declines to 10 or lower.

To the casual observer, apparently the insiders are "wrong" and those who sold at 15 were "right" as, indeed, from a short-term point of view they are. But consider the position of the insiders. They know that a UPB is underway that promises to boost earnings to $5.00 a share in the near future and, hopefully, to $10.00 a share eventually. In the eyes of the insiders, the stock is dirt cheap at 15. After all, most top management men aren't experts on the stock market—who is? Furthermore, if they are tending their shop, they don't follow the market closely—which is just as well. For all they know, the stock may not decline below 15. Yet they must own stock if they are to profit from the UPB they have engineered. So they start buying at 15. If a decline starts, fine. They buy more on the way down. They are the people who are buying when the stock sinks to 10 or below, where it turns out to have been a truly amazing bargain.

For many years, I wrote a regular article for *Barron's* on insider trading. From my files I will illustrate, in detail, how the above theoretical story actually worked out in practice for one company out of any number I could cite. The beginning of the Crown Cork & Seal story is now ancient history, but enough time has elapsed so that we know the sequel, whereas we don't yet know the outcome of more current examples that I could cite. The principle involved is timeless. It is just as valid today or tomorrow as it was ten or twenty years ago.

John Connelly once explained his philosophy to me after he had become president of Crown Cork. He expected his executives to be rewarded through ownership of stock that they had bought on the open market, rather than via lush salaries, bonuses, or advantageous stock options that could be exercised at a low price (and low risk) later on.

During the 1950's a succession of mediocre management teams had permitted the company to slide downhill. Crown's share of the total market for bottle caps had slipped from over one-half to less than one-third. Per-share earnings fell from $2.54 in 1951 to a loss in 1957, and the company was facing bankruptcy.

Connelly first became interested in Crown because his own firm—Connelly Container Corp.—although much smaller than Crown—was an active competitor. This is why he understood Crown's problems and thought that he knew how to solve them. In 1955 he began buying the stock, and in 1956 he was given a seat on the board of directors. During this period he acquired about 40,000 shares of common stock at an average price of 15–18.

By April 1957, the board, which had previously ignored Connelly's drastic suggestions for rejuvenating the company, finally gave in and elected him president. In this month he bought 1,800 shares, while three other officers also bought 1,800 shares. Thereafter, action came fast and furiously as the entire corporation was reorganized. For instance, the home office staff was cut in half; by 1959, the payroll had been cut by $10 million.

In June 1957, when Crown stock was selling around 15, Mr. Connelly took on a king-sized 28,900 shares, while three other officials added smaller blocks. In July and August he added another 19,400 shares, when the stock was selling between 15 and 16. Then the market crashed and the stock promptly slid to a low of 10½ by December. During the slide, Connelly and other insiders kept right on buying. By the end of 1957, he personally held 102,700 shares in which he had a paper loss of approximately $400,000.

This was the crucial point at which faith and fortitude paid off. The company was running a deficit and the stock was selling at a twenty-year low. The outlook could not have looked blacker to the average investor—not unless they knew that six different insiders had bought a total of 67,500 shares during the year just ended. Even so, this was certainly a time when insiders seemed to be "wrong."

However, these men who had bought all of their stock on the open market and who had heavy losses did not panic, like the average investor doubtless did, and sell out. They didn't even establish their losses "for tax purposes." They apparently were more interested in not losing their positions. They knew, of course, that the tide had turned, that lots of black ink was about to replace the red ink; more important, they knew that the company was now on the threshold of making a unique profit breakthrough, that continues right up until the present day.

During 1958, when the stock tripled in price, Connelly added another 55,900 shares, while other insiders bought lesser amounts. Here an important principle is involved, which most investors fail to comprehend because they are either too greedy or too fearful. The insiders at Crown Cork had large paper losses at one point. Did they try to "get out even" on the recovery? Or when they had a 100% or 200% profit? *No.* They bought still more because they had bigger profits in mind.

The really serious mistakes were made by investors who bought at, say, 15, only to watch the stock plummet almost immediately to 11. Even if they resisted the fear-inspired temptation to sell then, they were still throwing away a fortune if they sold when they could get out even. Almost as big a mistake was made by investors who bought at 12 and then took a 50% profit when Crown hit 18 on the theory (a favorite with brokers) that "You'll never go broke taking a profit." As long as the UPB continues to dominate the company's affairs and profits continue their rise, resist the impulse to take any profits at all—or, for that matter, resist the apparently desirable aim of selling before (or during) a general market decline.

In retrospect, it looks easy to sell before a big reaction and then buy back somewhere near the bottom. It isn't. Moreover, you invariably lose your position in the one big winner you have—the very one you need to offset your other more numerous mistakes. The stock market provides a continual test of character because no matter what you do, at some point after you do it, you appear to have made a mistake. In contrast, if you buy a house or a diamond, you don't know what its current value is until the day you actually sell it.

In 1959 and 1960, when Crown moved in a trading channel between 30 and 40, Connelly and the other insiders continued to methodically accumulate their stock. In November and December 1960, seven officials bought 24,795 shares. By this time, earnings had risen to $3.15 a share and it was clear to them that despite the recession then underway, earnings would approach $6.00 a share in 1961. Note that despite these gains, at no time did the stock appear to be especially cheap on a price to earnings (PE) ratio basis.

In January 1961 Connelly bought another 16,125 shares. By that time, the price was in the high 40's, so at least $700,000 was involved. By May, CCK was selling in the 80's and in this month three insiders bought another 13,645 shares. In July and August six officers added another 16,770 shares. At this point they stopped buying. Little wonder, since in August the stock moved from 90 to above 120.

Thereafter, no significant buying was reported until the spring of 1962. On that reaction, which started at 134 and ended below 80, three officers bought 18,700 shares. In the fall, when CCK was hovering around 100, eight officials (other than Connelly) added to their already huge holdings, which amounted to almost one-third of the shares outstanding.

Another characteristic of an authentic UPB is that it dominates a company's future for a long, long time. The Crown Cork trend of earnings for the past twenty years is worth pondering. They are adjusted to reflect stock splits totaling 20 present shares for one original share:

TABLE 6
CROWN CORK & SEAL

Year	Earnings	Year	Earnings	Year	Earnings
1958	$ .13	1965	$ .71	1972	$1.58
1959	.19	1966	.80	1973	1.81
1960	.22	1967	.91	1974	2.20
1961	.28	1968	1.01	1975	2.43
1962	.37	1969	1.11	1976	2.84
1963	.41	1970	1.27	1977	3.46
1964	.51	1971	1.43	1978	4.16

What about dividends? CCK paid a liberal dividend during the years it was floundering and finally almost went bankrupt. The unique profit breakthrough years began when it stopped paying dividends. Nor has the company paid a single dividend since 1957. This demonstrates an important point: *A UPB company may pay a small but steadily rising dividend: It never pays a liberal one.* The yield will never compare favorably with fixed-income investments—at least not if you look at the current yield. However, the yield, based on an investor's original cost may be much higher. IBM illustrates this point perfectly. It currently yields 4.4%. The yield twenty years ago was also 4.4%. However, the current yield for the investor who bought twenty years ago is 28%.

How did the investor who bought CCK twenty years ago and has received no dividend income at all during those twenty years fare? In 1978 CCK sold above 700 after adjusting for stock splits. This means that $15,000 invested in this essentially unglamorous company had grown to almost $1 million. Incidentally, the Crown Cork UPB did not develop out of its original bottle-cap business—at least not directly. Rather, management correctly anticipated the market for aerosol and beer cans and led the way in developing and marketing these lowly products.

What is to be learned from a study of past UPB companies? First, you did not need to know anything that was not available to anyone who read their annual reports or other standard sources of such information. What you needed was to share management's conviction that there was a great future in store for computers, beer and aerosol cans, copying machines, door-to-door selling, or whatever. In fact, I will have a few words to say about the fallacy and dangers of inside information further on.

Second, if new management has entered the picture, check to see whether or not they are buying their own stock. If management has founded the company you are investigating, they probably already hold a substantial amount of the stock and, at times, will do some selling for personal reasons (gifts, estate planning, etc.), which has no bearing on the company's future. Third, a UPB company never pays out a large portion of earnings to the stockholders. In the first place, they will own a lot of the stock themselves and don't want the income, which will be subject to double taxation. They reason—correctly—that they will gain far more if they reinvest earnings in the company, which will come back to them in the form of capital gains, when they sell their stock.

Meanwhile, if the earnings plowed back into the company boost the price of the stock, they are far better off to borrow the money they may need to buy a yacht or a villa on Capri, using some of their stock as collateral for the loan. After all, the interest is tax deductible, whereas if they used money paid out in the form of dividends, it is taxable—and at a high rate at that. This is one main reason a growth stock is a growth stock.

To sum up: If you want to beat inflation, place a placard over your bed which reads *"Never buy a stock with a high yield."*

THE IBMs AND XEROXes OF THE FUTURE

High-technology companies always seem the most likely candidates for UPB honors. After all, most of them are engaged in esoteric activities which few of us can even understand. It ain't necessarily so. A firm devoting its life to the collection of garbage may better fill the bill—especially if it finds a better way to convert garbage to methane, fertilizer, and other profitable products. Nevertheless, there are, without question, future IBMs to be found among the younger and smaller high-technology stocks of today.

How do you recognize such a company at a sufficiently

early stage to let it turn you into a millionaire? The surest way is to be plain lucky—which is another way of saying that you are able, at least occasionally, to correctly appraise the impact of a corporate development, which most investors misjudge, despite the fact that it has been widely publicized.

The key word here is *occasionally.* Obviously there will be only one big winner among a barrel of lemons. How to recognize it depends, first, on pure luck, for want of a better word. Second, on the amount of risk you are willing to assume. Only you can decide that, and you must decide it for yourself, rather than relying on someone else's judgment.

This problem continually confronts those of us who are always looking for the UPB stocks of the future. For example, during the late 1960's, when high-technology stocks were all the rage, several of the top men at Fairchild Camera departed to form their own new company, which they named National Semiconductor. I had followed Fairchild for many years (one of my clients had made a modest fortune in it) and felt that these men had the ability and contacts to make a success of their new venture. Yet I felt there was more risk involved than I cared to assume. After all, Fairchild itself was a leader in transistors and semiconductor components. Moreover, there were any number of other highly competent competitors in the field; including the Japanese, who were coming on strong.

It seemed for a while that my reasoning—or reluctance to take the risk—was justified. After a brief flurry of activity on the news, the new stock found few takers, even though it was priced below 5 in the over-the-counter market. As it turned out, these men knew what they were doing; not only from a technical standpoint, but they also had the necessary customer contacts. Before long the stock was listed on the New York Stock Exchange and sold (after adjusting for subsequent splits) above 250. Thus a $10,000 investment snowballed to $500,000 in a relatively short time. National Semi was one of few long shots which actually paid off. This did not mean that my judgment was at fault, it was simply a longer shot than I cared to gamble on at that time.

This illustrates an important principle. The greatest misconception of all is that you need access to inside information if you hope to get in on the IBMs of the future at an early stage. The fact that Atlantic City had legalized gambling and that Resorts International would be the first to open a casino there was certainly no secret. Yet more than a year passed before the casino stocks finally took off. Then Resorts A stock moved from 15 to 210 in less than a year.

All summer long, lines of gamblers waited to enter the sacred precincts, where they could, at last, legally throw away their money. Many must have tired of waiting and opted for even faster action—buying shares in the casino itself. Many who made such a decision fared far better than those who made it into the packed casino itself.

The Resorts profit breakthrough was certainly a unique one (earnings soared from $.26 to $4.57 a share in one year), since the company enjoyed a temporary monopoly on casino gambling along the East Coast. Will this head start continue to pay off for Resorts in future years, or is the UPB a temporary one? You have just as good a chance of answering this question correctly as anyone else—including the top management of the casinos involved.

My advice regarding inside information is unequivocal: never act on it. It will wipe you out faster than almost anything else. This has nothing to do with the accuracy of the information passed on to you. You gain the intestinal fortitude necessary to hold a potential UPB candidate through thick and thin only when the decision to buy it is yours and yours alone—after you have studied all the available information on the company and know as much about its present position and future outlook as any other owner or prospective owner knows. As a matter of fact, at this point you will probably know more about the company than anyone outside of the company and be in a more objective position to make a decision about it than most of the people inside the company.

This takes time, but only such an investment in time supplies the confidence needed to back your judgment with your life's savings. If you don't have the necessary time, then I would recommend investing in the closed-end trusts discussed in the previous chapter, where you will do about the same as the market averages. While it eliminates any chance to participate in the big winners, I think it will enable you to beat inflation by a good margin in the years ahead.

Inside information may enable you to realize a short-term windfall profit, if you have a direct pipeline to the top policy-making executive in the company concerned. Since not one investor in a thousand has such an exclusive source of information, I will discuss the type of inside information most of us hear almost every day that we enter a broker's office. This is not to suggest that all of the second-, third-, or tenth-hand information you hear will turn out to be wrong. But you can be sure, that by the time *you* hear the news, it will be much too late to profit from it.

There is another hazard. All too often, inside information may be intentionally misleading. Someone who wants to bail out of a mismanaged company (perhaps it is facing bankruptcy) before it is too late, will spread a rumor about an impending takeover, at a price far above the current market. These rumors are always attributed to the most impeccable sources. So when you are presented with inside information that is almost irresistibly appealing, remember that UPBs require years to develop and that to participate in one requires sound judgment on your part, rather than exclusive information.

How about investment counselors? After all, they devote all

their time to seeking out the great growth stocks of the future, don't they? No, they don't. Your own spare time, diligently applied, will probably add up to more hours devoted to original research and thinking than that of the average investment counselor. Their aim, like everyone's, is to increase their income. If they can't do it by producing superior results, they will devote their time to drumming up new business by whatever other means they find they have a talent for. This may range from entertaining stockbrokers to advertising. If they don't even have a talent for this, they go back to bartending or working for a bank.

This is how it works. An investment counselor usually gets started in one of two ways. First, he may have a say in managing family funds. He may also persuade other guileless members of the family or their friends to let him manage their accounts. Second, he may have worked for another investment counsel firm and gotten on a sufficiently friendly basis with some of its customers to be able to persuade them that he could do a better job for them than his boss is doing. Ordinarly, this would not require very much persuasion.

However he starts, let's assume that he is managing $5 million. If his fee is 1% his take is $50,000. That's not much after paying the rent and telephone. He discovers early on that finding new money to manage is a much more reliable way of building up his business than depending on achieving a superior track record. One reason is that in practice, often he just duplicates the buying and selling being done by the fellow down the street. The end result is not average—but less-than-average—performance. Now he becomes desperate and begins to take foolish chances. (After all, he is playing with someone els's money.) Usually this takes the form of overtrading—or churning—his clients' accounts. Remember: he is talking to his brokers every day, and the more action he takes, the more money they make. From his standpoint, this produces a positive result. His brokers tell their customers that the counselor is a financial wizard and urges them to place their accounts under his management. How can anyone lose (except the customers)? The broker now sits back and just counts his transaction tickets. When things go sour he is not to blame.

The lesson to be learned here can be boiled down to simple common sense. Ordinarily, those who are proficient in their own art don't need to teach it. Anyone who has the flair, astuteness, judgment, intuition or whatever else you may choose to call it necessary to recognize the big winners can make far more by managing his own money (even if he starts with very little) than he can by taking a pittance for managing the money of others. There is no example on record that I know of where an individual who was able to consistently make a lot of money for himself in the stock market, ever could be bothered managing the accounts of others. In fact, the objectivity necessary for success is immediately destroyed if you have to justify your actions to others. This is especially true if those others are paying you to do it.

Now that I have buried inside information and investment counselors as sources of instant wealth, let's get back to high-technology stocks. Which of the relatively new names in this field will turn out to be the IBMs or even the National Semiconductors of the future? Some big winners may emerge from the companies listed in table 7.

These twenty-three companies all have two things in common, besides operating in an area of high technology, where their products reduce costs—especially labor—at a time when labor and other costs are soaring. First, they are all relatively small, yet well-established companies; thus their potential for future growth is virtually unlimited. Second, they have all posted solid gains for four consecutive years.

All very well. But, since you can't buy all twenty-three, how do you determine which one (or two or three) you should

TABLE 7

HIGH-TECHNOLOGY COMPANIES

Company	Listed	Earnings Per Share				Principal Business
		1975	1976	1977	1978	
Amdahl Corp.	ASE	def.	$1.21	$1.68	$2.81	Computer Systems
Augat Inc.	ASE	$ .69	.88	1.37	1.99	Electronic Equipment
Calif. Microwave, Inc.	OTC	.29	.45	.78	.96	Microwave Components
Communications Ind.	OTC	1.04	1.20	1.39	1.66	Communication Equipment
Compugraphic Corp.	NYSE	1.58	1.83	2.08	2.82	Computer Typesetting
Computervision Corp.	NYSE	def.	.46	1.14	2.07	Automation Designs
Data Terminal Systems	NYSE	.25	.55	1.45	2.91	Computer Systems
Four-Phase Systems	NYSE	1.16	1.67	1.85	2.60	Data Process Distributor
Harris Corporation	NYSE	.03	1.10	1.63	2.11	Communications, Graphic Arts
Intel Corp.	OTC	.83	1.27	1.59	2.16	Semiconductor Circuits
King Radio Corp.	ASE	.35	.76	1.23	2.66	Communications, Navigation Equipment
Kulicke & Soffa Ind.	OTC	def.	.99	1.41	2.53	Semiconductor Manufacturing Equipment
Lanier Business Prods.	NYSE	1.14	1.38	1.60	2.14	Word-processing Equipment
Management Assistance	OTC	.55	.96	1.52	2.06	Computer Systems
Micro Mask, Inc.	OTC	def.	.45	.54	1.35	Microcomputers
Molex Inc.	OTC	.69	1.30	1.75	2.60	Electronic Equipment
Nicolet Instrument	OTC	.55	.67	.81	.99	Electronic Measure Instruments
Plantronics	NYSE	.61	.80	.97	1.27	Telecommunication Equipment
Rogers Corp.	ASE	.05	1.37	1.41	2.58	Polymeric Electronic Components
Scope, Inc.	OTC	1.36	1.78	2.20	3.08	Communication Equipment
Teradyne, Inc.	NYSE	.12	.71	1.50	2.03	Electronic Testing Equipment
Volt Information Sciences	OTC	def.	.02	.45	2.25	Photocomposing Systems
Waters Associates	OTC	.64	.87	1.37	1.57	Chromatography Systems

buy from this list—or, better still, from a new up-to-date list, which you have compiled for yourself? After all—and above all else—you must have confidence in the stocks you buy.

You must be convinced that new developments (exciting ones, if possible) will sustain a rising profit trend for several more years, so you must thoughly investigate the outlook for the company and the best way to do this is to carefully study recent annual reports, as well as the prospectus if any have been issued recently. Then, if possible, meet with at least one or two top management people; not in an effort to learn things not included in the annual reports and news releases, but rather to appraise their ability and integrity.

Obviously, no one has the time to do this with twenty or thirty companies, and few readers will have the time to do it for even one company. Therefore, do the next best thing. Locate a security analyst who does have the time and whose ability you respect. If this means opening an account with a new broker do it. The large brokers have specialists in each industry, and these lonely people are there to share this sort of information with you.

Over the years I have followed the recommendations of dozens of analysts. I eliminated most as being no better than average when it comes to picking winners. The others I have found do have a superior record. Moreover, they seldom issue more than one or two recommendations a year, thereby avoiding the buy, buy, buy, advice that reduces the effectiveness of most analysts.

Three of the high-technology stocks listed in Table 7 were chosen from recent reports issued by these analysts, and I want to quote a few paragraphs from one of them, to demonstrate the type of information that I find helpful when it comes to identifying potential UPB candidates.

The company is Volt Information Sciences, Inc. However, please bear in mind that this is *not* a recommendation to buy, since you will be reading these paragraphs about a year after the report was issued. The first bit of confidence-building information comes from William Shaw, Volt's president, in his 1978 annual report:

As a young man I wanted most to build a hundred-million-dollar business. Some people want to climb Mount Everest, others to win a Nobel prize. My ambition was to create a big corporation.

Last fiscal year Volt's revenues reached $100,711,000, a 57% increase over the prior year's $64,054,000. It took almost 30 years to reach my goal.

One of the typical analysts I've referred to (who is a friend of mine) says:

Volt Information Sciences provides temporary and permanent personnel for industry and commercial activities. It also performs automated data management services and produces the world's fastest phototypesetter from its subsidiary, Autologic. In addition, it provides the telephone industry with a variety of systems and services.

After divesting itself of several unprofitable operations during the past several years Volt is now developing substantial earnings gains. For the fiscal year ended October 31, 1978 revenues amounted to $100 million up from $64 million in the corresponding period a year earlier. Earnings rose substantially reflecting increased sales and much greater efficiency to $2.25 a share from $0.73 the year before. For the first quarter ended January 31, 1979 earnings rose 50% to $0.76 a share, from $0.50 in the corresponding period a year ago. For the current fiscal year ending October 31, 1979 we expect revenues to exceed $130 million and earnings to be in the area of $3.25–$3.50 a share.

Prospects for future growth are excellent. Autologic's backlog is at the highest level in its history. Worldwide sales of computer composition equipment including automated phototypesetting and copy processing systems, should reach $1 billion by 1982. In the process, more than 90% of traditional U.S. typesetting equipment will be replaced by automated equipment of the kind made by Autologic.

Volt, founded over a quarter of a century ago to provide technical services in support of various military and industrial programs, has from the beginning been recognized as a leader in this field. The field, however, has undergone a radical change.

In the early 1950's Volt's staff of technical writers, editors, illustrators, parts catalogers and typists used simple tools. By today's standards, the equipment they were supporting was also simple. Their output—technical manuals, drawings, illustrated parts breakdowns and the like—could be produced on printed pages. This was the pre-computer age.

The present-day resources of Volt's Technical Services Division extend to the full range of Autologic electronic photocomposing equipment. The Division's staff, enhanced by the addition of systems analysts, programmers and terminal operators, uses computer-storage devices and microfilm and microfiche in addition to the printed page to record technical information. Systems developed by the Volt organization can now merge graphic artwork with text material in computer-indexed files for storage, display and transmission in a variety of modes.

Technical writing, illustrating and parts cataloging—Volt's original business—are now accomplished by means of video display of the data base. The efficiency with which technical material can be updated and edited through computer terminals has been significantly enhanced by Autologic's new text-management system. Volt's technical publications division installed this system in its operations late in 1978 and immediately put it to use in the preparation of quick reaction proposals for customers bidding on government contracts. Now it is also being applied to the processing of large complex data bases, such as those involved in the preparation and updating of operations and maintenance manuals for defense and aerospace products.

Volt believes its directory systems, which are continually being refined and adapted to each telephone company's method of generating data, to be the most advanced now in use. Telephone companies benefiting from these systems realize substantial savings in production costs and higher directory advertising revenue.

In systems being developed by Volt for telephone companies, the key feature is distributed processing. The telephone company processes changes to its tariff structure and transmits them to the master data base maintained by Volt. These changes are further processed by Volt to produce updates to the many telephone network documents affected by tariff modifications. The first long-term contract for these services was signed in 1978.

Volt's Contract Services Group provides its clients with technical and professional personnel for assignments anywhere in the world.

These engineers, designers, draftsmen, systems analysts, programmers, computer operators, technical writers, editors and illustrators (to name a few representative classifications) remain in most cases Volt employees throughout the period of their assignment. Volt takes care of all administration, salaries, payroll taxes and fringe benefits. The client pays only a fixed dollar rate for each hour actually worked.

Volt's Temporary Personnel Group is a source for all kinds of temporary office and industrial personnel. Clerks, secretaries and word processors, keypunch operators, bookkeepers and accountants, communication and marketing specialists, truck drivers, forklift operators, welders, assemblers, stockroom clerks—Volt provides these and many other skills for assignments varying from days to weeks to months.

Last year was a good one for the industry, with revenue growth of about 17%, well ahead of normal. There are now more than 2,000 temporary-help offices around the country, ranging from domestic industry leaders like Kelly Services, Inc. and Manpower, Inc., 85% owned by Parker Pen Co., to tiny local firms. Right now, nearly all of them are making money. The best estimates are that the industry earned about $100 million last year, up about 30% from 1977.

Return on total capital runs from 23% to 33%—more for privately owned firms—and the industry leaders have good balance sheets. For example, Olsten ($100 million sales) has nearly $10 million in cash and virtually no long-term debt. Kelly has $15 million in cash and Manpower can lean on Parker's nearly $17 million. A number of sizable fortunes have been created by the temporary-help business, including the Kelly family's $30 million and over $15 million for Manpower's founding families.

Volt's Electronic Pre-Press Equipment Division is incorporated in subsidiary, Autologic, which designs, manufactures and sells the "APS" line of phototypsetting equipment.

The APS-5 is the world's leading digital CRT (cathode ray tube) typsesetter, with output speed up to 3,000 lines a minute. Technologically, the APS-5 represents the state of the art in cold-type composition.

More than 400 phototypsesetters of the APS-5 and earlier APS-4 models have been sold in the United States and abroad to newspaper, magazine and book publishers, to commercial compositors and printers, and to government agencies and other organizations having internal publishing facilities.

Volt itself uses APS equipment to photocompose telephone directories, technical documents and other publications produced by its various service divisions.

In pursuit of its vision of the future, Autologic in 1978 entered into an agreement with a major customer to develop and deliver an integrated system for scanning, screening, sizing, cropping and positioning graphic material and merging it with text material for phototypsesetting.

This system includes a new flatbed laser scanner, a new interactive visual display terminal and the APS-5 typesetter. The scanner electronically screens photographic and other continuous tone material (in order to prepare it for the printing process) at full scanning speed—as little as one minute for an 18-by-21-inch page.

The result will be the most advanced system of its kind for photocomposing complete pages of integrated text and graphics, including logos, line art, unscreened photographs and computer-generated drawings.

The worldwide computer composition market will increase 11.1% a year through 1982, with the U.S.–Canadian market growing at a 15.3% rate. This worldwide market is estimated at $1 billion by 1982; a major potential market for such equipment, after the newspaper composition market is saturated, will be the 74,000 commercial printing and in-house print shops. This market is seen as growing at a 14.2% annual rate through 1982.

Within the equipment field, editing and pagination (which allows an operator to electronically position ads, pictures and text on a page electronically) products are expected to lead industry sales with growth of about 18.6% through 1982.

As of October 31, 1978 the company had current assets of $27.4 million compared with current liabilities of $12.3 million. Long-term debt amounted to only $1.5 million and there were 2,746,525 common shares outstanding, of which about 1.6 million were closely held. Because of the high cash flow being generated, the company has no need for financing of any kind.

Prospects for the current fiscal year are excellent. One of the reasons for our expectation of higher revenues and earnings is the highest backlog in the company's history. Volt's phototypesetter is the world's fastest with a record of 8,000 characters per second. Its speed is exceeded only by its reliability—only three moving parts. Its many options include, microfilm recording, logo and line-art scanning, on-line media processing, etc.

The equipment made by Autologic helps provide telephone company service throughout the nation. The five-year contracts are at record levels with many of Bell Telephone subsidiaries. Moreover, the temporary help service in competition with Manpower, Olsten, and Kelly Services, is now providing contract services around the world. This division should do a record level of business as people change jobs more frequently than ever before and as more women work on a part-time basis.

In short, all phases of Volt's business should continue to do well throughout this year and into next. We believe the company's strong financial condition will help facilitate new products and acquisitions and in view of its excellent prospects for future growth we strongly recommend the common stock to the investor interested in capital gains.

Once you identify and buy a stock which you think has UPB potential, how long should you hold it? When should you sell it? Advice is generally the one commodity that there is always plenty of. The one exception is selling advice. For every recommendation to sell, you will get 500 to buy. Why is this so? The answer is simple enough if you are a stockbroker. For every investor who owns any given stock, there are 500 who don't. Therefore, your buy recommendations have about 500 times more chance of generating business than do your sell recommendations.

Hold UPB stocks indefinitely as long as their earnings continue to rise at an above-average rate. (That is, unless you prefer the faster action described in the next chapter.) Should you continue to hold during a bear market or business depression, such as we will undoubtedly experience as an aftermath of runaway inflation? The history of UPB stocks conclusively shows that you should hold them regardless of all other considerations. You may ask with ample justification: "But won't even a UPB stock decline drastically during a bear market?" The answer, of course, is yes. However, investors who attempt to time market tops and bottoms are sure losers—because it can't be done. In contrast, investors who buy and hold UPB stocks are sure winners; UPB stocks will decline less than the average stock during bear markets and may actually rise.

For example, in the early 1930's, many gold stocks proved to be ideal UPB issues. Homestake, for one, fell from 92 to 65 in the 1929 crash, but passed 100 early in 1931 and subsequently soared to over 500. Another example from that era was the emergence of talking pictures as the nation's favorite amusement; the movie companies became classical UPB vehicles. Loew's, for instance, boosted earnings from $7.91 a share in 1929 to $9.65 in 1930, when earnings elsewhere were declining. As a result, the shares moved from a low of 32 in 1929 to a high of 98 in 1930. Investors who sold before the crash made a serious mistake.

More recently, in the worst bear market since the 1930's, any number of stocks chalked up new highs during the 1974 debacle, because their profits were rising at a rate which made them preferable holdings to cash or high-interest-paying savings accounts even during a bear market.

A few examples which might be cited include Air Products

and Chemicals, whose earnings went from $1.76 a share in 1973 to $3.94 in 1975 and has continued to rise each year since then; Albertson's Inc., Applied Digital Data Systems, Big Three Industries, Crane Company, Dresser Industries, Falcon Seaboard, Fluor Corp., Gearhart-Owen Industries, Harnischfeger Corp., Homestake Mining, International Minerals, Joy Manufacturing, Kaneb Services, Koppers Company, Miller-Wohl Company, Mapco, Inc. Pittston Company, Potlatch Corp., Rosario Resources, St. Joe Minerals, Southland Royalty, Southwest Airlines, Sunshine Mining, United Energy Resources, and U.S. Steel.

What conclusions can be drawn from this list? First, there is a noticeable absence of high-technology and institutional favorites in general. Since inflation was a worry then, too, we can conclude that these stocks were not viewed as offering a superior hedge against inflation. In contrast, those stocks countering the bear trend in 1974 were mainly special situations, owned primarily by individuals, rather than institutions—especially natural-resource-rich companies.

In short, it would appear that the 1974 period was dominated by a twofold fear of recession and runaway inflation; therefore, the traditional asset-rich, money-in-the-ground hedges were favored. As it turned out, the 1974 inflation rate of 11% was cut in half by 1976 and 1977—a successful inflation-fighting effort that is not going to be duplicated in the 1980's—or, at least, not to that extent. In either event (moderate or runaway inflation), those high-technology companies which manage to boost their earning power at a substantially faster rate than inflation should also prove to be superior inflation hedges.

Another observation: In several cases, the ability to score new highs during the worst bear market in forty-five years presaged even more sensational rises when the general market recovered.

10

The Six-Step Plan

When I was a stockbroker, my most successful client lived near Lisbon, Portugal. The climate and cheap living had attracted him, but not nearly as much as the tax situation; there were no taxes on stock-market profits. This is why he became a naturalized citizen of Portugal.

The coup Raymond engineered would have been much more difficult in his homeland. American tax laws are loaded against those who buy and sell capital assets, as contrasted to retail or manufactured goods. The latter can depend on a fairly consistent markup in bad years as well as good. Of course, they will make more money in the good years than in the bad years. If they suffer an actual loss in any year, they can reduce future profits, for tax purposes, by the full amount of the loss suffered. The fairness of such treatment seems obvious, but it does not apply to people who deal in stocks or any other asset that is traded, rather than consumed.

I am reminded of the brilliant owner of a computer programming firm located in the Stanford Industrial Park. He was intrigued by the challenge of the stock market and had worked out a system of trading which he figured would yield a steady 30% profit, or $30,000 a year on the $100,000 of capital he had available. His computer had tested the system over past markets, and it seemed foolproof. When I timidly expressed the usual tax-oriented warning against short-term trading, he replied, "To me the tax on stock-market profits is the same as any other business expense." (Unfortunately, nothing could be further from the truth.)

Admittedly, he could not have chosen a worse time to put his system to the test. The 1962 bear market was far more severe than a picture of the market averages would suggest. In any event, he hit his target right on the nose, but with a loss, rather than a gain. Now his capital was reduced to $70,000. The next year more than made up for the near catastrophe of 1962. He did some buying near the market lows, and wound up 1963 with a $35,000 profit for a gain of 50% on his capital at the end of 1962. His tax liability on his profit was $15,000 (it was mostly short-term). At this point, his trading capital totaled $90,000. Thus, following a year of losses and a year of much larger gains (on a percentage basis) his capital had still declined from $100,000 to $90,000.

Raymond had observed a recurring cycle in individual stock patterns: when a stock broke out of a narrow channel (or several-year trading range) on the upside, the ensuing move lasted, on average, about four years and carried the stock up 400% to 800% from its original price. Ray developed a plan that would capitalize on these major moves, but he was not greedy. In fact, he modestly figured that he would be lucky and satisfied if he could regularly capture only a fraction of each move; but also—and this is important—in only a fraction of the time required for the entire upswing to be completed.

He devised what he called the Six-Step Plan for becoming a millionaire. He methodically calculated how he could accomplish this by setting up several alternate possibilities, which looked like this:

Five-Step Plan	Six-Step Plan	Seven-Step Plan
		$ 7,825
	$ 15,650	15,650
$ 31,300	31,300	31,300
62,600	62,600	62,600
125,200	125,200	125,200
250,400	250,400	250,400
500,800	500,800	500,800
1,001,600	1,001,600	1,001,600

Ray's account with me totaled just under $50,000, so he was confronted with the decision of whether to operate in one stock, three stocks, or six stocks. With one stock he would need only five steps, but he would be placing his bets in a single basket. An attractive feature of this plan was that if his initial commitment resulted in a loss, he would have a reserve of almost $20,000 to combine with what was left of his original investment. With this he could try again. On the other hand, for the Five-Step Plan to succeed, he would need to pick five winners in a row. He was sufficiently experienced to know that the odds against accomplishing this feat were much too great.

Ray could divide his capital into six parts, which would

require an extra step or two, but certainly the chances of selecting the one or two winners needed would be improved six-fold. He decided against the Seven-Step Plan because he felt that he could not concentrate on six separate commitments to the extent he felt was necessary for success. Therefore, he decided on the Six-Step Plan, which required three initial positions. If he had two units that failed he would combine them into one new unit and proceed. When this unit doubled, he again split it into two new units.

Ray first bought 800 shares of Pacific Petroleums, 200 Owens-Corning Fiberglas and 900 Curtiss-Wright. As luck would have it, he hit two winners out of three, and this got him off to an auspicious start. He now had two legs on his way to completing the second step of his plan. The Curtiss-Wright resulted in a loss, which was eventually recovered and reinvested in a new step-one phase.

One of Ray's step-two selections was Tri-Continental warrants; the other was Hunt Foods (subsequently merged into Norton Simon). The Tri warrants performed handsomely for him, but not the Hunt Food. Although his failures outnumbered his successes in number, his strategy kept him going until two or three years later, when he hit the jackpot with Brunswick Corp. (good for two steps), and Fairchild Camera. In less than five years, his original $50,000 had grown to well over $1 million; therefore I think his philosophy of investing is worth examining.

Ray looked for what every speculator looks for: a favorable industry outlook—at least in the eyes and imagination of investors—combined with a steadily rising earnings trend. In addition, he watched for the stock to break out of its trading channel on the upside. But he concentrated on the forest rather than the trees: he ignored short-term news and trends. Ray also ignored all gyrations in the market averages. He made no particular effort to buy at intermediate bottom, nor to sell before or during the early stages of a decline, although his system often caused him to sell before major declines.

How did Ray recognize the all-important markup or break-out phase? He watched the volume leaders every day (in the Paris edition of the *Herald Tribune,* which among European newspapers has unequalled coverage of American financial and stock news). When a stock first appeared on the most active list, he added it to his list of candidates. When it made a new high for the year, he moved it toward the top of his list. He eliminated those companies which appeared on the list because of spot developments, rather than long-term fundamentals; an example would be merger candidates and the like.

Next Ray thoroughly looked into the fundamental outlook for the company and its industry. He used the technical approach to locate those stocks that might turn out to be in the markup stage. In addition, he realized how important it was to have confidence in the value behind the stocks he bought. This usually meant that they were growing at an above-average rate and seemed likely to continue doing so in the foreseeable future.

The resulting peace of mind was essential; it enabled him to hold on during the inevitable bear markets, when it seemed that everything was going down the drain. Under these depressing conditions, Ray was better able to resist the temptation to sell and try to buy back lower down. He felt that this was not only an impossibility (except by luck, and his plan did not rely on luck), but that any such attempt was nerve-racking and would divert him from his primary purpose.

If a stock qualified on all counts and also had an exciting aura of mystery, so much the better. Ray was a keen student of investor psychology. He knew that investors' dreams have a far more powerful influence on stock prices than does reality. For example, what did the French citizens, who were so avidly buying Mississippi shares, know about the tens of millions of acres of wilderness they were investing in? Nothing at all. And that is what lent glamour to the whole enterprise. Human nature was the same in the 1720's as in the 1920's, and will be no different in the 1980's. As the history of speculation proves and continues to prove, with dependable regularity, in today's stock market, people are willing to pay any price for dreams, but very little for reality.

When a company with a glamorous but unproven new product or service captures the imagination of the public, they will bid the price up to unbelievable heights on the basis of projected profits, that discount the millennium. And when, as sometimes does happen, some part of these dreams are realized (most such dreams quickly turn into nightmares), then the shares nosedive and there is no further interest in them.

At the time, I didn't realize how impressively simple arithmetic favored Ray's approach. As an engineer, who had progressed up the math ladder through differential equations, I should certainly have caught on sooner, but I was imbued with the soundness of the UPB approach and still am; especially if you live in America where capital gains are taxed and you usually profit most by *not* selling a good stock. But then I didn't have Ray's magic touch.

Ray asked me early on: "Would you rather own a stock which doubled in price six times or one that gained 1,000%?" Probably most people would answer as I did: "I'll take the 1,000% profit." I should have thought about this puzzle for a few minutes because the answer conceals the secret of his success. Because *a stock that doubles six times gains almost six times as much as a stock that increases 1,000% in value.* Consider one share of a stock selling at 10. If it doubles six times, it is worth 640; if it gains 1,000%, it is worth 110. And 640 is just a shade short of being six times as much as 110.

Ray had gone an important practical step further in his

reasoning than this mere arithmetic. Over the years, the superstocks have risen 400% to 800% on average in about four years. Between their lows and their highs, most of them gained 1,000% or even more. However, we have all experienced the futility of trying to buy at or near a market bottom and trying to sell at or near the high. It can't be done; at least, not very often. Moreover, you would need to own six stocks that gained 1,000% apiece to equal the results obtainable in six stocks that only doubled—provided, of course, that you reinvested in the second after selling the first, and so on.

Ponder this difference carefully and you may be well on the way to duplicating Ray's success. We all know that dozens of stocks double in price in a few weeks and, sometimes, in a few days. A glance at any chart book will confirm this fact. It will also confirm that upside progress was much slower after (and before) this markup stage. In view of this, Ray's strategy of holding a stock only during this fast, middle portion of its rise makes a lot of sense.

During the five years I worked with Ray, he held a total of about twenty-five stocks. About eight or nine of these actually doubled (he needed only six to fulfill his plan); the other two or three made up for the losses on his failures. So he was wrong at times, as we all are; and he got whipsawed at times, as we all do. This happened when a stock made a "false move" out of a channel on the upside, only to fall back and become dormant once again. When this happened, he switched into the next most promising candidate on his list.

This may sound as though Ray traded a lot. Actually, he had a great deal of patience: the most important virtue of all in the stock market. However, his patience was not the kind that causes investors to become wedded to their mistakes out of a sense of false pride. This kind of false pride is not caused by what others may think, but rather because investors are reluctant to admit their mistakes to themselves.

As a general rule, as long as the reasons for buying remained valid Ray held on, especially if the laggard performance following an upside breakthrough was in sympathy with a general market decline. In a bull market, he would act much more quickly to replace a laggard performer. Nor did he always sell automatically when a stock had doubled. If he felt that it had the potential of doubling again he held on (Brunswick was on example), but with the provision that if the upward trend reversed, *he would not hold the stock below the point at which it had doubled.*

Once a month Ray sent me an updated list of his candidates for buying. I airmailed information about each, which he considered to be important. This usually included the following:

1. *Insider trading:* He preferred to own stocks which a company's management was buying or else already owned a substantial percentage of the outstanding shares. He would eliminate from his list any stocks which showed a consistent pattern of selling by two or more insiders.

2. *Short interest:* Ray believed that short covering often helped a stock along during the markup stage, especially if the short interest was large—preferably several times larger than a normal average day's trading volume.

3. *Institutional holdings:* He avoided stocks heavily favored by banks and mutual funds. If institutions owned 25% or more of the outstanding shares, Ray felt they would be net sellers on strength and that, in any case, there would not be much further additional buying because of the reduced float. However, he might make an exception if such holdings were less than 15% and increasing.

Even then, Ray tolerated the company of professional investors only when he felt that a special situation was developing. Obviously, these funds, because of their size, can deal only in stocks of mature companies, where the daily volume of trading exceeds 20,000 shares. His policy, therefore, was to avoid the shares of established institutional favorites, such as General Motors, ATT, and IBM, and invest only in those issues that could conceivably become institutional favorites in the future.

4. *Stock charts:* Ray was not a technician in the sense that he acted on the esoteric patterns that are so dear to chartists—such as head-and-shoulder formations, triangles, and all the rest. However, charts helped him select stocks which appeared ready to break out of long trading ranges. Although he did not attempt to wait for and buy on general market reactions, when a stock broke out of a channel on heavy volume, he would wait for a low-volume reaction before buying.

When it came to selling, Ray reversed this tactic. Thus, if a stock was nearing his upside objective of, say, 40, he would sell on a further high-volume runup whether it enabled him to sell at 37 or 43. He felt that if volume of trading accelerated at roughly the same rate that a stock climbed, the uptrend would be sustained. But if volume declined as the stock moved up to new highs, it was a danger signal. He would then abandon his position and sell out because trading volume had not supported the advance.

In a sense, as far as daily contact with the market was concerned, Ray was living in a remote monastery. He had no telephone, and on the infrequent occasions when he phoned me, he had to go into Lisbon to do so. In short, he was effectively insulated against the mass psychology of the marketplace. And his isolation was a decided asset. He was fairly immune to a paraphrase of Newton's second law, which says that investors can depend on an equal amount of good and bad news. This causes them to continually question, not only the outlook for their stocks, but for the nation's economy and the entire world as well.

Ray felt that his original reason for buying a stock would not change, except over the long pull. It is only our emotions that are influenced by day-to-day developments. After all, even amid the despair of a bear market, virtually none of the companies listed on the NYSE actually go bankrupt. Similarly, when euphoria reigns supreme, even those stocks that stage the most sensational rises eventually come back down.

The best feature of the Six-Step Plan is knowing in advance what action to take. The most difficult problem confronting most investors is knowing when to sell. For example, if you buy a stock at 20 and it moves up to 40, should you sell or hold on for much larger gains? Ray was never in doubt. He sold. He maintained that if you didn't have such a plan, you might hold the stock for years, during which it moved back and forth between 20 and 40, or perhaps between 30 and 50. It might never make another big move.

Ray argued that investors ran the risk of losing out on two or three steps in his plan if they held indefinitely, since they could recognize a sustained new uptrend only well after its inception, and they had an even more difficult problem recognizing a final top after which a stock consolidated (or worse) for many years. Ray maintained that investors should aim to hold stocks only during the fast markup stage—at least to the extent that luck or natural ability permits.

I still think that Ray had an unusual—even uncanny—ability to find the right stocks and then take action at the right time. Not many of us have this ability, and I still think most investors are better off to buy into UPB companies in which they have great confidence and then hold them as long as the UPB factor continues to dominate the company's future—even though the results obtainable are far less impressive than with the Six-Step Plan.

However, times change, and I may not be changing with them. The chances of carrying through a Six-Step Plan to its triumphant conclusion should be many times better during the inflationary 1980's, than it was when Ray was operating in the late 1950's. The number of big winners is going to multiply and multiply again as the flight from the dollar gains momentum and seeks the only rational inflation hedge left. Moreover, the tax problem can be reduced and/or postponed by means of a number of devices that were not available in the past.

Let us explore these briefly, bearing in mind that the tax laws change continually and that you should check carefully with your accountant or tax attorney before taking action. (Who knows? Maybe a miracle will occur and that peculiarly American device—the capital-gains tax—will be abolished.) Let's assume that you have successfully arrived at Step 5. Up to now the capital-gains tax has slowed you somewhat, but not sufficiently to prevent you from getting this far. Now you are lying awake nights worrying about what to do with a paper profit of $250,000. (Success is an even greater strain on the psyche than failure, because greed is a stronger emotion than fear.) What if that big paper profit vanished? Or, even if it doesn't, you may see little prospect of the big winner that got you this far doubling again. Yet how can you achieve the final goal if you sell and have to pay out $50,000 or $60,000 in capital-gains taxes?

There are a variety of tax-shelter programs that will enable you to avoid the tax, while still having a good chance of reaching Step 6. These programs will be discussed later on. Meanwhile, there are ways you can continue the plan, while at the same time avoiding most of the tax on your profit. The only drawback is that your timetable will be set back by a few months.

One such plan is offered by some of the larger and better-financed brokerage houses, who will buy the stock in which you have a short-term gain and give you their note payable in installments over a period of years. This payout period can range from two up to ten years, depending on your own personal requirements. This means that you can reduce and defer the tax obligation to whatever extent will benefit you most in subsequent years. Meanwhile, they will pay you interest on the unpaid balance at, say, 1% under the prime rate.

Let's assume that you elect to receive your $250,000 in three installments, over a three-year period. With proper timing, you will still have most of this capital available for investment. Thus, if the first installment of $83,333 was paid in January, you would have the use of the full amount for fifteen months before paying the capital-gains tax.

If you don't choose to go the installment-payment route and you wish to nail down your profit before the end of the year, or protect a short-term profit until it becomes long-term, you can sell an equal number of shares of the stock you own "short against the box." If the stock goes down, as you had anticipated, you profit by the amount of the decline on your short sale, while retaining your original long position. If, on the other hand, your stock continues to advance after you set up the short hedge, you are assured of the profit which caused you to take out this insurance in the first place and which has now become long term. The main disadvantage to this procedure is that any profit realized when you cover the short sale in the new year is short term. However, a short-term profit is better than a loss, whether short or long.

Still another solution to the tax problem is to retain all of your capital intact as it builds up, while borrowing sufficient money to pay the tax on the profits you have accumulated. The stocks you currently own can be used as collateral for these loans. The interest on the money borrowed is fully tax deductible and will reduce your tax liability.

When you achieve the rarefied level of Step 5, you might also deviate from the original plan and sell only half of the position you took after Step 4, which would cut your tax liability substantially. You could then reinvest this money in the most promising of your remaining candidates. These funds would not be reduced by the tax payments for, perhaps, a year or even longer.

Instead, you may wish to raise the necessary cash to pay taxes or profits by using your margin buying power; i.e., borrowing from your broker rather than from a bank. Up to now I have not recommended the use of margin because it is a two-edged sword that cannot only double your losses (assuming you buy originally on the current 50% margin) but, even worse, adversely affect your psychological equilibrium. Should you or should you not meet a margin call? This dilemma can keep you awake nights.

In contrast, when you have a large profit cushion, any losses suffered will reduce your potential tax liability on paper profits as well as your actual tax liability on profits already realized. In this enviable situation, you don't really care all that much when the inevitable losses do come along. Moreover, the interest on your margin debt will reduce your tax liability, since it is a fully deductible cost of doing business.

Consider the arithmetic for a minute. At the conclusion of Step 4, you have a profit of about $125,000 after selling the stock responsible for this long-anticipated achievement. When tax time rolls around, let's assume you owe $30,000 tax on the profit.

As I write, the interest charged by brokers is about 12½%, or $3,750 a year on a debit balance of $30,000. If at Step 3 you had anticipated your successful arrival at Step 4, you might have decided to increase your commitment of $125,000 by another $20,000 borrowed on margin. Since this additional sum would double along with the original Step 3 commitment, when Step 4 arrived, you would already have made provision for the tax liability while maintaining the necessary capital to continue the Six-Step Plan on schedule.

In this way, if you continue to be successful, you are simply increasing your scale of operations through margin borrowing sufficiently to pay the taxes as you go. The end result will be the same as though you, like Ray, had no tax liability at all.

11

Renewable Natural Resources

The ideal inflation hedge would be one that combines the finite investment values of land ("they aren't making any more") with the ability to replace itself as used with little or no effort on the part of the owner. Timber alone combines these unique advantages. Furthermore the many uses of wood aren't even well understood. Most of us would be at a loss to name more than the three most obvious uses: (1) as a building material for houses and furniture; (2) as the raw material for paper; and (3) as a fuel, not only for the fireplaces of city dwellers, but also to heat rural houses. And wood still constitutes a major source of energy in this country as well as throughout the world. This end use is growing, rather than declining; as you might suspect. For example, paper mills are now using wood waste as a replacement for oil in their boilers.

There are thousands of other uses for wood. An especially important though little appreciated property is that it is the most versatile of all plastics. For one thing, we don't need to go to the expense of manufacturing it from expensive petrochemicals; instead, it comes to us in ready-to-use form. Rayon and related synthetic fibers are made from wood; their future looks promising, since competitive synthetic fibers depend on the diminishing supply and ever-rising price of oil. Many synthetic chemicals can easily be made from trees, starting with methanol (wood alcohol). Methanol can be added (10% to 15%) to gasoline to improve mileage without modifying present engines. With only a few alterations, the engine in your car can run very nicely on 100% methanol, as the Germans demonstrated during World War II. Wood waste can also be converted into oil and its derivatives without too much difficulty.

Trees also represent a virtually limitless potential supply of food since both sugar and protein can be made from them. Already cattle feed is being made from wood, and synthetic vanilla flavoring has been made from wood for many years.

Most of the major forest product companies manage their vast timberlands on a sustained-yield basis: For every tree they cut down, they plant several new ones. This is why, back in the 1950's and early 1960's, these companies were viewed as super-growth stocks. In those days, the big buyers were scrambling to pay 20 or 25 times earnings for them. Now that these farsighted policies are finally paying off, most of them are going begging at 7 or 8 times earnings. Hope is always worth twice or three times as much as reality. Then, too, fashions change. The vision of steady growth was replaced by the immediate reality of intense competition. As a result, the shares of the forest-product companies seem relatively undervalued as we enter the inflationary 1980's and drastically undervalued when the flight from the dollar into tangible assets gains momentum.

Not only are the timber holdings carried at costs far below replacement cost, but these lands often conceal a host of hidden values which are apparent only to the most dedicated reader of annual reports. Typically, such unstated values include agricultural land, often located near cities where land values are soaring, as well as underground treasures such as oil, coal, minerals, and geothermal resources.

To illustrate, International Paper has become the largest rice producer in the country, as well as a major land developer and a substantial producer of oil. Burlington Northern, another land-rich company, owns, in addition to 1.5 million acres of timber, another million acres of grazing land beneath which are buried 12 billion tons of proven coal reserves and probably much more. What does this mean to the owner of BNI shares? Since there are a little more than 12 million shares outstanding, this means that each share represents ownership of 1,000 tons of coal plus one-eighth acre of timberland. Or, in more familiar terms, 100 shares represents ownership of 100,000 tons of coal and 12½ acres of forest land.

Obviously, these timberlands vary in value depending on location and use, as well as what lies beneath them. For example, timber located in the South and Northwest is more valuable than timber located in the Northeast because it grows faster. The forests of Weyerhaeuser are located chiefly in the Northwest, while those of Union Camp and Westvaco are mainly in the South. Crown Zellerbach lands are concentrated in both areas, while those of Scott, Mead, St. Regis, Boise Cascade, and Great Northern are located mainly in the North and Northeast. Timber holdings of the remaining forest product companies are widely distributed.

All productive land is renewable: crops can be grown on it for the next thousand years, and grass on grazing lands will reappear year after year (if it rains) without any effort on the part of the owner. So why not go out and buy a farm or a few hundred acres of timber if you want the perfect hedge against inflation? Well, many investors are doing just that. But many who do are in for an unpleasant surprise. I know because I have been there. Absentee owners without previous experience in land management had better be in a high tax bracket, so they can write off the losses that seem to plague about 99 out of 100 who venture into these reef-infested waters.

The only way for the inexperienced land-lover to invest directly is to buy a small parcel where you can learn the rudiments of the business with a minimum drain on your capital. An outside source of income is still an absolute necessity during the early years. If you are willing to work hard while learning you should wind up with the ideal inflation hedge, since products of the land often replace money as the preferred medium of exchange during the late stage of every period of runaway inflation.

Another reason to tread cautiously when it comes to buying land directly is that farm values have already risen substantially, although at a much slower rate than urban and suburban real estate prices. Thus, between 1945 and 1970, farmland prices rose at the rate of about 10% a year. In 1973 and again in 1974, prices soared more than 20%. Since then the rise has slowed somewhat, depending on the type of land and its location.

It is apparent from these figures that land values have consistently, though moderately, outpaced inflation during the postwar years. This inflation, beating record seems likely to improve, if anything, in the inflationary years ahead. First of all, there is less and less of it in relation to the burgeoning worldwide hunger for food. Of more immediate interest, urban developments gobble it up faster than what little virgin land that is left can be developed.

Furthermore, in recent years, some investors disillusioned by their experience in the stock market have turned to land as a hedge against inflation. To some extent, then, this has contributed both to the sagging stock market and buoyant land prices. Could we have a future boom in both land and the stock market? Why not? Certainly, the potential funds available in savings accounts, urban real estate, Arab oil, and gold are sufficient to fuel a rise in rural land prices, as well as the stock market. Nor has the flow of such funds into rural land yet reached the proportions of a stampede. Farm and timberland brokers estimate that 90% or more of all rural land transactions are still made by bona fide farmers or ranchers and less than 10% by outside investors seeking an inflation hedge.

As far as opportunities remaining are concerned, the rise in land prices has varied greatly from one section of the country to another. For example, in recent years the average gain in the Midwest has exceeded that of California and the Southwest. Doubtless, this divergence reflects the recent drought years in the latter areas and, perhaps, has created a buying opportunity now that the rains have returned. At any rate, this is the reasoning of some brokers, who specialize in ranch. and farmland acreage; not only because prices are relatively depressed, but due also to improved methods of irrigating these arid lands.

But why assume all these headaches and risks when you can accomplish the same end in five minutes, rather than five years? You can buy the shares of companies that already own valuable land that the market values at only a fraction of the price they paid and of its current value—not to mention its future value. The low cost of this type of land is revealed in Table 8. Currently, the market places a value of only $43 and

TABLE 8
COMPARATIVE LAND VALUES

Company	Acres Owned	1979 Price	Market Value Per Acre (1)	(2)
Alico, Inc.	170,000	$30	$ 386	$ 361
AZL Resources	397,000	5	140	43
Brooks-Scanlon	230,000	33	329	322
Brown Company	520,000	15	465	195
Boise Cascade	2,700,000	32	501	348
Burlington Northern	2,500,000	43	600	217
Crown Zellerbach	3,415,000	33	328	240
Georgia Pacific	4,500,000	30	1,188	966
Great Northern Nekoosa	2,831,000	36	260	196
Hudson Pulp & Paper	500,000	26	131	122
International Paper	8,000,000	45	355	268
Louisiana Pacific	840,000	21	790	510
Mead Corporation	1,400,000	26	698	416
Newhall Land	148,000	30	1,640	1,114
New Mexico & Arizona	582,000	12	51	46
Pacific Lumber	165,000	45	3,445	3,432
Potlatch Corp.	1,293,000	36	530	424
Pope & Talbot	210,000	28	425	413
St. Regis Paper	3,200,000	30	300	211
Southern Pacific	3,700,000	30	435	216
Southwest Forest Industries	425,000	17	510	235
Tejon Ranch	270,000	40	226	210
Westvaco Corp.	1,121,000	30	623	450
Weyerhaeuser Co.	5,600,000	30	814	683
Willamette Industries	430,000	33	1,220	944

(1) Market value of common and preferred stock plus par value of funded debt divided by acres owned.
(2) Market value of common stock divided by acres owned.

$46 per acre on the grazing lands owned by AZL Resources and New Mexico and Arizona Land. This is before making allowance for the funded debt and preferred stock ahead of the common. If these obligations are included, the per-acre market appraisals increase to $140 and $51 respectively; thus leverage is greatest in the common shares of AZL, least in those of New Mexico and Arizona. Even the rich, irrigated farm lands of Tejon Ranch, after more than doubling in price recently, are still priced by the market place at only $210 an acre, which is only a fraction of what investors would have to pay if they bought comparable land outright.

Year after year the land owned by all of these companies steadily increases in value while, in most cases, the price of their shares languishes not too far above the lowest prices of the past ten to twenty years. Of course, these underlying values are appreciating at different rates, depending on the nature of the land and how it is utilized. For example, New Mexico and Arizona concentrates on developing rental and royalty income, rather than on conducting its own farming, mining, or cattle business. In contrast, both Tejon Ranch and AZL Resources are operating companies.

Tejon Ranch farms 30,000 irrigated acres in California's San Joaquin Valley. In addition, more than 5,000 acres are planted in row crops in the nearby Antelope Valley, while 8,000 acres of varietal grapes are now being crushed annually and retailed under the Tejon Ranch label. Another 4,000 acres of Tejon's San Joaquin land are covered with almond orchards.

AZL is primarily a cattle ranch; it grazes more than 40,000 head of cattle and feeds another 170,000 in the company's Arizona and Texas feedlots. To help feed all these hungry cows and bulls, the company grows and harvests 20,000 tons of forage crops each year. However, AZL has more strings in its bow than cattle. Farm equipment sales (Farmhand, Inc.) contribute about $40 million a year in revenues. The company is also one of the nation's major commodity futures brokers through its Chicago headquartered subsidiary, Rufenacht, Bromagen and Hertz, Inc.

The 148,000 acres owned by another Southwest company—Newhall Land and Farming—command a much higher price than do those of the three companies just discussed, and for obvious reasons. One 40,000 acre parcel of Newhall land is located in the heart of one of Los Angeles County's most rapidly developing areas. Newhall's Magic Mountain amusement park (which, as I write, may be sold any day) generates about $10 million in income each year. Despite these lucrative sidelines, Newhall's main source of income grows out of more than 60,000 irrigated California acres which produce bountiful crops of sugar beets, wheat, rice, cotton, alfalfa, and tomatoes.

James Dickason, Newhall's president, expresses optimism about the future of land investments: "The long-range agricultural outlook is for the value of farmland and the importance of efficient large-scale production expertise to increase dramatically as the world population doubles in the next twenty-five years."

Virtually every company surveyed has been confronted with the problem of how to best utilize land that is too valuable for tree growing or farming. They have all come up with the same solution: some sort of commercial, residential or recreational development. Such developments are obviously expected to produce above-average profits. However, except for Newhall and one or two others, these developments—especially the sale of lots and houses—resulted in large losses during the recession of 1974–75. Though the value of the land continued its uninterrupted rise, the ability of the buyer to pay for it did not. Understandably, most companies seem content to let others exploit the possibilities inherent in residential development.

Some land-rich companies not only own vast spreads of land, but have retained or acquired the mineral rights on still more. For example, New Mexico and Arizona Land owns the mineral rights on an impressive 1,350,000 acres. Several energy-hungry companies are searching for oil and uranium on NZ land. Burlington Northern holds all of the mineral rights on an incredible 5.1 million acres, plus partial rights on another 1.1 million acres.

AZL Resources also has an active mineral-exploration program underway on the 499,000 acres of land on which it owns the mineral rights. Currently, geothermal-energy possibilities are being evaluated on the 101,000 acre Baca Grant Ranch in Colorado, while General Electric is evaluating the "sizable" tungsten ore deposit located on the 132,000 acre Gamble Ranch in Nevada. An active search for oil is also being carried out. Commercial quantities of gold are known to exist on the Baca Grant Ranch, since twenty-three old gold mines on the property have produced gold in the past.

Land located in California and Florida obviously has more current and potential value than rural land located in less accessible areas. Thus, the land owned by Alico, Inc. is valued by the market at $361 an acre, even more than the rich farm and orchard lands of California's Tejon Ranch. This appraisal would seem to be amply justified since Alico's spread, located in central and south Florida, consists mainly of timber-covered land plus extensive citrus orchards.

An additional interesting aspect of Alico is that the company buys back approximately 100,000 of its own shares every year. Thus, between 1972 and 1979, the total common shares outstanding were reduced from 2,692,000 to 2,058,000, which obviously boosts the value of the remaining available shares.

I have purposely omitted from Table 8 several large land companies primarily engaged in building residential communities; examples include General Development Corporation (owned by City Investing), Horizon Corporation, and Deltona Corporation. Historically, urban and suburban real estate has not provided a good hedge against inflation when it reaches the runaway stage. There is no reason to assume that the inflationary 1980's will turn out to be any exception. On the contrary, in recent years prices have risen far faster than for comparable land and houses in rural areas, and risks have risen accordingly.

SCIENTIFIC MANAGEMENT

As Table 8 reveals, the major forest-products companies own even larger spreads of timberland, which today is being managed as scientifically as the highly efficient grain farms of the Midwest. Yields which are routine today would have seemed impossible a generation or so ago. Thus, when the first Europeans arrived in North America, the corn harvest averaged about 5 bushels an acre. Today, thanks to genetic improvements and intensive management, yields exceed 200 bushels per acre.

Similar progress is being made in tree growing. According to George H. Weyerhaeuser, president of the company which bears his name: "We have recently found means to stimulate early tree flowering, so that the time between successive generations of superior trees has been shortened dramatically. We also have developed methods to assess quickly the growth efficiency of the resulting seedling trees, making it possible to determine the success of a particular genetic breeding within weeks rather than decades." Even without genetic breeding, Weyerhaeuser's scientific management doubles and even triples the wood production attained by unmanaged forests.

Like all the forest product companies surveyed, Weyerhauser can cut timber on a lot more land than they own outright. Probably close to half of its timber requirements comes from cutting rights on national forest lands, as well as those rented from private individuals. Thus the "acres owned" figures in the table understate the natural-resource wealth of these companies. For instance, the figures exclude foreign timberland ownership which can be sizable. Westvaco, for one, owns 80,000 acres in Brazil. Back in the 1950's the company started planting loblolly pine seedlings (which are indigenous to the southeastern United States) on its Brazilian lands. Today more than 40,000 acres of these fast-growing trees serve as the basis for the most modern integrated papermaking facility in that country.

Westvaco is as progressive as Weyerhaeuser, although on a smaller scale; 280,000 acres of its land now consists of mature plantations of genetically superior pine trees, which according to president David I. Luke "yield as much as four times more fiber than natural stands of timber." Westvaco plans to add to its timberlands until it is able to supply at least 50% and up to 75% of its fiber requirements.

International Paper, the world's largest papermaker, also owns the most land; considerably more, in fact, than the entire area of the state of Rhode Island. In addition to those timberlands owned outright, IP has harvest rights on an additional 15.6 million acres and owns mineral rights on a total of 9.9 million acres.

IP has not neglected scientific management of its vast spread of forests. Each year more than 100 million seedlings are planted—five for every tree that is harvested. Nevertheless, what really intrigues management is the potential profit lying dormant in all this land that can be added to the present income derived from papermaking. This is why emphasis is being placed on the development of mineral resources. A major step was taken in 1975, when General Crude Oil was acquired so that its specialized technology could be put to work exploring for and developing these potential resources. Although these efforts have met with a high degree of success, in 1979, IP sold General Crude Oil at a profit of about $300 million.

Nor has IP neglected to develop lands suitable for commercial, residential, or agricultural use. One example will suffice: in only a few years IP has become a major rice grower; it produces 50,000 tons a year on company lands near Houston, Texas.

The value of timberlands varies greatly depending on their location and type. For example, the market places the highest value of all on the land held by Pacific Lumber because it contains the choicest remaining stands of virgin redwoods that are still in private hands. Obviously, an acre of redwoods is several times more valuable than an acre of pine trees used to make paper. Moreover, PL has extensive corporate activities other than its redwood lumber business. This nonlumber business accounts for more than 50% of sales.

Forest product companies are an ideal inflation hedge for precisely the reasons that cause stock prices to lag behind inflation during its early stages. Under these near-normal conditions, investor disenchantment seems justified because corporate profits reflect windfall inventory profits and to that extent are overstated—or so investors and accountants reason. Further uncertainty is added—and uncertainty is the thing investors fear most—by the difficulty of calculating costs and planning for the future. An even more adverse effect of inflation is inadequate depreciation charges and, to the extent that they are understated, income taxes are overstated and overpaid. Other things being equal, this is not good; but the distinguishing characteristic of runaway inflation is that past standards and relationships cease to be either equal or meaningful.

Of the two, this latter bookkeeping problem is the more serious. The IRS couldn't care less if corporations pay too much income tax because depreciation charges fail to reflect replacement costs. In fact, they oppose any change in accounting practice that will take inflated costs into consideration.

The problem of inventory profit overstatement seems valid only when inflation is temporary. When inflation continues and accelerates, inventory profits would appear to be justified and reflect the realities of the situation; at least for those companies which have a captive and inexhaustible source of raw materials. In this respect, the profits of General Motors are overstated whereas those of the large forest product companies are not. General Motors buys most of its raw materials from others, whereas the forest-product companies obtain the major part of their raw materials from their own forest lands.

The western railroads rank high on the list of the nation's largest landowners, and their far-flung acres produce more and more income for them every year. Still, revenues from land represent only a small fraction of freight revenues. Southern Pacific, for example, owns and manages more than 3.7 million acres of land, which generate annual sales exceeding $100 million. A substantial business, indeed, yet one that represents only about 5% of total SP revenues.

The productive potential of arid lands has been demonstrated by SP in Nevada—a huge area generally thought to be unsuitable for row-crop farming. However, SP has developed adequate water resources on several thousand acres. Yields of potatoes and beans are comparable to those in areas of Idaho and California, which specialize in these crops. And SP is a major factor in California agriculture, with special emphasis on cotton. Last year some 50,000 acres of SP land in the San Joaquin and Imperial valleys were planted in cotton.

The 2.5 million acres of land owned by Burlington Northern (plus mineral rights on another 6 million) conceals wealth that staggers the imagination. One gem already mentioned: 12 *bil-*

lion tons of proven coal reserves. To be sure, BNI is prevented by law from mining and selling this coal for its own account. However, BNI can and does license others to mine its coal and receives in return a royalty payment on every ton. Further, there is only one practical way to deliver the coal to the buyer—via rail—and there is only one carrier available—Burlington.

The potential of this coal traffic can be imagined from the trend since 1970. In that year BNI hauled 3 million tons. By 1978 this business had grown to more than 50 million tons. To visualize the extent of these reserves in still another way, if 50 million tons were mined each year, the Burlington reserves would last for 2,400 years.

In addition to coal, BNI is a major producer of lumber and related forest products from its 1.5 million acres of timberlands. Furthermore, it is constantly looking for new reserves of uranium and oil. The company refines oil into diesel fuel used by its fleet of locomotives.

Even if the land-rich companies discussed in this chapter don't find rich new lodes of minerals under their land, one conclusion seems as certain as death and taxes, to which runaway inflation must be added: In the long run, these natural resource-rich companies are bound to appreciate in value at least as fast as the dollar depreciates.

12

Nonrenewable Natural Resources

Twenty years ago, when actual inflation was negligible, fear of inflation was widespread. Consequently, and quite logically, the stocks of those companies with large reserves of non-renewable natural resources were in great demand. During the intervening years, as inflation fears gradually turned into reality, companies rich in natural resources were out of favor. Not until 1979 (when profits of the oil industry soared) did interest in resource-rich companies revive. Even now these stocks remain cheap both by traditional price-earnings measurements and even more so based on the value of reserves in-the-ground. This comparative neglect may be due in large part to the public's disenchantment with stocks in general. A more likely explanation is the implication of "nonrenewable." What happens when a company runs out of oil or copper?

Whatever the reasons, this still presents the investor seeking inflation hedges with what may very well turn out to be a once-in-a-lifetime opportunity. Because while a mineral may be nonrenewable, this does not mean that at some time in the future the supply will suddenly vanish. Instead, the price will rise in proportion to the reduction in reserves, which will never be entirely used up.

As we have seen in Chapter 4, owners of natural resources in Germany succeeded in beating the most devastating inflation ever seen because they had fundamental and psychological factors working in their favor. For one thing, domestic inflation made German exports (especially coal, chemicals, and machinery) cheap in terms of foreign currencies, since the exporting firms were paid in American dollars or British pounds, both of which were in great demand in Germany. Business flourished as never before.

Investors were aware of this situation and, as a result, the stocks of natural resource-rich companies (which in Germany meant heavy-industry companies) were in special demand. Strangely enough today, even with double-digit inflation, American investors prefer land or even savings accounts, where they lose more in purchasing power than they earn in interest. As for stocks, they apparently take the term "nonrenewable" literally when it is applied to natural resources. If oil companies are going to run out of oil, and mining companies are going to run out of minerals, then companies depending on such finite assets should be avoided; not only as a poor inflation hedge, but as a bad business risk as well.

I agree with the land lovers although, as mentioned previously, land tends to appreciate early in periods of inflation. It follows that real estate investors might prudently prepare for another roller coaster ride like that of the 1920's when the bull market in stocks got into high gear only after the real estate boom had died on the vine. Real estate investors were wiped out some years before stock market investors suffered a similar fate. This is why in the years to come, ten new fortunes will be made in the stock market for every one realized in real estate.

The currently fashionable idea that we will soon run out of oil and minerals because the supply is finite reflects superficial thinking. It makes more sense to reason that we will run out of gold and diamonds, which are the rarest natural resources of all. Certainly the supply is finite; yet gold has been mined for thousands of years. As it becomes more and more difficult to find large nuggets lying around on the ground, the price rises. And how it rises! Even teen-agers can remember when gold sold for $40 an ounce.

Similarly with diamonds. Every woman would like to own a dozen choice diamonds. If the price was ridiculously low, at say, $100 a carat, the diamond mines would have been depleted long ago. However, the price of diamonds, according to the latest reports emanating from Arkansas and South Africa, has risen quite a bit higher than $100 per carat. Predictably, as prices rise consumption and, therefore, production falls. This is precisely why the profits of DeBeers Consolidated Mines climb with every passing year.

In the final analysis, everything comes from the earth and the oceans. The only exceptions are the wind and direct solar energy. Even the most sophisticated computers are made of silicon, silver, and copper and are powered by electricity made from coal, oil, gas, or uranium. As we have seen, some of these resources have been wasted because they have been chronically undervalued. We are now experiencing the long-overdue upward price adjustment and this accounts, in part, for inflation.

This process of correction has much further to go. For example, many base metals are still deeply undervalued. Investments in companies with large reserve positions will turn out to be a much better inflation hedge than generally believed—if investors think of them in these terms at all. Moreover, some of the more exotic minor metals, such as cadmium, lithium, molybdenum, and beryllium could mushroom in value, when and if some of the promising new uses now being investigated become a reality.

First, however, let us examine our off-again, on-again energy "crisis" and ask two questions: Are we really running out of oil? Are we being blackmailed by a handful of greedy foreigners? The answer to both questions is *no*.

Oil—The popular idea that we are running out of oil is ridiculous. *We will never run out of oil.* World oil reserves will decline eventually. However, the total *value* (or price) of these reserves will *increase* at a faster rate than they will be depleted. This is elementary economics—the old law of supply and demand guarantees that we will never run out of oil. In fact, in the year 2000 those oil companies that currently own large reserves will earn far more *even in inflation-adjusted dollars* than they are earning today, because oil is much too valuable a commodity to be used for gasoline and generating electric power. There are other and potentially more economical ways to do these things.

Those young Arabs educated at Stanford and Harvard were the first to realize this, or at least they were the first to be in a position to act upon their knowledge—as we learned when they quadrupled the price of oil in 1973. They did the whole world a favor, if you take the long view, and they certainly did a very special favor for the foolish, shortsighted oil companies.

Higher prices notwithstanding, the absolute magnitude of domestic oil reserves will doubtless continue to decline due to our spendthrift fuel habits, which we, like all addicts, find hard to change. After all, if an American, down to his last dollar, was faced with the choice of spending it on food or gasoline, can anyone doubt which he would choose? However, it is less certain that worldwide reserves will decline by very much, if at all, by the year 2000. Huge new fields have been found in Mexico and reportedly in China. More will doubtless be found elsewhere.

Meanwhile, the new psychology of scarcity will prevail and thereby drive prices higher and higher until eventually oil will become too expensive to burn and, instead, will be used only as the raw material for an endless list of chemicals, plastics, and synthetic fibers. When this day arrives, what will replace gasoline in our fuel tanks? There are many possibilities which are feasible right now and will become practical when car manufacturers finally design cars that will operate on the most readily available fuels, rather than vice versa. Some of these possibilities, such as methanol or hydrogen, have already been mentioned.

In due course, new and more efficient power sources will replace the gasoline engine. One promising possibility is the fuel cell—also powered by methanol or hydrogen—which has the added advantage of not polluting the atmosphere. A battery-powered car is still another possibility, when the new lightweight lithium-sulfur batteries are perfected.

An exhaustive analysis of the oil industry is beyond the scope of this book. However, there is an all-important consideration: How much oil in the ground does each company own? Therefore, in Table 9, I show the dollar value of proven oil and gas reserves per common share after deducting long-term debt and preferred stock, which have prior claims on the corporation's assets. To obtain these values, I have used a price of $5 per barrel of oil, 50 cents per 1,000 cubic feet of gas, and $1 per ton of coal. (Several companies have a stake in coal that is not shown because their reserves are either small

TABLE 9
ENERGY RESERVES

Company	Oil (millions of barrels)	Gas (billions of cubic feet)	Coal (billions of tons)	Debt (millions, including preferred stock at par value)	Common Shares (millions)	Value Per Common Share
Amerada Hess	962	2,800	—	$1,400	26.4	$182
Atlantic Richfield	2,800	12,500	—	4,300	108.0	147
Cities Service	644	3,700	—	990	27.7	142
Continental	2,100	6,200	14,800	1,750	107.3	249
Getty	2,400	2,800	—	225	82.1	160
Occidental	1,100	400	4,300	1,610	70.0	77
Shell	1,900	6,900	—	1,600	143.8	79
Standard Oil of California	2,000	8,500	—	2,500	170.6	69
Standard Oil of Indiana	1,900	8,600	—	2,550	146.3	77
Sun Company	990	4,300	—	1,100	51.4	118
Union	565	6,900	—	1,100	44.0	118

or not available.) Whatever the merit of these assumptions, the relative values will still be meaningful, although they must be adjusted from time to time to allow for consumption vs. new reserves added.

Let's look at some other energy sources.

Uranium—I worked with this radioactive metal as a young chemical engineer on the Manhattan Project. In those days, the only source of the ore was Africa and, for security reasons, the ore was shipped to us labeled "cocoa"—which it resembled. Since then I have followed the development of nuclear power with intense interest but with growing dismay.

In the first place, the Atomic Energy Commission concentrated on weapon development, while other nations, which started out far behind us, concentrated on the development of efficient nuclear power. We opted for light-water reactors, which use the enriched uranium necessary for the production of bombs. Such plants have serious disadvantages. In contrast, England, Japan, and Germany all developed reactors fueled by natural uranium and, later on, fast-breeder reactors, which have numerous advantages over our horse-and-buggy light-water reactors.

What are the disadvantages of light-water reactors? First, they are dangerous. Second, they produce plutonium, a by-product which can easily be made into atom bombs. There is also a more fundamental drawback, which is more difficult to prove. In spite of the enormous amount of energy released by the fission of uranium 235, I am not convinced that more power is gotten out of it than is put into it. And, after all, that's the reason power plants are built in the first place. In the first place, the efficiency of a light-water reactor is incredibly low. They work as well as they do because when mass is converted to energy, a tiny amount of mass produces an enormous amount of energy.

The plutonium bomb that leveled Nagasaki contained fissionable material that weighed about as much as the nail on your little finger. Natural uranium contains less than 1% of uranium 235. To separate it from uranium 238, the government operates three giant gaseous-diffusion plants which gulp incredible amounts of electric power. Then, too, the uranium oxide or yellowcake from which the fissionable uranium 235 is extracted in the diffusion plants requires an expensive refining process before it is ready for the diffusion step.

It would seem that the outlook for a power system that uses up as much power as it produces is not very promising—especially not when it also creates a whole new bunch of safety and contamination problems that would otherwise not exist at all and which appear to be largely insoluble. In short, the opponents of nuclear energy are right but mostly for the wrong reasons. Whatever the future of nuclear power, the outlook for light-water reactors seems doubtful at best.

Meanwhile, inflation watchers should note that a couple of years ago, the Bureau of Mines predicted that yellowcake would rise from $8 to $17 a pound by the year 2000. But they were wrong. They hardly had time to get this sample of bureaucratic wisdom in print before the price was $40 a pound. Apparently, the present generation of nuclear power plants require uranium regardless of theoretical considerations concerning their efficiency. Only a handful of companies have appreciable reserves. These include Kerr-McGee, which controls perhaps 25% of known reserves in this country, Denison Mines, which has huge reserves in Canada, Atlas Corporation, Ranchers Exploration, and UNC Resources.

Coal—There is more energy locked up in the proven coal reserves of this country than in all the oil of the Middle Eastern countries combined. When oil prices quadrupled, it seemed the time had finally arrived for coal to recapture its steadily declining share of the energy pie. This has not happened—at least not to the extent that the Department of Energy envisioned. Nor to the extent that the price-per-BTU advantage enjoyed by coal would logically suggest should happen. There are a number of reasons for this laggard performance.

Coal is dirty—dirty to mine and dirty to burn—as almost every householder past middle age can vividly remember. To awaken in the morning with the temperature outside below zero and the fire in the furnace out (after you so carefully banked it before going to bed) is not an experience you quickly forget. Perhaps this is why coal lost practically 100% of the space-heating market and why it seems doubtful that coal will ever regain this market—even if it was delivered to your front door free of charge.

When it comes to underground mining, the record of coal is even worse than that of uranium, perhaps because it has had a longer history in which to establish a bad reputation. As everyone knows, over the years the mining casualty list reads like something issued by the War Department. Personally, if I had to choose between working in a coal or uranium mine, I would be hard pressed to select the lesser of the two evils.

It is easy for the Department of Energy to direct large users of energy to convert from oil and gas to coal. It is not very easy or economical for these users to comply with such directives. For example, diesel locomotives, which consume a lot of energy, cannot readily be converted to coal; even if they could, formidable air-cleaning problems would have to be overcome. This is why we see Burlington Northern diesel locomotives pulling 100-car trains loaded with coal. This low-sulfur coal is rolling toward coal-burning electric power plants which prefer it because it can be burned without making the expensive modifications in their plants required to scrub out the sulfur.

But these trains can roll only so far before they boost the

price of the coal beyond that of its fossil rivals, oil and gas. The problem is that the low-sulfur coal is in the Northwest, and the largest potential customers are in the East, Southeast, and California. This makes the outlook dim, indeed. Most eastern coal is not only high in sulfur, but is also located too far below the surface for strip mining. (And strip mining has plenty of problems of its own.) These are a few of the points to check out before rushing out and buying coal stocks as an inflation hedge.

Looking further ahead, one promising new use for coal is as a raw material for the manufacture of an almost endless list of chemicals ranging all the way from nylon to aspirin. (Coal-tar chemicals have long been a byproduct of steelmaking.) Also, I might add from firsthand knowledge, vitamins. I helped develop the first plant to synthesize a vitamin—nicotinic acid—from coal.

However, the truly mind-boggling potential for coal (and one that is economically feasible at last, thanks to the ever-rising price of oil) lies in the production of synthetic gas and oil. The necessary technology is well known and proven. Remember, at the turn of the century, most cities were lighted by gas manufactured from coal. Not so long ago, one major-league baseball team—the St. Louis Cardinals—was known as "the gas-house gang." The name referred to the city's gas plant, which could be plainly seen and smelled from the ball park. And remember that Hitler's Panzer and motorized divisions ran on oil and gasoline made from coal.

The essential step in the coal-to-gas-and-oil process is the addition of hydrogen, so those companies with large hydrogen-producing capacity and technology may well be prime beneficiaries of the oil from coal boom that lies ahead. Specialists in hydrogen production include Big Three Industries, Union Carbide, and Air Products and Chemicals.

Most major oil companies have acquired coal reserves in

anticipation of just such an eventuality and are actively working on increasing the efficiency of coal-to-oil technology. Burlington Northern is also at work in this area, and with proven coal reserves of 12 billion tons, seems well situated to participate in this inevitable development. Confirming such a conclusion was a recent announcement by Burlington that it had formed a joint venture to convert coal; "to products now made from natural gas and petroleum, such as ammonia fertilizer, methyl fuels, synthetic diesel fuels and possibly other products."

A great deal of basic research on coal gasification has been carried out by the Koppers Company in conjunction with its venerable business of producing chemicals from coal tar. Allied Chemical, another producer of coal-tar chemicals, is also doing research along this line.

The catalytic combination of coal with hydrogen produces methane, which is the principal ingredient of natural gas. Methane, of course, can be piped from the coal fields, where the gasification plants should logically be located, in the already existing network of natural gas pipelines. This is a far more economic method of delivering energy than coal cars or copper wires; that is one reason why natural gas has always been a relatively cheap source of energy.

Gasification plants also have the option of oxidizing methane to form methanol (methyl alcohol or CH_3OH). Methanol is the source of formaldehyde, which is the building block for a host of valuable chemicals. One exciting possibility: With only minor modification, our present car engines will operate nicely on methanol or on a combination of methanol and gasoline. Methanol also shows promise as a fuel for fuel cells. The future of fuel cells is another story, which I will condense into one sentence. There is a good possibility that eventually fuel cells, rather than the much publicized solar energy, will provide heat and electricity for our homes.

Another possible byproduct of coal gasification is ethanol (ethyl alcohol or C_2H_5OH) which can also be produced from almost anything organic. Our car engines will also operate nicely on ethanol. In fact, back in the 1930's, a fuel was marketed in the Middle West with the brand name Agrol, which was a blend of gasoline and ethanol. The same blend is being reintroduced today in several areas of the country. The world will not end when we can no longer afford to make gasoline from oil.

This is why so many companies which have not previously had any interest in energy have staked out a position in coal. To name only a few: Kennecott Copper, AMAX Inc., W. R. Grace, Gulf Resources, International Paper, Georgia Pacific, and Anaconda. Most are also diversifying into oil, usually by acquiring small independent oil operators.

To participate in the oil-from-coal boom that appears to be just over the horizon, funds should be concentrated in the major companies, rather than in the small independent coal and oil companies, which do not have either the necessary technical know-how or the capital resources necessary to finance synthetic-oil plants.

Oil shale—I first became interested in the possibilities of obtaining oil from shale way back in 1956. The first thing I learned was that the substance known as oil shale contains neither oil nor shale. Oil shale consists of a sticky rubbery substance known as kerogen and a rock known as marl. Unfortunately, the two have a tenacious affinity for one another, which makes them very difficult to separate. When they are separated, the kerogen yields a black, fishy-smelling material resembling crude oil.

My interest was stimulated by the annual prediction of the oil-depletion lobby that we would run out of oil in fifteen or twenty years and even sooner, if the sacred depletion allowance was tampered with. (It was and we didn't.) In fact, I became sufficiently intrigued to travel to Rifle, Colorado, to look at the pilot plant recently started up by the Oil Shale Corporation. They showed me around and explained their process with the usual enthusiasm of dedicated scientists. Fortunately, as a chemical engineer I could grasp at least part of the problem of producing oil from shale. However, at the time I don't think any of us fully understood the environmental and water availability problems, which then seemed pretty remote if, indeed, they were considered at all.

The lunar landscape of western Colorado and eastern Utah conceals some 600 billion barrels of potentially recoverable crude oil in the form of kerogen dissolved in rock. To release it, the rock must be crushed and heated either above or beneath the surface. In the first method, the oil-shale rocks are mined in the conventional way, crushed and then heated in a rotating kiln, similar to those used in making cement. The resulting crude oily product then goes to a refinery, where it is converted into gasoline, diesel oil, and other prodcuts. The most promising above-ground process is still the one developed by Oil Shale Corporation (now Tosco) with the original assistance of Rockefeller money.

To begin with, the huge quantities of treatment water needed were evidently taken for granted. Not any longer. The oil-shale facilities are located in the watershed of the upper Colorado River, where the water is already fully committed. Therefore, a reliable alternate source must be found and developed before a full-scale plant can be started up.

By 1974 the Colony Development Corporation (a consortium of Arco, TOSCO, Ashland, and Shell) completed plans for a commercial-scale plant using the TOSCO process which—and here I quote from the 1977 and 1978 TOSCO annual reports—"will mine some 66,000 tons per day of oil shale to recover 55,000 barrels per day of crude shale oil for further refining on-site to produce up to 48,000 barrels per day of petroleum products." In 1977 an updated estimate placed the production costs at $1 billion which "will amount to $8.63 per barrel of oil produced having a value in excess of $15." Despite the apparently favorable profit margin—at least on paper—the consortium decided to shelve the project. Water was one problem.

Then, too, the entire concept of oil-shale exploitation caused Sierra Club members and their friends to climb the canyon walls of the Colorado. Not only because mining the shale may play havoc with the underground aquifers; but also because you wind up with twice as much spent shale as you start with. Probably the best solution is to build artificial mountains with it—a solution that is not popular with nature lovers. If you spread it around and plant grass or something, you need large amounts of topsoil, fertilizer (made from oil and gas), and still more water.

It all adds up to the same nagging problem that increasingly worries the nuclear-power industry: Are you putting more power into the system than you are getting out of it? People who have devoted the best part of their lives to the project are not likely to embrace such a conclusion with much enthusiasm. Meanwhile, I doubt that any of us will live to see the day when our cars are running on gasoline from shale oil.

However, some experts disagree with me. So does Dr. Armand Hammer, chairman of the board of Occidental Petroleum, who is the leading champion of the underground, or "in situ," process. His technique involves removing enough shale rock to create an underground room, about the size and shape of a subway station. A powerful explosion is set off, which collapses the roof and in so doing crushes the rock. The room is then sealed off, and a controlled fire is started which liberates the shale oil. It flows out of the cavern and into waiting Occidental tank trucks. The Occidental process was publicized with much fanfare a few years ago by the flamboyant Dr. Hammer, but not much has been heard about it since.

Once our preoccupation with turning everything into energy subsides, we will recognize the fact that oil shale represents an enormous storehouse of essential chemical products that are far more valuable than gasoline. As such, it represents a *long-range* hedge against inflation that could benefit younger readers. Table 10 lists the net oil-shale acreage controlled by the oil companies listed. These are the largest private holdings in thousands of net acres as calculated by the author.

TABLE 10
OIL SHALE HOLDINGS

Atlantic Richfield	20	Standard of California	40
Cities Service	10	Standard of Ohio	10
Equity Oil	10	Superior Oil	7
Exxon	12	Texaco	19
Getty Oil	24	Tosco Corp.	9
Mobil Oil	20	Union Oil	30

Tar sands—The largest deposits are located in northern Alberta and contain an estimated 500 billion barrels of heavy oil. If you take a bucket half-filled with heavy crude oil (or asphalt), fill it up with dirty sand, mix thoroughly, then freeze it to the consistency of concrete, you will wind up with pretty much the same material that lies below the barren muskeg swamps of northern Alberta.

Extracting this material and separating the oil is almost as difficult as separating kerogen from marl—but not quite. After mining the sand, separating the oil from it involves a comparatively simple flotation process. The problems are logistic.

In the summer, the entire area is a quagmire which breeds clouds of mosquitoes. In the winter, the temperature falls to 40 and 50 below zero, and the frozen sand wears out the steel teeth of the giant bucket excavators after only a few hours of use. On the positive side, there is no such thing as a dry hole, so exploratory costs are virtually nil; this is an offsetting advantage of considerable importance to oilmen.

After years of agony, the pioneer company—Great Canadian Oil Sands, Ltd. (80% owned by Sun Company)—now produces 50,000 barrels of oil a day at a nominal profit. Syncrude—a consortium including Gulf, Imperial, Cities Service, and Arco—recently brought a similar-sized operation into production and plans to expand it to 125,000 barrels a day by the early 1980's. Such ventures do not come cheap. Cities Service, which has a 22% interest in Syncrude, has invested $460 million in the project.

Copper—The red metal has been known and valued since the beginning of recorded history. In ancient lands it was used to make tools, weapons, water pipes, and to prevent the growth of barnacles on the bottom of ships. Tin and zinc combine with copper to form bronze and brass, alloys with which everyone is familiar. As a conductor of electricity, copper reigns supreme. The only competitor worth mentioning is silver, which has become much too expensive for such prosaic use.

A majority of copper producers have reserves of ore that should last well beyond the year 2000, so there is no danger of a shortage developing. Nevertheless, with demand steadily increasing, copper would appear to offer a superior hedge against inflation. Furthermore, so many copper mines have been shut down in the recent years of low prices that a shortage of above-ground copper seems certain. This situation favors price rises exceeding the inflation rate and, for this reason, I predict much higher prices for copper by 1985. As an inflation hedge, my preference would be those companies which are primarily producers of other metals, which promise to be in short supply, but also produce substantial amounts of copper. Companies that qualify include Freeport Minerals, AMAX Inc., Inco Ltd., Ranchers Exploration and Texasgulf Inc.

Molybdenum—Molybdenum is used mainly as an additive to toughen steel; no other material has been discovered which threatens to replace it. In addition, molybdenum has other uses for which there are no effective substitutes, so future demand seems assured. The largest single deposit, located at Climax, Colorado, is owned by AMAX Inc., although smaller amounts are produced by other companies as a byproduct of copper mining. Currently there is a worldwide shortage of molybdenum which cannot fail to benefit AMAX.

Cadmium—This relatively rare silvery soft metal has a number of promising outlets, especially in electroplating, in newer types of batteries, and as an alloy with silver for electrical uses. Cadmium compounds also have the unique ability of being able to convert sunlight into electricity; this could have a promising future if the efficiency of conversion can be improved. Cadmium is also used in nuclear reactors as a neutron absorber.

Cadmium seems to have an affinity for zinc; at any rate, it can be obtained only as a byproduct of zinc production. This is why the major zinc producers are the only source of the metal. These include AMAX Inc., Gulf Resources, Cominco Ltd., Asarco, Inc., Texasgulf, and St. Joe Minerals.

Lithium—Lithium is the lightest metal known. While present demand is not large, it could expand spectacularly if any one of several developments is successful. For example, one of the most urgent needs of our technological society is for a more efficient storage battery. Such a battery would have innumerable uses, ranging from battery-powered automobiles to the storage of off-peak electric power by electric utilities. The most promising combination for such a battery appears to be lithium and sulfur.

Theoretical considerations also point to the use of lithium in nuclear fusion reactors. In such a reactor, neutrons from deuterium (obtained from heavy water) convert lithium into tritium—an isotope of hydrogen with an atomic weight of 3— plus unimaginable amounts of power. In the process lithium is used up, which if fusion ever reaches the commercial stage, means that the market for lithium would explode. Of course, success in harnessing power like that of the sun appears to be a matter of decades—rather than years—in the future.

Two companies—Foote Minerals and Gulf Resources—control most of the world's known reserves. It has been estimated that the Great Salt Lake, where Gulf Resources has an extraction plant, contains enough lithium to supply the electric energy needs of this country for the next 2,000 years.

Titanium—The worldwide demand for this relatively new metal is expanding rapidly. Its strength-to-weight ratio exceeds that of steel and, unlike steel, it resists corrosion very well. Long before it was first used as a pure metal (in 1948), titanium dioxide was—and still is—used as a pigment in paints.

Titanium has a potential new use which may boost the demand for it enormously. Hydrogen is an ideal fuel for ordinary reciprocating engines, as well as for jet engines and fuel cells. Not only is it more efficient, it also eliminates air pollution. It would also be the ideal fuel for space heating since it burns without giving off objectionable byproducts, such as smoke and carbon monoxide. This means that a hydrogen furnace— unlike one fueled by gas or oil—would not need any venting system, and this would improve efficiency by about 30%.

The critical problem with hydrogen is how to handle it without getting blown up. The simple solution is to store it in the solid hydride form. It can then be released as needed by gentle heating. The best hydrides are mixtures of iron and titanium. Admittedly, such developments are still in an early stage. However, cars and buses fueled by liquid hydrogen have been running for several years after only minor alterations have been made in their original gasoline-burning engines.

Titanium is obtained from the mineral ilmenite; presently, there is only one logical way to participate in the future of titanium: by investing in NL Industries, which controls about 50% of world reserves.

Since this chapter was written, President Carter has announced a huge crash program to develop gas and oil from coal and oil shale. This program in no way alters the conclusions expressed in this chapter. If not insoluble, the environmental problems will certainly slow down development of these programs, especially in the arid West, where most of the suitable deposits of coal and shale are located. Large quantities of water are required for treatment, and one wonders where it will come from when all available water is already committed. So don't hold your breath until these plants are built and producing.

Meanwhile, nothing at all has been said by the Administration about what may turn out to be the most promising future source of energy: the oceans. The surface of the sea is a giant solar collector: it is much warmer than the water beneath the surface. In the tropics and subtropical regions, the surface temperatures average 80°F., while the temperature 3,280 feet beneath the surface averages 40°F. If these cold and warm layers are brought together by pumping the cold water to the surface, the latent heat released is equivalent to the same volume of water falling 90 feet.

As we all know, the cheapest electric power is generated by hydroelectric plants which use the energy of falling water to turn their turbines. However, unlike the limited amount of falling water available on land, the 40° temperature difference in seawater represents more potential energy than this country consumes in a century.

The transformation of this energy into electricity works on the same principle as the refrigerator in your kitchen. In your refrigerator, a fluid (usually freon) having a suitably low boiling point is compressed by electric power; when vaporized, the heat inside the box is absorbed and dispersed to the outside. In a seawater conversion plant, the process is reversed: electric power is taken out of the system rather than put into it. The warm seawater vaporizes the fluid and in the process produces energy, which turns a turbine and produces electricity. The fluid is then condensed by the cold water, and the cycle is repeated. In either case, a chemical condenses and vaporizes within the temperature spread available. In a seawater plant, common chemicals can be used, like freon, propane, and ammonia.

Several problems immediately come to mind. Very large heat exchangers are required for the efficient extraction of the latent energy. In addition to the usual problem of keeping their surfaces clean, corrosion is a problem. Then, too, a barge on the surface with a pipe extending 3,000 feet down into the ocean depths would, by its very nature, be vulnerable to storms and other problems.

Moreover, again there is the problem of net energy input vs. output. The most practical heat-exchanger material from the standpoint of economy and corrosion resistance would appear to be aluminum, which requires large amounts of energy to produce. Should it turn out that the heat exchangers need to be replaced frequently, the end result might be a net energy *loss*. This is a possibility because the efficiency of a thermal energy conversion plant will be low, at best—probably between 5% and 10%. Since electrical transmission losses are high, plants would have to be located as close as possible to shore.

At least two corporations think that these problems are surmountable. They are currently operating a thermal-conversion pilot plant in Hawaii using a closed ammonia system. This pilot plant generates only 50 kilowatts of power, all of which is used to pump the water to the surface, lifts the cold water through a 24-inch-diameter polypropylene pipe. But what size pipes would a 500,000-kilowatt plant require?

13

Low-priced,
High-risk Hedges

In Chapter 8 we saw how one investor became a millionaire following a method he referred to as the Six-Step Plan. His idea was simple enough: If you can double $15,650 six times, you wind up with $1 million. He started with almost $50,000, or three units of $15,650 each, which tripled his chances of success or reduced by one-third the time required to reach his goal.

If you are more aggressive, or have less to invest than this basic unit of $15,650, it is possible to make one dollar do the work of two or three by investing in speculative low-priced stocks. The desired end result can often be achieved much more quickly, but with greater risk than if you concentrate in investment-grade issues. Better still, you can invest in warrants where the potential gain may be still greater than in low-priced stocks, while the risk need not be as high if you follow the basic rules and suggestions spelled out in this chapter.

Warrants are a strange and little-understood world. Warrants are considered by most investors to be the most risky of all investments; *yet some warrants are actually guaranteed against loss.* In this one respect, at least, some of them have the same advantage over stocks that bonds have. First, however, we must distinguish between warrants and options which, in recent years, have gained enormously in popularity and respectability.

Warrants are options, but options are not necessarily warrants; yet both represent the right to buy one share of a common stock at a fixed price for a specified length of time. Unlike options, warrants are issued by a corporation as a part of its capital structure. Options are sold by individuals who own a common stock to other individuals who anticipate that the stock will eventually sell at a much higher price. Warrants represent the right to buy a stock; options can represent the right to either buy a stock (in which case they are called "calls"), or to sell a stock (in which case they are called "puts").

The attraction of both warrants and options derives from the fact that investors can control a much larger investment than they can afford (or choose) to buy outright. Option buyers purchase this right for only a relatively short period of time (usually three, six, or nine months) and this time limitation represents their greatest drawback. In contrast, warrants usually have a life, when issued, of at least five years, and more normally ten years or even longer. Back in the 1960's, when I was writing and publishing stock-market reports, I also wrote (or sold) options against the stocks in my investment portfolio. The option buyer would pay me, on average, 12% to 15% of the price of each stock that he fancied, depending on its popularity and the length of the option.

How did this work? The option dealer maintained an up-to-date list of stocks that I and other writers owned. When a buyer wanted an option on a stock which he thought was about to soar into the wild blue yonder, the dealer would sell him a call for, say, $600 on a $40 stock. Simultaneously, he would offer to buy the option from me (if it was one of my stocks) for, say, $550. The difference represented his commission.

In those days, there was no aftermarket for options. The buyer either had to exercise his option, which meant putting up sufficient cash to purchase the stock (the price at which the option can be profitably exercised) even if he planned to sell it immediately, or else let the option expire. Today, in contrast, the owner who changes his mind during the life of the option can sell it at any time to someone else, providing there is an active market for that particular option. Today options are traded on the Chicago Board of Trade and on several stock exchanges.

I continued to write options for a number of years. It prevented me from selling good growth stocks on the emotional news that needlessly triggers most of the transactions that take place on the stock exchanges. In addition to the dividends, I was realizing another 10% or 12% on the value of my portfolio, which was a pretty good return at a time when interest rates averaged 6% or less. True, occasionally I missed out on a large profit when a big winner was called away from me. Nonetheless, in the long run, I confirmed the fact that the odds in the option business favor the seller rather than the buyer—and by a pretty wide margin.

At this point you may wish to take time out to study Chapter 18, in which the psychology of successful speculation is discussed, because the emotional pressures on the option buyer are unrelenting. The seller of an option has only one decision to make: to sell the option or not to sell it. Thereafter, the decision making is out of his hands and in the hands of the buyer, who has a decision to make every day (even if it is to do nothing) until the option either expires or is exercised. Time and patience work powerfully in favor of the seller. To illustrate, suppose I write a six-month call on Ford Motor at 40, for which the buyer pays $600. Perhaps he thinks that Ford's new models are going to be a great success, or simply that Ford is deeply undervalued at only four times earnings. Paradoxically enough, I must agree with him on both counts, even though I am selling the call, or I wouldn't own Ford stock in the first place. While we may agree about the outlook for Ford, otherwise our psychological positions are miles apart.

After writing the call, I have a 5½ point *profit* on my 100 shares of Ford *no matter what happens*. Moreover, there is no further action I can take during the life of the option. In contrast, the buyer of the option will reach the breakeven point only when Ford rises to 46. Let us assume that after three months Ford has risen to 50—a pretty substantial gain for an institutional stock. At this point, the option owner has a paper profit of 4 points. Will he take it? Not likely. He is looking for a much larger profit.

Then Ford backs off to 43 a month later. The option owner could still exercise his option, sell the stock, and salvage half of his investment. Will he do it? Again not likely; hope springs eternal. After all, two months still remain during which Ford could soar above 50. By the time the option expires, Ford has retreated to around 40. The buyer loses 100% of that particular investment. The problem is that, contrary to popular belief, wide moves either up or down within a six-month interval are the exception rather than the rule.

While most options are never exercised, they have gained steadily in popularity because (1) they limit possible losses and

(2) the buyer can control more stock for less money. He can make more per dollar invested if he is right—in time. For instance, if a $40 stock doubles, the owner of 100 shares has a profit of 100%. In contrast, the option buyer realizes a profit of $3,400 on his $600 investment for a gain of 560%, or almost six times as much. How often do stocks double within six months? Apparently often enough to keep alive the hopes of those who buy options. Looking ahead, if the scenario outlined in Chapter 9 unfolds on schedule, the stocks that double in six months will become the rule rather than the exception, and the extravagant dreams of option buyers will come true.

The idea behind option buying makes a lot of sense even now for a person with a limited amount of capital. However, the danger lies in paying too much for too little—too little time, that is. The time element defeats the option buyer. This disadvantage can be overcome by buying warrants, rather than options. If the cost is comparable, why buy an option that expires in six months when you can buy a warrant that expires in six years?

I have discussed options at some length to show why they are not suitable for the inflation-hedge investor who wants to get maximum mileage out of his fast-depreciating dollars. Fortunately, much better opportunities do exist if one searches diligently for warrants. Warrants are long-term options, and those are what we are looking for. Not only does the longer life strengthen the strategic position of the owner, but an option with a life of several years may cost little more than one with a life of only three or six months.

Warrants are cheaper because they are usually created as a byproduct used to "sweeten" a new issue of debentures. No value is assigned to them when they are issued, no price when they are first traded. Few investors know what warrants are, let alone what they are worth. This is why the best time to buy a warrant is shortly after it has been created. The new owners of the debentures to which the warrants are attached may not want to be bothered with the relatively few warrants involved and may sell them immediately for whatever they will bring. This initial price may be unrealistically low, simply because few investors are even aware of their existence, while still fewer have the long familiarity and experience with warrants necessary to recognize if they are over- or undervalued. Later on, the warrant will continue to be attractive if the common stock sells substantially below the conversion price.

Another rule of thumb: Warrants are attractive only when they sell for no more than one-third the price of the common and they are still more attractive when they sell for no more than one-fourth the price of the common. Even when the latter condition is fulfilled, warrants which expire in less than two years should be avoided. If the common stock remains below the conversion price as the warrant expiration date approaches, the warrant will gradually lose its value and will finally become worthless. As the record shows, this has been the ultimate fate of a majority of all the warrants ever created. Obviously, then, the longer the remaining life of the warrant the greater its value.

Equally obvious, a warrant cannot be any better than the underlying common stock. I need not stress the importance of investigating the financial condition of the company and the outlook for the common stock before even considering buying the warrants. Warrants—like other options—must also have sufficient leverage to enable a small amount of money invested in the warrants to accomplish what a much larger sum would accomplish in the common stock.

Warrants with a leverage of less than 2-to-1 (a fixed amount of money will gain twice as much in the warrants as in the common stock) should not be considered. After all, if you can make almost twice as much in the warrants, what more do you want? You want to make three times as much. The greater the potential, the stronger is your psychological position; therefore, your determination to hold the warrants until their ulti-mate potential is realized. You need all the encouragement you can get during those long months or years of waiting when the common stock may be paying dividends which you, as a warrant owner, are not receiving.

Consider the following table of typical warrants, all of which are traded on either the American or the New York Stock exchanges.

TABLE 11
TYPICAL WARRANTS—1979 (Fourth Quarter)

Company	Price Common	Price Wts.	Purchase One Common at	Warrants Expire
American Airlines	10	3½	14	4-1-84
American Broadcasting	40	35½	16	1-2-82
Atlas Corp.	20	7	31.25	perpetual
Braniff International	8	6½	22.94	12-1-86
Charter Company	40	31	10	9-1-88
City Investing	18	1½	(1)	7-15-83
Chrysler Corp.	8	3	13	6-15-85
First Pennsylvania	10	1½	20	5-8-83
Frontier Airlines	10	4	11.37	3-1-87
Kidde (Walter) & Co.	35	1¼	(2)	4-29-81
Loews Corp.	55	27	40	11-29-80
Mattel, Inc.	7	4	16.25	4-1-86
Rapid-American	20	4	35	5-15-94
Resorts International A	27	13	53	8-1-84
Sterling Bancorp.	7	1	15	12-31-83
Total Petroleum	19	12	10	12-31-80
U.S. Air Inc.	7	1	15	12-31-83

(1) Right to purchase one share GDV, Inc. at $27.70.
(2) Right to purchase one cum. CV. "C" preferred share at $90.

Look at the relationship between warrant price, common price, and the price at which each warrant can be converted into common. There is no hard-and-fast rule determining such relationships because there are too many variables involved including, most importantly, the life expectancy of the warrant. Equally important and unpredictable is the often irrational behavior of the public who trade in warrants without fully understanding them. This state of affairs creates endless opportunities for investors who make the effort necessary to understand these relationships. Fortunately, they are not really mysterious; they are only a matter of simple arithmetic.

To illustrate this arithmetic: Total Petroleum warrants represent the right to purchase one common share at 10 until December 31, 1980, so the warrants have little more than a year of life as this is written. Nonetheless, recently with the common at 19, the warrants sold at 12. This means the warrants had an intrinsic value of 9 (19 minus 10) so they were selling at a 3 point premium, which seems difficult to justify in light of their relatively short life expectancy. True enough, if the common doubles to 38 the intrinsic value of the warrants would be 28, so the upside potential is 133%, or one-third more than for the common. However, by the same token, if the common falls 50% to 9½, the warrants would lose twice as much, since in the past when the common sold at 9½ the warrants sold around 3. Then too, with the expiration date fast approaching they would no doubt sell even lower than 3.

Consider the relationship between the Chrysler and the Braniff warrants. Their expiration dates are only six months apart, so in this respect they are comparable. Moreover, the prices of the common stocks happen to be identical, so this is another variable which can be eliminated. Furthermore, in making such a comparison, the future prospects and problems of the two companies can be ignored, since these imponderables are presumably discounted (to whatever extent this is possible) by the current price of each stock. Notwithstanding all these similarities, the market places a wildly different evaluation on the warrants. Thus, the Chrysler warrant represents the right to buy the common at 13, or only 5 points above the current common price. Historical experience indicates that the price of 3 for these warrants lies within the area which might be considered "normal." This normal area might vary a point on either side of 3.

A very different relationship exists between the Braniff common stock and warrants. At 8 the common sells 15 points below the conversion price. When and if the common rises to that point ($22.94) the intrinsic value of the warrants will be zero. Yet the warrants are selling at 6½! Why the huge premium—more than twice that commanded by the Chrysler warrants? For one thing, the Braniff warrants are unique in that each one of them represents the right to buy 3.18 shares of common for $73 (or one share for $22.94). These unusual terms may confuse many buyers and encourage them to pay a premium which seems to be unrealistically large. There is another possible explanation for the large Braniff premium. Very often a group seeking to gain control of a company that has warrants outstanding will accumulate the warrants to reinforce their eventual position in the common stock. Whether or not the new group gains control, their investment in the warrants may appreciate sharply in value when their intention to gain control becomes public knowledge. These theoretical explanations are intriguing, but need not cloud the practical conclusion. Statistically the Chrysler warrants are a much better buy.

The most sensational performer on the New York Stock Exchange in recent years was the Charter Company warrant. In the ten months between December 1978 and September 1979 these warrants skyrocketed more than 4,000% (from 1 to 45¾). The history of this performance warrants careful study on the part of speculators who hope to participate in future bonanzas of a similar nature.

In the fall of 1978 Charter Company marketed a $50 million issue of 10⅝% debentures. Each $1,000 debenture had 75 ten-year warrants attached representing the right to buy 75 shares of common at $10 through September 1, 1988. At the time, Charter common was selling around 6, so what were the warrants worth? The answer depends on how optimistically prospective buyers viewed Charter's future, as well as on speculative sentiment at that time.

Charter was at that time a relatively obscure company whose main assets were a string of service stations in the South, plus a 70,000 barrel-a-day refinery in Houston, Texas. In 1978 such properties were considered to be more of a liability than an asset. Therefore, we can safely assume that few investors were even aware of the existence of Charter, let alone of the new warrants and that not many of those who were aware of the warrants were familiar with their provisions. On the other hand, no doubt most of the new owners bought the debentures because of their liberal yield (at that time) and were not interested in owning the highly speculative warrants. In short, there were potentially more sellers around than buyers and therein existed an unprecedented opportunity for those investors with sufficient courage and vision.

When trading commenced on the New York Stock Exchange the highest price recorded for the warrants was 1⅝, with a majority of trades taking place at 1½. During October-November 1978 the market turned acutely weak, causing the Charter common shares to decline from 6 to 4, the warrants from 1½ to 1. During December 1978 the average price for the common and warrant was 5 and 1¼ respectively. As I have pointed out, a warrant is most attractive when it sells for from one-third to one-fourth the price of its common. The reason is obvious in the case of Charter. In the warrants you could control four times as many common shares as by investing the same amount of money directly in the common.

Consider the possible reasoning of an investor seeking an inflation hedge who visualized the Dow-Jones Industrial Average reaching the 5,000 level during the 1980's. This would be a six-fold gain based on the then prevailing level of 800. If Charter common only managed to duplicate this performance (low-priced stocks usually gain much more than the market averages) then it would sell at 30. At that point the warrants would have an intrinsic value of 30 minus 10 or 20. A $5,000 investment in the common would appreciate to $30,000, whereas the same amount invested in the warrants would be worth *a minimum* of $80,000.

Should the common outgain the Industrial Average by a modest margin and rise to 50, then the warrants would have an intrinsic value of 40, which means a $5,000 investment would grow to $160,000. In short, the higher the common rises the greater the relative percentage gain by the warrants. As it turned out, these projections were actually realized in less than a year and the gains in the warrants were considerably greater than these projections, because in practice warrants always command a premium which persists until their expiration date draws near. For example, when the common reached 12 the warrants sold at 6, and when the common hit 18 the warrants sold at 13. When the common reached the 25 level the warrants were not far behind at 21. As Charter climbed from 12 to 25 the premium on the warrants actually *widened* from four to six points, which is contrary to what might be expected. Ordinarily, the further the common climbs above the striking price the less the premium investors are willing to pay for the conversion privilege enjoyed by the warrants. How then can the extraordinary action on the part of the Charter warrants be explained? This can only be a matter of conjecture. However, the events that occurred in the spring of 1979 go a long way toward explaining it.

During the spring and summer Charter was negotiating to take over the bankrupt Cary Energy Corporation, which owned 65% of a 500,000 barrel-a-day oil refinery in the Bahamas. Imaginative investors correctly anticipated that, if successful, the acquisition would have a dramatic impact on Charter earning power. Therefore, they were willing to pay a sizable premium for the warrants because by buying them they could control a greater number of common shares for the same dollar investment.

To illustrate, when the common and warrants sold for 18 and 13, respectively, any investor who correctly envisioned a move in the common to 50 was assured of realizing a larger profit in the warrants (177% vs. 202%) even if the premium had entirely disappeared by then. Actually, when the common sold at 50 the warrants were selling at 45¾, or at a premium of 5¾ points. At that point the gain in the warrants amounted to 251%, compared to 177% in the common.

Moreover, as the warrants climbed to 20 then 25 and beyond, they evidently looked "too high" to many traders who proceeded to sell them short. This is hardly surprising since only a few months before they had been selling between one and two. The short interest soon averaged about 12% of the total number of warrants outstanding. Since all warrants sold short must eventually be bought back, this short position represented an important support for the warrants. Considerations such as these must have contributed to the 5¾-point premium when the common sold at 50, since at that point the potential profit for new buyers was greater in the common than in the warrants.

Finally, to get back to my rather unbelievable statement that there is such a thing as a "high-risk speculation guaranteed against loss." Sometimes warrants are not as risky as they look. Not if the issuing corporation guarantees to buy them back at a definite price and time. Why would a corporation deign to do this? Your guess is as good as mine. Possibly to avoid having a lot of warrant owners mad at them if the warrants turn out to be worthless when they expire. More seriously such a provision obviously makes the warrants, and therefore the debentures to which they are attached, more attractive to prospective buyers. Whatever the reasons, the importance of this provision should not be overlooked by those who are looking for warrants to buy and would like to have their investment guaranteed against loss.

To illustrate, the prospectus describing the debentures and warrants issued by The Charter Company reveals that the warrants are guaranteed against dilution should the stock be split, or should the common share holders receive rights offerings at less than the current price, or receive spin-offs of assets. This is an important consideration and warrants that do not enjoy this protection against dilution should be avoided. Here it should be pointed out that the odd conversion prices in Table 11 reflect such adjustments.

Furthermore, as we read on we learn that: "The warrants may be tendered to the company, at the option of the holder thereof, for $1.25 each in cash during the 10 trading days ending September 1, 1983 and, if the expiration date has not been accelerated, during the 10 trading days ending September 1, 1988." In short, if the warrants have not been previously exercised, the company will buy them back before their expiration on September 1, 1988, and also reserves the right to make a similar offer five years sooner, which the warrant owner may accept or reject as he chooses.

This means that the buyer of the warrants late in 1978 when the price was 1¼ was guaranteed against loss of principal providing, of course, that Charter is still a going and solvent concern five or ten years from then, and also providing he is willing to forego interest income on the money invested in the warrants during the intervening years. This latter drawback seems relatively minor in comparison with the size of the gain potential inherent in warrants if they are bought when the common stock is selling well below the price at which the warrants may be converted, and if the leverage in favor of the warrants is at least 2 to 1 and, preferably, 3 to 1 or even higher.

The longer you study the table the more you realize that the price of common stocks vs. warrants is an extremely complex relationship due to the numerous variables involved. For example, the Loew's warrants expire in less than a year. With the common selling at 55 the warrants have an intrinsic value of 15, yet they are selling at 27, or for a 12-point premium. Is this option over- or under-priced? You can muster a persuasive argument either way. Thus, if Loew's doubles in price before the warrants expire, an equal dollar investment in the warrants will yield a 60% larger gain than the same investment in the common would. I personally don't think that the extra gain is sufficiently large to justify the risk, but this is a matter of opinion (and by the time this is published I may very well be proven wrong).

At least one reason can be cited that might explain a higher price for the Loew's warrants than seems justified, in view of the fast approaching expiration date. Like most warrants, these were created to make an issue of debentures more attractive to prospective buyers, while at the same time reducing the interest cost to the company. The Loew's debentures are due in 1993 and pay annual interest at the rate of 6⅞%. Without the attached warrants the interest rate necessary to attract investors would have been appreciably higher, perhaps 8 or 9%.

At the moment, the debentures (without the warrants attached) sell for 68, i.e., a $1,000 par value bond can be purchased for $680. This is an important consideration for the warrant owner who is considering converting the warrants into common stock because the newly issued common stock he receives can be paid for either with $40 in cash or with the debentures at their par value. That is to say, by using the debentures rather than cash, the buyer reduces the effective price he must pay for the common stock from $40 to around $27 a share, This potential windfall may account for a considerable part of the premium commanded by the warrants.

By now the place of warrants in the inflation fighter's arsenal should be apparent. If you decide to adopt the Six-Step Plan, or some similar approach, and have only limited funds, an investment in warrants enables you to make one dollar do the work of two or three invested in common stocks. Let us assume that one Six-Step Plan investor, whom we will refer to as "A," liked the outlook for Charter. Perhaps upon investigating the company he discovered that the trustees of the Alfred du Pont estate had invested heavily in Charter (the estate owns about 23% of Charter common stock) and he figures what is good enough for the du Ponts is good enough for him.

However, he does not even consider the Charter warrants, because he shares the prejudice of most investors that warrants are much too risky for conservative investors to even consider buying. Instead he invests one unit ($15,650) in Charter common at 5, which means he buys 3,130 shares. Furthermore, when and if Charter doubles in price, thereby fulfilling the first step in the Plan, the stock will still only be selling at 10. When this occurs, he diligently searches for a better way to invest the unit now concentrated in Charter common. As it turns out the outlook for Charter still seems promising to him and the stock still appears cheap at 10, so he decides to keep his funds in Charter during Step 2, which, incidentally, saves a considerable amount of money in brokerage commissions.

Inflation hedger "B" shares A's positive attitude toward Charter but unlike A he has no prejudice against owning warrants. If they can help him accomplish his objective. This is fortunate because he has less capital to invest than A. He manages to scrape together $7,125 and with this he buys 5,700 warrants paying 1¼ including commissions for them. When and if Charter reaches 20 his $7,125 will have grown to $62,700 and he will have successfully completed step 2 of the Six-Step Plan with less than half of the investment needed by A. Such is the magic that the leverage of warrants can accomplish.

From a more practical point of view it means that you can start out with more units because, after all, not every stock is going to move from 5 to 20 and even those that do usually require long periods of time to do it. You can buy more units with warrants and the more units you have the quicker you may realize our goal of pyramiding $15,650 into one million. This disclaimer is amply warranted in today's sluggish stock markets, when a real bull market has not been experienced in ten years or more. However, when the psychology of hyper-inflation dominates the market place, it will be possible to complete the Six-Step Plan in a matter of months, rather than years, especially if you concentrate your units in new and attractively priced warrants shortly after they are issued.

How will you be able to learn about new warrants when they are issued? Especially those that are guaranteed against loss? The research department of your stock broker's firm is in the business of locating such situations and they will be happy to call them to your attention if they are aware of your interest in them.

Of course, the issuance of new warrants is a comparatively rare event. Still, many opportunities can be found among warrants that are already issued. So let's compare the relative merits of four of the warrants listed in Table 11: First Pennsylvania, Sterling Bancorp, Rapid American, and Resorts International. In each case, the common sells at about half the price at which the warrants may be converted. So, other factors being equal, you might logically expect their warrants to be selling at about the same price. However, other factors are seldom equal in the esoteric world of warrants.

At first glance the most attractively priced of the four warrants would appear to be those of First Pennsylvania and Sterling Bancorp. However, they expire in about three years, a less desirable feature than if they enjoyed a longer life. Then too, a warrant is attractive only if its common stock has substantial upside potential. These bank holding companies can hardly be classified as dynamic performers, whereas both Rapid American and Resorts can.

Rapid American is one of the largest retailers in the land and also owns Schenley Distillers. However, the dynamic aspect lies in its highly leveraged capital structure which tends to make per share earnings fluctuate widely. As was demonstrated a couple of years ago, Resorts moves in dynamic fashion because of the nature of its gambling business. While the two companies are hardly comparable, let us assume you feel they have similar upside potential. If the common stocks double (the warrants would then have an intrinsic value of zero) it is difficult to imagine the Resorts warrants selling at a much greater premium than its present price of 13. In contrast, if Rapid American common doubles the warrants could conservatively be expected to sell at a 7- or 8-point premium. In this event the upside potential of the warrants would be twice that of the common. Looking further ahead, assume that the common doubles again to 70. If by then the warrant premium has narrowed to 5 points, the gain in the warrants would be 1,400% compared to a gain in the common of only 200%. Moreover, these warrants have the longest life of any of those listed with the exception of the Atlas warrants, which are perpetual. These, then, are some of the intangibles which make the study of warrants so fascinating and, occasionally, so profitable.

PART III
Traditional Inflation Hedges

14

Precious Metals

If you are a "gold bug" [12] with high blood pressure, you may
wish to skip this chapter. What I have to say in the first part of
it may make you unhappy. Yet, not so long ago, I was beating
the drums for gold as fervently as any French peasant. That
was a decade ago, when it was against the law for American
citizens to own gold bullion and before there was a futures
market in gold. Then I advised clients to buy gold stocks, as
well as gold and silver coins, as a hedge against inflation.

In my book, *Reality in the Stock Market* (published in 1965),
I summed up the gold bug position as forcefully as I could:

A flight from the dollar will develop due to a speeding up of inflation
and fear of still more inflation. The perfect hedge is still readily

available—but not for long. I am referring, of course, to our silver coins.

The dimes, quarters and halves now in circulation contain 90% pure silver so that 10 dimes, two quarters and any half dollar contains 47 cents worth of pure silver. Undoubtedly, if the price of gold is raised, a similar increase will occur in the price of silver. In fact, there is a good chance the price of silver will rise above its monetary pegged price of $1.293 an ounce, even without a change in the price of gold. Certainly few comparable investments, i.e., diamonds and the like, have the universal acceptability of silver coins. Since about 750 B.C. silver coins have been readily accepted in exchange for goods, when base metal coins and paper money were not accepted. Finally, what other investment is guaranteed against loss? After all, in an emergency you can spend these coins.[13]

Those were the days when you could walk into just about any bank, hand the teller a piece of paper with "one dollar" printed on it and walk out with a silver dollar. Or, if you had a strong back and $1,000, with a bag containing 1,000 silver dollars. Moreover, such bags often contained many coins worth far more than one dollar due to their numismatic value.

On one memorable occasion, the floor of my office was littered with twenty bags of silver dollars. Those bags which cost $1,000 apiece are today worth $30,000 in circulated condition and much more uncirculated. It was like Christmas Eve when my children sorted through these bags and found many Carson City dollars. Since those never-to-return days, gold has soared 2000%, silver 3000%. So the gospel of the gold bugs has been vindicated. However, all this is ancient history. What now?

THE GOLD BUBBLE

The gold lobby maintains that a return to the gold standard will solve the problem of government irresponsibility, which is the basic cause of inflation. This is clearly not true, as a study of monetary history repeatedly demonstrates. No matter what the nature of the currency, governments have always found ways of debauching it. Admittedly, these ways are simpler when you can create billions of new dollars simply by writing a check rather than by adulterating the coinage, as the ancients did. Or, should we return to the gold standard, raising the price of gold in terms of paper money as the gold bugs advocate? However, in every case the outcome is the same: inflation.

All governments attempt to implement inflation in whatever way is least obvious to their subjects. The result is a never-ending battle between the political right and left over the role of gold as backing for the currency.

If you are a conservative, you favor gold above motherhood and the national defense. If you are a liberal, you oppose gold as the cross upon which those who don't have it are eternally crucified. John Maynard Keynes, the patron saint of liberals, called gold a "barbarous metal." Herbert Hoover, who, while not the idol of all conservatives, was nevertheless about as conservative as you can get, called it "the unalterable standard of value." Neither sentiment bears close analysis. Nevertheless, we know that Keynes saw gold as the greatest of evils while Hoover viewed it as the solution to every problem.

The conservatives argue vehemently that if money is backed by gold, it will prevent inflation (providing that those who advocate an astronomical increase in its price do not prevail) because we can't inflate faster than we can mine new gold. This is not a only a slow process, but one that benefits the Communists, who do not rate very high on the conservative totem pole. However, this unpalatable fact is more than offset by the fact that it would also benefit some of those who do rank high—notably South Africa.

Liberals argue just as heatedly that gold not only prevents

inflation (theoretically), but that it also causes deflation, which is even worse. No wonder the gap between conservatives and liberals is unbridgeable: It comes down to whether you own gold or don't own it. The argument that gold represents an indestructible store of value which will always serve as a medium of exchange is countered by the liberals, who maintain that any commodity has intrinsic value only so long as the ordinary citizen is willing to exchange his labor for it.

To illustrate this point, when crossing the Atlantic in a small sailboat, I ran out of fresh water and would gladly have exchanged my hoard of silver dollars (I always carried some with me when traveling) for a glass of fresh water. Happily, I came across a freighter, whose crew gave me five gallons free of charge.

The liberal argument boils down to this: Money represents so much labor rather than a store of value. Therefore paper serves better than such primitive forms of money as iron, wampum, or gold. Their idea is that the money you receive for working entitles you to the product of someone else's labor at some future time. This, of course, presupposes a stable economic system; if the system breaks down, it doesn't matter whether paper or gold is the accepted form of money. From this definition it is not hard to see why those who have money tend to be conservative; those who don't, liberal.

The liberals further argue that we venerate gold for the very same reason that the Israelites worshiped the golden calf, the Egyptian cats, and many moderns believe in astrology: because we are superstitious. The psychology involved is precisely the same as that Tom Sawyer used to get his fence whitewashed. We value gold not because it is useful, but rather because we are convinced that someone else will give us something we want for it at some future time. If they won't play the game according to the rules we have learned, then what?

GOLD AND TULIPS

In 1970 the official price of gold was $35 an ounce—a price that was considered sacrosanct. After all, it had been raised only once in the previous 136 years. That was in 1934, when Franklin Roosevelt raised the price from $20.67, where it had been pegged a century earlier. However, the entire concept of gold as money (or backing for money) was in the process of disintegrating. In 1971, as a result of devaluation of the dollar, the price was boosted to $38 an ounce; and with the devaluation of 1973, to $42.22 an ounce. That was the "official" price: the price at which governments bought or sold gold to each other.

During these years, there was a second market for gold under the peculiar "two-tier" gold system then in effect. This free market reflected the price level set by users of gold and, more importantly, by gold speculators. The free market in London averaged two or three dollars an ounce higher than the official market. Moreover, the official price was itself a pure fiction, since convertibility of the dollar was suspended as part of the 1971 devaluation; that is, Washington raised the price to $38 an ounce, but refused to sell any gold at the new price, nor at the new price of $42.22 set in 1973.

This government refusal to sell had a predictable effect on the world price, which quickly jumped to $100 an ounce in 1973 and $180 in the following year. Of course, the price in this new free market fluctuated down as well as up. However, by December 1979, gold soared through the $500 level and early in 1980 was nearing an unbelievable $1,000 an ounce. By fall 1979 gold reached the $420 level—the long campaign of the gold bugs had succeeded beyond their wildest dreams.

Could it turn out, however, that the gold bugs are as deluded as speculators with an overwhelming obsession have always been deluded in the past? After all, during the early seventeenth century in Holland, tulips were regarded as being infinitely more valuable than gold. It was not uncommon for a Hollander to trade his house and land for one tulip bulb. Nor was it unusual for a rare tulip to sell for the equivalent of $50,000 in our money.

A brief dissertation on tulipmania seems warranted, since there is a much closer analogy between it and our current reverence—if not lust—for gold than between our Gold Bubble and the Mississippi or South Sea Bubbles.

The tulip was introduced to Europe from Turkey around the middle of the sixteenth century. Early in the seventeenth century these flowers began to catch on to such an extent that it became fashionable to own them. A wealthy person without a tulip collection was roughly equivalent to a present-day millionaire who does not own a yacht, art collection, or Mercedes-Benz. The fashion spread as fashions do in every age— from the top down—and soon people of moderate means began to build up collections. In short, demand rapidly outstripped the supply of the exotic bulbs. (Quite a contrast to the supply-demand situation today. Recently I saw an advertisement offering to sell tulips at a price of 4 cents each.)

In 1636 tulip bulbs were admitted to trading on the Amsterdam and Rotterdam stock exchanges. This event was no doubt heartily applauded by the stock jobbers of that day, who were already adept at manipulating prices. Tulips were ideal for such antics: which bulbs were truly rare and which were relatively common? This sort of speculative excitement proved contagious, and soon all classes of Dutch society were busily engaged in buying and selling tulip bulbs. Fortunes were made in short order, as prices leaped ahead at a breathtaking pace.

Everyone assumed that the Dutch passion for tulips would

not only last forever, but would soon spread throughout the world. Obviously, potential demand on such a grand scale could only be filled by those who managed to accumulate a sufficiently large inventory of the bulbs. In short, speculators believed implicitly that the wealth of the world would flow into Holland as foreigners came to appreciate the unique beauty of these unusual flowers, and they acted accordingly.

At first the mania caused other prices to fall as speculators sold land, houses, and other possessions in order to raise cash to buy tulips. Then, as anticipated, many foreigners also succumbed to the mania, capital flowed into Holland, and the cost of living soared. This inflation was reflected most noticeably in land and luxury items, since the Dutch who sold tulips abroad used the proceeds to buy land, houses, jewels, and other valuables at home.

Predictably, tulipmania ended when the bulbs were being used exclusively for trading rather than growing, just as we hoard and trade gold rather than use it today. By then bulbs were worth far more than their weight in gold and would soon be worth their weight in diamonds or emeralds! Then, too, a futures market had been established in bulbs and this contributed to the ultimate and inevitable collapse. As Mackay explains:

A had agreed to purchase ten *Semper Augustines* from B at 4,000 florins each (a florin was worth about $15), to be delivered in six weeks. B was ready with the flowers at the appointed time[,] but the price had fallen and A refused to pay the difference or receive the tulips. Defaulters were announced day after day in all the towns of Holland. Hundreds who, a few months previously had come to doubt that there was such a thing as poverty in the land, suddenly found themselves the possessors of a few bulbs, which nobody would buy. . . . Many, who for a brief season, had emerged from the humbler walks of life, were cast back into their original obscurity. Substantial merchants were reduced almost to begging, and many a representative of a noble line saw the fortunes of his house ruined beyond redemption.[14]

Finally, in order to avoid civil strife, the government was obliged to step in. The Provincial Council decreed that all contracts made prior to the height of the mania (November 1636) were null and void; those made after that date could be settled for 10% of the agreed-upon contract price. Those who had cashed in before the crash were allowed to keep their profits. So the canny (or lucky) speculators in Holland were fortunate indeed, compared to those who made fortunes out of the South Sea and Mississippi Bubbles, only to have their fortunes confiscated later. But the economy of Holland suffered a severe setback from this attack of tulipmania, from which it did not recover for many years.

While many flower fanciers would consider tulips to be more beautiful than gold, they certainly could not consider them to be more durable, and historically durability has been one of the chief attributes of gold. Yet there are numerous base metals that are about as durable as gold though most of them lack its color and malleability. (A single ounce of gold can be drawn out into a thread 50 miles long.)

Why, then, the premium people are willing to pay for gold? Gold jewelry is attractive. In some industrial applications, gold has unique advantages. As a young chemical engineer, I spent considerable time inside glass-lined tanks patching holes in the glass with an alloy of gold, which was highly resistant to the corrosive chemicals we were using. However, these highly specialized applications absorb only a small fraction of annual world production and even less of the total world supply.

Gold is no more essential and useful than tulips were in seventeenth-century Holland. We need coal, oil, timber, wheat—you name it. We don't need gold—or tulips, which is why bulbs are now selling at the rate of 10 or more for a dollar. Today's gold market, like the tulip craze in Holland, represents a speculative bubble which will be punctured because it does not produce wealth or represent tangible productive assets.

Gold's value is due solely to the game of musical chairs that has grown up around it. If you pay $800 an ounce, can you find a fool who will pay you $1,000 for your ounce? Meanwhile, the gold you hold produces no income at a time when other more productive assets are earning 15% and more a year. Moreover, in addition, the owner of gold is saddled with the expense of storing and insuring his hoard.

Let's look in more detail at the reasons why I am convinced that the current mania for gold will go down in history along with the other famous bubbles, which we have already examined at some length:

1. The South Africans use what amounts to slave labor to dig gold out of the ground at the cost of incalculable human misery and suffering. They refine it and ship it to America or Europe, where it is promptly buried once again. This whole procedure is as irrational as was the tulip craze, even allowing for the beauty of both gold and tulips. All the buried gold in the world could disappear and nothing would change. It might just as well never have been dug up in the first place because a majority of owners never see it and probably never will.

Who looks at the tons of gold bars stacked in the vaults of the New York Federal Reserve Bank or the Bank of England? Only the guards who must be paid to guard it. When it is bought and sold, it is simply switched from a bin marked "France" to another one with the name "Italy," "Switzerland," or some other player. Clearly, if all of this gold disappeared without the owners' awareness of the fact, nothing would change. The same cannot be said about useful commodities.

2. The total worldwide supply of gold is about 4 billion ounces.[15] Perhaps 1.2 billion ounces of this amount is owned by national governments. Most of the remaining 2.8 billion ounces is buried in backyards or locked up in bank safe-deposit boxes. Certainly less than half of it is circulating in the form of jewelry, dental work, industrial uses, and so on.

The total world supply increases each year by about 40 million ounces; the exact figure depends on how much we estimate the Russians produce. Thus the total world supply is being added to at the minuscule rate of about 1% a year. Furthermore, this rate does not increase appreciably as the price of gold rises. In fact, production was higher at times when the price was $35 an ounce than it is today when the price has risen 2,000%; this apparently defies the law of supply and demand.

There are several reasons why the usual economic laws do not apply to gold. First, in most areas other than South Africa, gold is obtained as a byproduct from the production of base metals. Second, the rich South African veins are running out, and costs rise as poorer grade ore is mined. This is why new facilities are not being brought into production in response to sharply higher prices.

Third, the escalation in operating costs—especially labor—combined with the fast-rising capital costs of new facilities, discourage new production even when the grade of ore available remains constant. Fourth, it seems improbable that any rich new ore bodies will be discovered, since for several centuries just about every square inch of the globe has been combed for gold.

3. Therefore we can safely assume that production of new gold will not increase significantly; a factor which would seem to assure higher prices for the existing supply. This, of course, is exactly what has been happening; not, however, because of the failure of current annual production to expand, but rather

due to substantial new sources of demand. In 1975 it became legal for citizens of the richest nation in the world to own gold, which added heavily to demand. Then, too, during these same years, millions of dollars of Arab oil money has sought the presumed safe haven offered by gold.

However, eventually the supply side of the gold equation will certainly prove to be the deciding factor. After all, where has the gold come from to supply the above and, perhaps, nonrecurring demand? The answer: mainly from central banks which still own more than 1 billion ounces. This is equivalent to about 30 years of worldwide production. The U.S. government has become a large and regular seller, which may foreshadow similar future action on the part of other large holders, such as the International Monetary Fund, West Germany, and France. After all, what good are these hoards when gold is no longer used as money or for settling international trade payments?

Needless to say, the millions of private speculators and hoarders who own more gold than all the nations of the world put together constitute an enormous source of future supply hanging over the market.

4. The demand for gold originates almost entirely from speculators. Although about 80% of annual production is fabricated, the largest part of this goes into jewelry, commemorative coins, and the like which is bought, in part, at least, as a hedge against inflation. When evaluating jewelry, bear in mind that pure gold is designated as 24 karat, while a 12-karat object is half gold and half some other metal—usually copper. White gold is the most valuable type since it is alloyed with silver and nickel. Most gold jewelry sold in this country is 14 karat, which means it is 58% pure gold.

About twice as much gold is consumed by the jewelry trade as by industrial users. Only about 3 million ounces a year—or less than 10% of annual production—is consumed by industry;

chiefly for use in semiconductors, connectors, and integrated circuits. As might be expected, currently high prices seem likely to discourage any significant expansion in industrial and dental demand.

There can be only one conclusion: How sound is the market for any commodity where perhaps 50% of the demand comes from hoarders who are inspired by fear? Fear of inflation and fear of some undefinable catastrophe, such as a revaluation of the currency which might cause a breakdown in our complex system? While I think that their fears are well grounded, I also think that there are far better ways to hedge against them than by owning an essentially worthless metal. How much is one ounce of gold really worth in terms of 1980 dollars? $100? $500? $1,000? My own guess is around $500 currently and $1,000 only after many additional years of accelerating inflation.

Today the market places the same value on 5 ounces of gold as on 100 shares of Crown Zellerbach common stock. Can there be any doubt which makes the more sense as an inflation hedge? The owner of 5 ounces of the yellow metal receives no return on his investment and must pay to store it or run the risk of losing it from theft or fire. In contrast, the owner of 100 shares of Crown, which cost $4,500 in early 1980, owns scientifically managed timberlands worth at least $10,000 today— and they are increasing in value every year—plus paper mills worth at least as much more. Moreover, he receives an income of $210 a year from a dividend that has been regularly boosted over the years.

Crown, as well as all the other forest-product companies, supplies a necessity—paper—which is used once (except for the small amounts that are recycled) and then destroyed. Yet the raw material from which it is made is constantly being renewed. The difference between gold and timber is that gold is not being destroyed as fast as it is produced. In fact, probably 95% of all the gold ever produced since prehistoric times is still in existence. The other 5% has been lost through fires, industrial consumption, maritime disasters, and the like. Thus a truly enormous supply of gold exists which, I am willing to wager, will someday be thrown on the market regardless of price.

5. The OPEC nations have been large buyers of gold. What happens when oil from coal replaces oil from the Middle East? This country has the coal and the capability of producing gasoline and fuel oil from it for centuries to come. When the capability is finally transformed from talk into reality—an inevitable development—the Arabs will be forced to spend their gold rather than their oil. Let's assume that when that long-awaited day arrives—in 1990, or whenever—the Arab oil money has been invested more or less equally in gold and tangible income-producing assets, such as real estate and corporate stocks. Will they then choose to liquidate their worthless gold or their wealth-producing assets? What would you do in their place?

The answer is obvious. The time will come when those speculators holding gold will stampede to get rid of it just as the Dutch scrambled to sell their tulip bulbs, when the last of the greater fools could find no one left to sell to. This has been the history of every speculative bubble. If you think gold will turn out to be an exception, it simply proves that you, too, are a captive of the speculative mania and mystique that surrounds gold.

Moreover, the idea that gold has always represented a timeless, universal store of value is simply not true. The native people encountered by the European explorers were baffled by the great value they placed on gold. To those primitive people, one iron nail was worth more than a ton of gold. Or again, to those American Indians who used seashells for money, seashells were worth more than gold. In short, gold has been highly valued in the Western world because it has been used as money in the past. Obviously, whatever is designated by the power of the state as money will have value in the eyes of the citizens of that state. If it is silver (India and China), silver will have the greatest value. If it is wampum, wampum will have value. When gold no longer functions as money, its value is as illusory as was the value of tulips in Holland—although both may retain some residual value as ornamental objects.

Nor does this mean that gold might not sell for $2,000 an ounce, or even more if inflation attains the devastating proportions I envision. The danger in holding gold is the same as in holding any other commodity—only more so, because it is a commodity that no one *needs* other than psychologically. This is why the demand for gold is so elastic—much more so than for any other commodity. For example, the demand for wheat is fairly inelastic; price fluctuations are volatile because the supply is dependent on such largely unpredictable future developments as the weather.

Price fluctuations in oil are inelastic because supply and demand are relatively fixed, and this relationship is largely unaffected by price changes. In 1973 and again in 1979, this was demonstrated in memorable fashion when a minor reduction in supply resulted in shortages and long lines at the filling stations. Just about everyone needs—in fact, must have—gasoline and fuel oil. In contrast, virtually no one needs gold; the supply is unlimited in relation to the need for and use of it. Yet, since 1973, gold has risen in price ten times more than gasoline. The difference is that gasoline won't decline in price because of the inelastic supply-demand relationship, whereas gold can and may decline in price by 50% or more.

These, then, are a few of the reasons why I do not recommend gold bullion as an inflation hedge. Buy or hold gold coins only if they have numismatic value independent of their gold value, and only if you collect them independent of their investment value. Unless you collect coins out of a love of collecting, why bother? Even then you need to be an expert or have the advice of an expert because the gold-coin market has been flooded with counterfeit coins. This tends to cast doubt on the entire rare-coin market.

The same line of reasoning applies to collecting stamps, beer cans, antique autos, or paintings. Buy them because you like to look at them and own them, not in anticipation of realizing a profit. Have you tried to sell a stamp collection or painting lately? All such collectibles have the same drawbacks as gold, with one exception: they are much less marketable. They are a good hedge against inflation only for dealers who buy at wholesale (from you when you want to sell) and sell at retail (to you when you want to buy).

Whatever the merits of gold as an investment may be, its merit as a barometer of future inflation remains unchallenged and that barometer has been telling us, of late, that inflation in the 80's will be much greater than individuals and governments alike anticipate.

BETTER THAN GOLD

After reading the above diatribe against owning gold, you may say to yourself: "He is full of hogwash because people will always want and have faith in gold, especially if inflation continues to gain momentum. After all, hasn't gold always been the best inflation hedge of all?"

Fair enough. You might well be right and, in any event, I respect your opinion because there wouldn't be a market (i.e., price fluctuations) unless opinions differed. However, before you buy gold, or if you already own it, I suggest that you consider buying (or switching into) the two white metals which are cheap compared with gold and which are in such great demand for essential industrial uses that higher prices are almost assured regardless of speculative supply-and-demand considerations.

I am referring, obviously, to platinum and silver.

The mystique surrounding gold which accounts, in large part, for its artifically high price, is most dramatically revealed when we examine its price relative to that of platinum. Since the early 1970's the price of gold has chalked up a gain of more than 2,000%, platinum only 500%.

As a result, platinum is no longer more expensive than gold; yet the total world supply of gold exceeds that of platinum by at least 10,000%—platinum is at least 100 times scarcer than gold. Moreover, virtually the entire annual production of platinum is consumed by industry, whereas, as we have seen, industrial use accounts for only a small part of gold production.

Platinum is relatively cheap because the ancient habit of regarding gold as the money of last resort has never been extended to platinum. Probably because it has always been too scarce, perhaps 99% of the world's population doesn't even know what platinum is, whereas everyone knows that normal people are supposed to value gold above anything else. Even that 1% who are aware of platinum probably are not aware that it is as beautiful and durable a metal as gold and, in addition, has many unique and useful qualities not possessed by gold.

Platinum functions as an irreplaceable catalyst in many chemical reactions—especially in the upgrading of petroleum to produce high-octane gasoline. In recent years, the largest single use in this country and Japan has been in the antipollution devices required on all automobiles. It also has many uses in the space program: e.g., the protective outer coating on space vehicles and in fuel cells.

Clearly, either gold is drastically overvalued or platinum is drastically undervalued, or—more likely—both. In my opinion, in due course, platinum will command a price several times higher than that of gold.

The U.S. government plans to triple its current stockpile, which amounts to 450,000 ounces. This compares to the 250 million ounces of gold held by the Treasury. This country consumes about 40% of world platinum production while producing practically none. Roughly 90% of the world's platinum is produced by Russia and South Africa. Therefore, it is certainly not difficult to imagine developments which could cut off all of our platinum imports overnight. Such a development would cause the price of platinum to skyrocket. In contrast, our supplies of gold are so huge—not even considering the millions of ounces held privately—that a cutoff of gold imports would have only negligible effect on its price for a long time to come.

One-ounce bars of platinum can be purchased from bullion dealers or from most coin dealers. Fifty-ounce lots can be purchased for future delivery in the futures market conducted by the New York Mercantile Exchange.

15

Silver's Silver Lining

I may as well deliver my bombshell right away and then justify it later. As I write, the price of gold has topped $800 an ounce and silver $40.00 an ounce. That is, gold is selling for 20 times more than silver. Speculators currently are willing to back their judgment with hard cash that this is the correct relationship. I disagree with them. I predict that gold and silver will eventually sell at the same price!

When is "eventually"? Probably too far in the future for me to see my judgment vindicated, but not too far for a couple in their thirties to profit from such a drastic realignment of comparative values. My target date, which was arrived at after

242

consultation with my favorite astrologer, is the year 2000. However, changes of this nature have a way of materializing faster than we expect. For example, only a few months ago the gold to silver ratio was 30 to 1, so the gap has been closing rapidly. Meanwhile, any further closing of the spread will enable alert speculators to avoid losses in gold and realize profits in silver.

At first glance, this prediction looks more irrational than the various irrationalities I have been poking fun at in this book. After all, people worship gold, and the golden calf is not going to be cast aside without a struggle. Furthermore, the world production of silver exceeds that of gold by a wide margin. Then how can I conclude that silver is potentially as valuable as gold?

Before answering that question, let's look for a moment at the historical background of silver. It has been used and valued both as money and for ornamental purposes at least as long as gold. Ornamental objects have been found in tombs dating back 6,000 years. Moreover, even in those days, silver was being used in a variety of practical ways such as for drinking goblets and other utensils where gold is not suitable.

Silver has also served as money since this convenient concept was invented around 750 B.C. in Asia Minor; in many societies, silver has been more highly valued than gold.

If gold and silver eventually sell at the same price does that mean gold will decline in price? Does it mean silver will rise? Or both? I think both, especially if inflation is held in the modest range of 10% a year. If, as appears inevitable, runaway inflation confronts us, then the price of both metals will rise, but silver will rise at a much faster rate than gold—a trend that has already developed in recent months.

Currently, world production of silver is almost seven times greater than production of gold (270 million ounces vs. 40 million). From the standpoint of current scarcity, this would suggest a gold-to-silver price ratio of 7 to 1 rather than 20 to 1. However, there are persuasive reasons to conclude that even a 7-to-1 ratio is far too favorable for gold.

Not only does silver share with gold the mystique associated with serving as money, but, unlike gold, industry uses far more silver than is produced each year. The shortfall is made up from a rapidly diminishing inventory that is concentrated largely in the hands of individuals. The numbers involved tell their own story.

In 1979 about 270 million ounces were mined and refined throughout the world, while an estimated 420 million ounces were consumed by industry, plus another 45 million which were used for coinage. The shortfall of 195 million ounces was filled as follows: About 95 million ounces were recovered from photographic processing, tableware scrap, and the like, while the remainder, or about 100 million ounces, was supplied from government inventories, foreign imports, melted coins, and private hoards of bullion. A substantial amount of the foreign imports came from India, where silver has long served as the average family's only form of material wealth. However, this source of supply, which exists mainly in the form of jewelry, has rapidly dried up due to government restrictions on exports. So also has the melting of domestic coins, which may amount to only 10 million ounces annually in recent years.

On June 30, 1979 the world's total above-ground stock of silver bullion and coins was about 700 million ounces. However, the largest part of this potential supply will never reach the industrial user because it is held by governments as a strategic reserve. For example, the U.S. Treasury holds 180 million ounces which, if Congress has anything to say about it, will never be sold. After all, silver is an essential component of missiles as well as of numerous other military devices.

In addition, it seems certain that fewer and fewer of the remaining silver coins will be melted. Certainly the major portion of those coins—400 million silver dollars—will never end their days in the melting pots because even the common dates are selling from 50% to 150% above the value of the silver they contain.

I estimate that the total above-ground supplies that will be attracted to the melting pots by higher prices amounts to only 150 million ounces, or enough to make up the annual shortfall for only 18 months. What happens after that? There is only one answer: Prices must rise far enough to encourage new production and discourage coinage and industrial consumption.

Production from new mines is not the answer because there are very few new mines. For centuries prospectors have searched as diligently for new deposits of silver as for gold—and with equal lack of success. Moreover, production of silver may actually decline even if prices rise still further and faster because 75% of newly mined silver originates as a byproduct of zinc, lead, and copper production. If output of these base metals falls during a recession, so will the output of silver.

Of course, if the price of silver rises high enough, no doubt presently unprofitable low-grade reserves will be brought into production. Similarly, spectacularly higher prices would probably encourage the Indian government to relax export restrictions, and it would also coax more of the old silver dimes and quarters into the melting pots. However, these sources of supply are limited, at best. The ultimate resolution of the silver-shortage dilemma will probably be a combination of steeply higher prices and a drastic reduction in usage by fabricators of coins and tableware.

These conclusions are supported by the inelasticity of the supply-demand balance for silver. On the demand side of the equation, the fabricators of silverware are the only consumer whose product contains a large percentage of silver per unit. Even this traditional silver monopoly has felt the impact of inflation. Today's brides are lucky if even the handles of their place settings are sterling silver. In hundreds of vital industrial products the total amount of silver per unit produced is negligible: The cost of the silver in the finished product is very small, and few electronics companies will stop using silver even if the price doubles or triples. Thus, industrial demand will not be reduced appreciably by higher prices.

On the supply side, the readily available above-ground supply is very small in relation to consumption, while new supplies are inelastic for the reasons stated. These, then, are the fundamental reasons why the price differential between silver and gold must narrow. The only questions are when, and by how much. To repeat the critical question: Will gold decline or silver rise? In the coming inflationary years I look for gold to hold in a trading range or rise moderately, while silver rises at a *much* faster rate until eventually the two metals are selling at the same price.

HOW TO BUY SILVER

Basically there are five ways to invest in silver:

1. Buy silver in the ground.
2. Buy $1,000 bags of pre-1965 silver coins.
3. Buy silver bullion outright.
4. Buy $1,000 bags of coins for future delivery.
5. Buy bullion for future delivery.

1. You can buy silver in the ground. For those of us who do not have a mule, pick and shovel, and plenty of time, the practical way is to buy the stocks of silver-mining companies. They usually own ore reserves that are worth considerably more than the price of their stock. There are only a few of them that have a proven record of earnings and ore reserves:

Hecla Mining Company—Hecla, which is listed on the New York Stock Exchange, produces over 4 million ounces of silver a year plus copper, lead and zinc from four separate mines in northern Idaho. One of these, the famous Lucky Friday, traded as low as 10 cents a share at one time (about fifty years ago) and a few years later had shot up to $25 a share. (This was before it was acquired by Hecla.) Hecla also owns one-third of Sunshine Mining, another silver producer.

Callahan Mining—Callahan's silver revenues come from its 50% interest in the Galena Mine in northern Idaho. ASARCO, Inc. (formerly American Smelting and Refining) owns the other 50%. Callahan's share of production amounts to about 5 million ounces a year. Considerably more than half of the company's revenues are derived from manufacturing operations, which have no connection with silver mining.

ASARCO, Inc.—ASARCO is the largest custom smelter of nonferrous metals in the world. Total annual production of silver amounts to about 10 million ounces a year, or more than 10% of sales. In addition ASARCO refines some 35 million ounces for other producers.

Noranda Mines—This Canadian company is one of the largest silver producers, with an annual output of about 30 million ounces. However, Noranda is a major producer of most other metals, as well as coal and oil, so that silver represents less than 15% of sales.

Sunshine Mining—Sunshine operates the largest single silver mine in the country, which produces around 4 million ounces of silver a year. A subsidiary—Anchor Post Products—generates about 75% of Sunshine's annual sales.

Gulf Resources and Chemical—Gulf produces 15% of the nation's silver, or some 10 million ounces a year. As I noted above, silver has always been a byproduct obtained from ore which, in the past, has been processed for its lead and zinc content. This concept and priority is changing. In past years, the value of the silver produced by Bunker Hill—Gulf's base-metal mining subsidiary—ranged between 20% and 30% of the combined value of the lead and zinc. Currently, however, silver accounts for nearly 50% of Bunker Hill's revenues. If the current rise in silver continues, lead and zinc will soon be the byproducts rather than silver. Historically, the market has always disdained the base-metal mining companies—an attitude that may be about to change.

Earth Resources—ERC owns two oil refineries: one in Alaska and one in Memphis, Tennessee. It also owns about 300 hundred service stations in the Southeast. ERC's refinery is the only one in Alaska. The company also owns 52½% of a silver mine in Idaho, with current production of around 2.5 million ounces a year. This mine has proven reserves of 50 million ounces.

2. and 3.   You can buy and pay in full for either bullion or bags of coins, depending on which form appeals to you. Bullion is easier to store, but coins would be more acceptable for barter during future periods of upheaval, which the prophets of doom predict will occur at any moment. Any reputable coin dealer can supply either and will charge only a small commission (about 2%) for doing so. The advantage of buying outright is that you have the silver in your possession in case of famine, revolution, or other disaster. The disadvantages to physically holding silver in your possession seem formidable to me, since I think the prophets of doom are wrong. America is fortunate in having the most stable political system and society in the world. If I am wrong and the prophets of doom are right, then there might be some advantage to owning silver coins.

In the meantime—which I hope will stretch out indefinitely—holding large quantities of coins has certain disadvantages. If you store them in your basement, you run the risk of fire and even theft, if the thief is muscular. If you store them in safe-deposit boxes you will discover that it requires a surprisingly large amount of space to store, say, ten bags of coins —even if they are rolled and fitted in individually.

As for bullion, if you buy 5,000 ounces (troy weight), you will receive five ingots weighing 83.3 pounds (troy) or 62½ pounds in our ordinary everyday measure. These ingots are easier to store, but harder to spend. An additional disadvantage is that when you sell them you must have them re-assayed. Meanwhile, you are immobilizing a substantial amount of capital—a disadvantage which the futures market has been specifically designed to overcome.

4. and 5. Options 4 and 5 are essentially the same, in that you are buying or selling contracts for future delivery: the difference is that if you are buying and decide to take delivery when the contract expires, you would receive bags of silver coins or silver bullion. In the case of bullion, a futures contract represents an option to buy or sell 5,000 ounces of silver when the settlement date rolls around at the price you paid for the futures contract. You usually pay 10% or less of the full value of one contract, which is referred to as the margin required to pay for the option. Some 95% of all futures contracts are closed out before they expire without taking delivery.

My advice in this book has been to buy the stock of companies which own undervalued natural resources or have made a Unique Profit Breakthrough and avoid commodity trading even though—at first glance—commodities may appear to provide an ideal hedge against inflation. I'm referring here to the major commodities, such as corn, wheat, soybeans, cotton, and cattle. (The more exotic commodities such as cocoa, coffee, pepper, sugar, and eggs are completely out of bounds. Consider the experience of a trader friend of mine who had a carload of eggs delivered to him.) It is true that they will rise at least as fast as inflation and, perhaps, a good deal faster. However, by their very nature, they are trading vehicles— even when the basic long-range trend is up.

The basic reason for their volatility—for major moves both up and down—is that they respond to future events over which you have no control and, worse yet, about which you are unable to obtain any advance knowledge. The weather is the main culprit, and futures prices attempt to discount weather developments—not only in this country, but also in Russia, Argentina, and wherever a commodity is grown. A good example was the impact on cattle prices due to the severe drought a few years ago in the Southwest. Similarly, during the life of every grain futures contract there will be several wide moves caused by fear of too much rain, too little rain, an infestation of insects, and so on.

In contrast, the supply-and-demand situation in silver does not change unexpectedly. In fact, the basic supply-demand relationship for silver, discussed in this chapter, will not change appreciably during the next year or longer, although we can safely assume that the opinion of speculators regarding the correct price for silver will change.

One advantage of buying silver futures, rather than the bullion itself, is that you avoid all of the personal inconveniences mentioned above, although the cost of storing and insuring the bullion during the life of the contract is included in the price you pay. For most people, a much more important consideration is that you need to put up less than 10% of the value of the bullion represented by the contract.

The arithemetic involved seems to be irresistible to the thousands of otherwise ordinary people who trade in silver and other commodities. One study revealed that these speculators ranged all the way from dentists and preachers to nurses and housewives. Consider the profit possibilities during some recent years when the price fluctuations in silver were hardly spectacular. For example, from 1974 to 1978, silver prices swung several times between $4.00 and $5.00 an ounce. Astute or lucky traders could have profited several times by buying at $4.00, then selling and selling short at $5.00. Each such trade would have resulted in a $5,000 profit, or more than 200% on the initial margin requirement of $2,000.

However, timing with such precision is just about impossible. If you had been wrong instead of right about each swing, you would have lost your initial investment several times over. Needless to say, the latter result is far more probable than the former. On the other hand, let us assume that toward the end of 1974 you concluded—as I have done in the above analysis—that silver was destined to sell much higher over the long pull. Acting on this conviction, you purchased one contract at $4.50 an ounce. Three years later, the price was about unchanged and you were saddled with the periodic commission charge of switching from the current contract before it expired into a more distant one. Moreover, during these three years, you received no return on your investment.

If your patience was sufficiently great, it finally paid off in 1978, when silver broke out of its long trading range on the upside and quickly moved to $8.00 an ounce. At that point, your profit on one 5,000-ounce contract amounted to $40,000 less your cost of $22,500, or $17,500. Even after allowing for commissions, you multiplied your original investment of $2,000 by more than an eightfold margin.

Currently, (January 1980), with silver above $40 an ounce, the value of one contract exceeds $200,000 and the margin required to finance it averages, perhaps, $25,000, although this requirement varies greatly from broker to broker. Moreover, the silver market has now become so volatile that, more often than not, the price fluctuates the daily limit of $1 an ounce. From a practical standpoint this means that you may not be able to make a transaction for several consecutive days.

Such a state of affairs can prove fatal to the small investor. For example, if you buy one contract at $40 and the price declines to $35 before you can liquidate your position, your paper loss amounts to $25,000. However, your loss will not be confined to paper, since you must replace your original margin whether or not you are able to close out your original commitment. This is why I advise against speculating in the futures market under such conditions unless you assume a hedged position as discussed below.

Obviously, this process also works in reverse. If you buy a contract at $10, silver need decline only to $9.40 to wipe out your investment. And before that, your broker will demand more margin; probably when it drops to around $9.75. (Margin maintenance requirements vary from broker to broker.)

Nonetheless, the futures market provides a valuable service to the adequately financed long-term investor in silver. Consider the alternatives. You can buy 5,000 ounces at the spot market price of $40 and take physical possession of it as the prophets of doom advise doing. You must pay for storing it— presumably at your bank—or run the risk of losing your entire investment. When your upside objective is reached and you decide to sell, you must then have your ingots re-assayed before you can sell them. If before that long-anticipated day arrives, silver declines to $35, you have a paper loss of $25,000. This loss, even though on paper, is just as real as a similar loss is for the buyer of a futures contract who buys on margin. (I should point out that when referring to "margin," you are not paying any interest on the difference between your initial margin and the full value of the contract. Charges comparable to interest when buying stocks on margin are included in the original cost of the contract you buy.)

At this point, the margin buyer would have received margin calls totalling $25,000, in addition to his initial margin requirement of $25,000. However, when the price recovers to

$40 the margin buyer can, if he wishes, withdraw the additional $25,000 he was required to put up as the market declined. In short, the loss potential is just as great for the buyer who pays in full as for the margin buyer.

To carry this comparison a step further, the investor who buys 5,000 ounces at $40 and pays for it in full is tying up $200,000 for as long as he holds it. Moreover, he receives no return on his investment until he sells it—if he sells it at a profit. In contrast, the margin buyer with the same amount of capital available can free $175,000 of the $200,000 both have earmarked for silver, which can then be invested elsewhere; perhaps in the stock market or even in Treasury bills, which would yield him about $20,000 a year. Meanwhile, he is in a position to realize as great a profit (or loss) as the investor who has paid for his silver in full.

When the settlement date approaches, the margin buyer can:

1. Take delivery by paying the difference between his equity in margin and the full price. In this event, the broker will hold his five ingots for safekeeping. If he is short and owns 5,000 ounces outright, he could deliver it, rather than cover his short position.

Or 2.—If a long-term investor thinks that silver prices have substantial further upside potential, he may decide to sell his contract a day or two before the settlement date. Since it was a contract that expired in one year his profit would be long-term. He then buys a new contract for settlement one year in the future, and his position as owner of 5,000 ounces remains unchanged.

THE SILVER-GOLD STRADDLE

At this point, the prospective silver buyer might be thinking: "If the price differential between gold and silver seems likely to narrow, why wouldn't it make sense to reduce my risk exposure by selling gold futures short and at the same time buy an equivalent dollar amount of silver futures? After all, gold and silver tend to move together, so the chances of suffering a severe loss would be greatly diminished."

In my opinion, this reasoning makes a lot of sense especially following a period during which both metals have risen substantially. You could add spice to your basic investment objective of owning silver by trading in and out of your gold contract on reactions. To illustrate, suppose you sell one gold contract (100 ounces) short at $800 and the market sells off to $700. You then decide to cover your short position and thereby realize a profit of $10,000. The silver side of your spread would presumably decline by a similar amount. By covering your gold commitment, you would, in effect, be reducing the cost of your silver commitment by $10,000.

In conclusion, I want to issue a warning. Very few speculators are temperamentally attuned for trading in even such relatively predictable commodities as gold and silver. A majority will sleep better if they own one of the above-mentioned silver producers which has large reserves of ore in the ground. However, even this conservative approach has drawbacks: ore in the ground is not at all comparable to already refined silver above the ground.

Even during an inflationary period, when silver prices are rising, the profits of a mining company may not rise by an equivalent amount. After all, the cost of mining and refining the ore will also be rising—conceivably, even faster than the inflation rate.

16

Diamonds

Good *investments* are never advertised.

I stress the word "investments" because many good products such as automobiles are advertised, but not even the seller claims that they are good investments. A good investment does not require advertising—the word will get around fast enough without it. In fact, when a *really* good investment is involved, every effort will be made to keep it a secret. Therefore, when you see an investment being repeatedly touted on TV—beware.

To illustrate, whenever I look at the evening news, I see a commercial which informs me that diamonds have appreciated at twice the rate of inflation. A gentleman with a British

accent adds that several years ago you could have purchased a
house or four gem-quality diamonds for $40,000. Today the
house is priced at $110,000; nonetheless, the same diamonds
would buy that house plus a Mercedes-Benz, a camper, and a
vacation home! He then gives me a toll-free telephone number to call for details on how to buy similar bargains in diamonds right now.

It is true that the price of diamonds has risen at twice the
inflation rate, or even more. However, it does not follow that
the buyer of those four diamonds at retail could have resold
them at the indicated profit. As this example suggests, the
largest part of this inflation-inspired rise has taken place since
1972. If the four diamonds were bought in that year, it means
each stone must have weighed around three carats, depending
on quality. Gemstones of this size are very difficult for an
individual to sell at all, let alone at a price anywhere near
their retail value (currently $40,000 to $50,000, depending on
quality).

In recent years, perhaps as many as 100 "wholesale" dia-
mond-selling firms have materialized out of nowhere to take
advantage of unwary investors eager to buy diamonds at
wholesale. They resemble the "bucket-shop" oeprations of a
happily bygone era in the stock market. "Boiler room," the
equivalent expression today, is a term used to describe an
office filled with telephones and salesmen who follow up TV
commercials, such as I heard, or who methodically make a
pitch to rented lists of potential investors. The chances are
practically nil that you will get what you think you are paying
for from such firms.

The fact is that there is no way for an individual who is not
in the diamond business to buy at wholesale—except indirectly, as I shall explain presently. The problem confronting
investors who want to own diamonds as a hedge against inflation is that the spread between wholesale and retail averages
around 100%. Thus, even if you buy diamonds at a time when

the price is rising at the rate of 25% a year, you will have to hold them four years before you can expect to break even, let alone realize a profit. This resale problem is especially acute if you have purchased diamonds as gifts, with the idea in the back of your mind that they will also turn out to be a good investment.

For example, my wife had some diamond rings and a necklace appraised for insurance purposes by a prominent jewelry firm in San Francisco. Their retail value was appraised at $23,000. Shortly thereafter, I saw an announcement in the paper saying that a buyer representing a leading diamond merchant from Los Angeles would visit the Bay area to buy diamonds "of every description." Out of curiosity, I made an appointment and took along these same pieces to see what we would be offered for them in actual money. The buyer offered $8,000 for the lot. This seemed unrealistic—not to say unethical—because, according to the appraisal sheet, the five largest stones were of good quality and averaged .65 carat each.

The point of this story is that when you buy diamonds as an investment, buy only unmounted stones. When you buy mounted stones, you pay a disproportionate percentage of the value of the stone for the mounting, which no one else may want. Then, too, a diamond in a setting cannot be appraised accurately.

Furthermore, I am convinced that the best policy is to buy from the most prestigious gem dealer in your area. You can rely on getting what you pay for and, if you are investing a sizable sum, each stone you buy will be graded and certified by the Gemological Institute of America as to its color, clarity, cut, and weight. These certificates are accepted throughout the world as giving the most accurate possible description of a diamond. In fact, a GIA certificate identifies a diamond as readily as a photograph identifies a person.

If you want not only an inflation hedge, but also a hedge against revolutions or other catastrophes, there are persuasive reasons to choose diamonds. A substantial investment in gold or silver weighs more than you can conveniently carry around. In contrast, a packet of diamonds worth several hundred thousand dollars will fit inconspicuously into a wallet or the change pocket of a lady's purse, and will weigh less than a package of cigarettes (into which it would also fit).

What size diamonds are we talking about? The ideal size for investment purposes ranges from 0.5 to 1.0 carats. The next most desirable size would be from 1.0 to 1.5 carats. While it is true that value increases in an almost geometric relationship with size, for this very reason large stones are less desirable because they are much more difficult to sell on short notice.

In the past, demand for diamonds has come almost entirely from the jewelry trade and industry. In contrast to gold, 80% of the diamonds mined are used for industrial purposes such as cutting edges, grinding wheels, and drills, as well as hundreds of other uses where extreme hardness is a requirement. While diamonds are the hardest-known substance, they do wear out when used to drill through rock or cut steel and therefore, unlike silver, cannot be recycled. This disappearance factor represents another bullish aspect of the long-range supply-demand balance, especially since the presently known reserves of diamonds will be exhausted in about twenty-five to thirty years.

However, since 1972, investment demand for diamonds has soared along with inflation, which no doubt accounts to a large extent for the bull market in diamonds. It seems probable that this addition to the demand side of the equation will persist and expand at least as fast as the inflation rate, thereby promoting a more liquid market than has existed before. There is no reason why GIA-certified gemstomes should not be traded on a central exchange similar to the stock exchanges. Such a development would make an investment in diamonds infinitely more attractive.

HISTORICAL BACKGROUND

Diamonds were created in the depths of the earth millions of years ago by the action of enormous heat and pressure on carbon molecules. In later ages, they were carried to or near the surface via eruptions of lava. Today, as much as 200 tons of this lava rock or gravel must be processed to obtain a single rough stone.

Diamonds were prized in the ancient world, especially in India, where Bombay is still an important diamond-cutting center. Greece and Rome imported diamonds from India. The Romans valued diamonds for their magical and medicinal powers. They believed that an especially brillant stone would protect a soldier in battle; the powder of a flawless diamond was believed to cure many diseases and other human defects. The Romans, who were superstitious, to say the least, also believed that the powder of a *flawed* diamond was a deadly poison; many notorious murders of that era were attributed to this source.

Even though diamonds were prized by the ancients, they were never mined systematically; nor was knowledge of how to cut and polish them developed beyond the most rudimentary stage. In fact, the diamond of fiery brilliance that we prize today was not developed until the late seventeenth century, when a Venetian lapidary invented a scientific cut with 58 facets, which permitted a gem to sparkle with maximum intensity. The 58-facet cut has never been improved upon and continues to be the industry standard to this day.

The individual who did the most to popularize diamonds was King Louis XIV, who, happily, reigned when the new 58-facet stones were introduced. Like most people who owned gems, he wore diamonds in the daytime and colored stones at night; presumably because the crudely cut stones of his day sparkled more enticingly in daylight than in candlelight.

However, Louis, who paid close attention to such matters, observed that the new stones attained their mysterious peak of seductive splendor (as every diamond owner has since observed) in response to the soft glow of candlelight. From then on, the Sun King wore his diamonds at all times: a preference that has endured to our day and shows no signs of weakening.

Most of us think of diamonds as ranging from colorless or "blue-white" through various shades of yellow because most of us own small stones. Actually, color increases markedly with size; some of the most famous and valuable diamonds in the world are anything but colorless.

The Hope diamond (44½ carats), which can be seen in the Smithsonian Institution in Washington, D.C. has a unique deep-blue color. The Hope is said to bring bad luck. It was discovered by a French adventurer in India who, the legend says, was torn apart by a pack of dogs. It was then sold to Louis XIV in 1668. He had the diamond, which then weighed more than 100 carats, recut to 67 carats.

Another victim of the Hope diamond curse was Marie Antoinette, who owned it until she was guillotined during the French Revolution's Reign of Terror. Shortly after her death, the stone was stolen and did not appear again until 1830, when Sir Thomas Hope bought a 44½-carat blue diamond for his wife. Thieves had evidently had it recut in an effort to disguise its origin. The Hope changed hands many times thereafter, until finally in 1911 Edward McLean, a mining magnate, bought it for his wife. A few years later, he was committed to a mental institution, their son was killed in an auto accident, and their daughter committed suicide.

The Dresden diamond (41 carats) is as green as an emerald and, like the Hope, came from India. It can be seen in the Green Hall in Dresden, where it successfully survived the fire raids of World War II.

The Tiffany diamond (128½ carats), an amber-colored stone, was found in South Africa's Kimberley Mine a hundred years ago. Tiffany had it cut to less than half the size of the original rough stone.

The world's largest diamond, the Star of Africa, was discovered in South Africa's Premier Mine in 1905. It was presented to England's Edward VII on his sixty-sixth birthday. This pear-shaped stone now graces the royal scepter, where it dominates the incredible collection of British crown jewels in the Tower of London. The original rough stone weighed an unbelievable 3,106 carats. Several other famous diamonds were cut from it. The most outstanding is also the second largest stone in existence (317 carats), which is set in the band of the imperial state crown. The queen's crown contains two more stones cut from this near-perfect, giant rough diamond: a pear-shaped diamond weighing 95 carats and a square stone of 63 carats.

The queen's crown also contains one of the world's most famous diamonds: the Koh-i-Noor or "Mountain of Light" (109 carats) and the Jonker. The Koh-i-Noor has been traced back 700 years to India, where it changed hands many times along with the fortunes of war. In 1849, when the Punjab region of India was conquered and added to British India, among the trophies captured by the East India Company was the Koh-i-Noor diamond. In 1850 it was presented to Queen Victoria to commemorate the founding of the company in the year 1600.

The Jonker diamond (726 carats) was found by a South African, Jacobus Jonker, in his garden one day in 1934. He sold it for $315,000 and it was then resold to the New York jeweler Harry Winston for $700,000. It was the first large stone ever cleaved in this country, and the Belgian cutter chosen for this nerve-shattering job studied it for more than a year before he struck his fateful blow. Happily the giant stone split as planned into 12 emerald-cut diamonds. The largest weighed 126 carats and may be the finest in the world. The Jonker was purchased (on time) by King Farouk of Egypt and was then repossessed when he failed to pay as promised. It was later purchased for the Queen of Nepal.

THE DIAMOND SYNDICATE

If you could buy an interest in a large hoard of gem-quality diamonds at a price that was far below wholesale, would you do so? Most people would, especially since, as we have seen, the individual investor has no chance whatsoever of buying at wholesale through the usual channels. Yet just such an opportunity awaits anyone who wants to take advantage of it.

There is only one catch: You must have at least $9. That is the price of one share of DeBeers Consolidated Mining common stock. DeBeers owns the world's richest diamond mines and also markets 85% of all the diamonds sold. Not even OPEC has a monopoly like that enjoyed by DeBeers. This monopoly is so secure that even the Soviet Union—the second largest producer next to South Africa—finds it to their advantage to market its stones through DeBeers. This monopoly is so secure that DeBeers has never found it necessary to reduce prices: it only raises them.

When demand slackens (which has not happened in recent years), diamonds are withheld from the market until demand picks up. When demand is brisk, the quantity of rough diamonds supplied to merchants is increased, but not enough to prevent prices from being raised sufficiently to enable one of the world's most profitable enterprises to become even more profitable.

The DeBeers monopoly is successful because it controls virtually the entire output of a commodity desired by virtually every woman in the world. Furthermore, its marketing methods are unique. Its marketing arm—the Central Selling Organization, or "the Syndicate"—has become a favorite subject of suspense novels.

The Syndicate holds ten "sightings" a year at its London

headquarters. About 200 of the most important buyers throughout the world are invited to attend. They are each handed a packet of rough diamonds and its price. There are no negotiations; buyers can choose to reject the offering. However, this seldom happens because the Syndicate is known to have very sensitive feelings which are easily wounded when its offerings are turned down. Buyers who commit such a social blunder are seldom invited back. The effectiveness of this system is hardly surprising: being black-balled by the Syndicate is tantamount to being put out of business.

DeBeers may be the most profitable operation in the world; I'm not aware of any other billion-dollar business which regularly brings more than 50% of sales down to after-tax net income.

TABLE 12
DeBEERS CONSOLIDATED MINING

Year	Diamond Sales (millions)	Other Sales (millions)	Earnings per share	Dividends per share
1979E	$1,200	$ 350	$ 2.60	$ .90
1978	1,100	303	2.36	.83
1977	864	220	1.99	.48
1976	519	127	.98	.37
1975	286	84	.70	.29
1974	352	145	.81	.38
1973	491	122	.98	.29
1972	263	80	.58	.20
1971	140	62	.37	.18

E—Estimated by author.

While DeBeers may be immune to price reductions, it is not immune to economic adversity among its customers. Thus, sales and earnings fell substantially as a result of the economic recession of 1974–75. It also seems certain that the millions of stock-market investors, who suffered staggering losses—at least on paper—during the 1974 bear market were in no mood to buy diamonds. No doubt sales and earnings will suffer similar setbacks in the future. However, it is also possible that speculators seeking an inflation hedge will cushion such setbacks in the future.

Meanwhile, an investor who buys 1,000 shares of DeBeers common stock for $9,000, which is equivalent to the wholesale price of a one-carat diamond, owns an investment which is backed by $4,000 in cash (and equivalents other than diamonds), plus another $1,000 in the form of an inventory of diamonds that are already mined and located, incidentally, in New York and London.

These quick assets do not take into account diamonds in the ground. How much are these reserves worth? Estimates are not available, but the value of these reserves is certainly substantial and far in excess of the remaining $4,000 investment of the buyer of 1,000 shares.

Another favorable development that augurs well for the future of DeBeers is indicated by "other sales." DeBeers is using its huge reservoir of cash to aggressively diversify into related mining activities, such as gold, copper, coal, and platinum.

Despite all this, investors fear that racial tensions in South Africa will explode into revolution someday and that DeBeers would be a tempting target for expropriation by a new black government. About the only rejoinder is that every investment involves risk, and that if this particular risk did not exist DeBeers stock would be selling much higher than 3 times earnings.

Why buy diamonds at retail when you can buy stock in DeBeers Consolidated Mining? I hope that the answer is self-evident now.

LAZARE KAPLAN INTERNATIONAL

If you are put off by the political uncertainty surrounding DeBeers' mining activities in South Africa, you may wish to investigate a much smaller New York-based diamond wholesaler whose shares are traded on the American Stock Exchange. Lazare Kaplan International buys rough diamonds—mainly from DeBeers—polishes and cuts them, and sells the finished stones to retail jewelers throughout the United States and abroad.

Lazare specializes in producing American "Ideal Cut" diamonds, in which the 58 facets are precisely placed and angled to bring out all the natural brilliance of the stone. The company founded Puerto Rico's diamond industry in 1917 and still operates diamond-polishing plants there. The Lazare Kaplan firm successfully cleaved and cut the 726-carat Jonker diamond mentioned previously. It was also instrumental in developing the grading standards used by the Gemological Institute of America.

In 1978 earnings soared to $3.48 per share, reflecting the recent strong demand for diamonds as an inflation hedge. Based on the recent price of around 13, the shares were selling for only 4 times earnings. Moreover, there are only 1.3 million shares outstanding, and Lazare has no senior debt outstanding. Net working capital, which is almost entirely in the form of diamond inventories, equaled $20.60 on February 28, 1979, or about $16 a share.

┌─────────┐
│   **17**   │
└─────────┘

Art as an Investment

Many recent books have celebrated the merits of art, stamps, antiques and oriental rugs as investments. The first words on the first page of one of these books make the rather sweeping claim: "Art can be the most rewarding investment in the world." I think this is unadulterated nonsense. The statement would come much closer to reality if "least" were substituted for "most."

When I use the terms "art market" and "investment," I am referring to art objects that are bought primarily in the expectation that they can be resold at a profit: paintings and sculptures selling for more than $1,000. I am not referring to art that is bought for aesthetic or decorative purposes.

While I am qualified to discuss only one of these "collectibles"—art—I am quite certain that what I have to say about art applies with equal validity to other areas. I, too, embraced the exciting gospel that "Art can be the most rewarding investment in the world." During the 1960's, when I wrote and published a biweekly report titled "New Horizons for Investors," I analyzed the art market in an effort to identify which of the various schools and periods were the best buy and which artists within each classification had the best chance of appreciating in value in the future.

To gather material for these reports, I diligently studied the international art scene, and devoted special attention to the auctions held in New York and London. I just as diligently trudged through a hundred or more galleries in San Francisco, Los Angeles, Chicago, New York, and London. I got carried away to such an extent that I not only wrote about the art market, I also bought what I wrote about. In due course, I had filled my home—all 3,500 square feet of it—to overflowing with paintings and sculptures of every description. Eventually, every room and hallway, including bathrooms and kitchen, were filled with art objects and paintings.

In short, I became an "art bug." To finance all this activity, I sold my large collection of silver and gold coins. From the point of view of aesthetics and personal pleasure, this was fine. After all, my family and friends could enjoy our art collection at any time. In comparison, how often did any of us go down to the bank to view the coins—the rolls all looked alike anyway.

From an *investment* standpoint, this switch from coins to art was a serious mistake—and for the very same reason that I warned against buying diamonds as an investment. The rule to follow is simple: buy art, oriental rugs, diamonds, antiques, and similar beautiful objects for pleasure and adornment only—never as an investment.

People who tell you otherwise have an ulterior motive: they hope to sell you the commodity they are touting. To excite your interest, they tell you about a picture by Cézanne or Monet that recently sold for a million dollars or more at Sotheby's. I know all about these techniques: they were my stock in trade when I was recommending art as an investment.

Fortunes have been made in art, but more often by the *descendants* of the collector. In the art market, decades rather than years must pass before you can hope to garner big profits.

To illustrate this point, I have always been fascinated by the stories about Ambroise Vollard, the Parisian art dealer who "discovered" Paul Cézanne in 1895; if discovered is the right word, since Cézanne was fifty-six at the time. Before then he had been unable to sell any of his paintings and, as a result, they were scattered among the gentry of the village of Aix, where he lived and painted the nearby and now-famous Mont Ste. Victoire.

Vollard was astute or lucky enough to recognize Cézanne's genius. In the hope that other people would also appreciate it eventually, he quietly began accumulating Cézanne's canvases. Cézanne, like many artists, was in the habit of paying his debts with pictures; so Vollard devoted many a day to going around the countryside, knocking on farmhouse doors and looking in attics and other places, where peasants were likely to discard something they didn't want or value.

Today, Vollard is remembered because he successfully sponsored Cézanne and other painters; but how many nonentities did he also sponsor? It was not until a generation later that Cézanne's work began to bring prices that would have made Vollard rich, had he lived that long—instead, Cézanne made Vollard's children rich. Anyone who bought a Cézanne when the artist was thirty would have waited two generations to cash in. And I stress the importance of patience in the stock market! You can make a million in the stock market in a fraction of the time it takes in the art market, assuming you have equally good luck.

I know of only a few documented cases of investors who managed to realize even a modest profit in art. I am not referring to a windfall profit on a single investment, but rather a net profit after allowing for losses, as well as profits over several years. One much-publicized example was Allen Funt, who decided in the 1960's that the nineteenth-century Academic School was due for a comeback after being out of favor for nearly 100 years.

The leading practitioners were Meissonier and Bouguereau in France; Burne-Jones and Alma-Tadema in England. These artists were popular in their day because they painted classical themes in which it was permissible to portray voluptuous nudes which catered to the prurient tastes of the Victorians.

Funt began to accumulate the paintings of Alma-Tadema, an artist whom *Larousse Encyclopedia of Modern Art* dismisses with the rather obscure comment: "He painted dry archaeological pictures." In any event, after a few years, Funt had accumulated 35 Alma-Tademas at a total cost of $264,000, or about $10,000 per picture. Funt correctly judged that the market for academic painters was about to revive—or perhaps it revived because of his buying.

At any rate, when Funt decided to sell, he wisely did so at Sotheby's in London and realized $425,000 for his collection. After several years, Funt's profit amounted to about 60% before taxes. After taxes it must have amounted to considerably less than 10% a year, which is better than a loss, but far less than hundreds of thousands of investors realize in the stock market—and in one year, rather than several.

When I was an active collector and hopeful investor, I was

especially attracted to the School of Paris painters. While making the rounds of the London galleries, I bought three paintings by artists whom I (as well as the dealers I bought them from) felt had a promising future. The paintings were top quality, and the brochures illustrating the shows were most impressive. I bought them because I liked them. I still like them. One is in the primitive style (Ghiglion-Green), one contemporary (Yutrides), and one in the impressionist style (Margarite Airs).

As investments, I might as well have bought the stock of a buggy-whip manufacturer just before the automobile caught on. Subsequently, I recommended these artists to my subscribers, and I fervently trust that they ignored my advice—that is, unless they bought the artists' work for its own sake rather than as an investment. This is the frustrating aspect of art, especially for the artist. For every famous artist whose works sell for astronomical sums, there are hundreds of unrecognized artists producing work of equal or better quality who are starving.

The last time I was in London I thought of selling, so I looked up the dealer from whom I had bought the Yutrides and learned that he was no longer in business. The second dealer said that he had lost track of Margarite Airs and had no interest in trying to sell my painting on consignment. By chance, the third dealer was holding a show for Ghiglion-Green, who had caught on; his paintings were selling for several times the price I had paid. "Well," I thought, "one winner out of three isn't too bad." I was beginning to realize that the prime function of the art market was to enrich one aesthetically, rather than monetarily.

As soon as the dealer learned that I was a collector of Ghiglion-Greens, he was effusively friendly. But when he learned that I wanted to sell rather than buy, his attentive attitude vanished. He reluctantly offered to give me a little more than I had originally paid for the painting, which was about one-third the price he was now asking for pictures of similar size and quality. Or, if I preferred, he would take it on consignment and give me half of whatever he could sell it for. How long did he think it would take? He had no idea. Possibly one day, possibly one year. I refused. I didn't really want to sell my Ghiglion-Green, anyway.

I think my experience is typical of most owners of art who wish to sell. In contrast, in the stock market you can sell almost any amount of stock in five minutes, and at approximately the going market price.

The entire price structure of the art market is fictitious and misleading. It is built on a pyramid of "wash sales," to use a now-obsolete stock-market term. Back in the days of pools and bucket shops, "wash sales" were used to create interest and buying demand on the part of the public in a stock until eventually it bought all of the stock offered by the pool at unrealistically high prices.

A pool would be formed among friends or business associates who had a large block of stock which could not be sold by ordinary means at a high enough price. Often the pool would be bound by a written contract designed to prevent one member from double-crossing others by selling prematurely. It might also specify how the profits would be split up, how much each member would contribute to the kitty, and so on.

Since there were no legitimate buyers—or, at least, not nearly enough—the pool members would buy and sell to each other at higher and higher prices. Each of these spurious transactions would appear on the ticker tape and would generate intense excitement among the pigeons in Peoria and elsewhere, who got the impression—as intended—that "they" were buying the stock because of yet-to-be-announced favorable developments. It is true that "they" (the pool members) were probably forced to buy more than they sold if their campaign to raise the price was to succeed. However, their objective was not to take advantage of some favorable piece of inside information, but rather to unload on the public when the pool's selling-price objective was reached. At this point, when the public had taken the bait, the pool buying would end, but their selling would be stepped up until they had "distributed" their entire holdings to the public.

Often the major portion of this selling was accomplished after the stock had topped out and started to decline. If the pool started its operation when the stock was at 50 and its plan was to sell at an average price of 80, it would drive the price to 100 and then sell most of its stock on the subsequent reaction. On the way up, the stock appeared to the public to be "too high" or "too expensive" at 80. But after reaching 100, it then appeared cheap after it had declined to 80. The pool manager knew from experience that he could unload bushels of the stock at that level.

The same basic procedure is followed by the professionals who manipulate prices in the art market. The main difference is that a stockbroker would go to jail for doing the same things that are considered normal in the art market. For instance, wash sales are considered to be perfectly legitimate—in fact, desirable—by the biggest names in the art business. How do they work?

Consider the case of Joel, a struggling young artist. He in no way differed from thousands of other undiscovered artists who were typically unable to get even a second-rate gallery to display their work. However, Joel had more imagination than most of his colleagues. In addition, he was in tune with current trends in the always-trendy market for contemporary art. He had enviously followed the smashing success of two previously unknown artists who rose to fame and fortune by painting filling stations and soup cans. Now they were paid from $20,000 to $30,000 for producing especially fine examples of filling stations and soup cans. They pioneered in the genre known as photorealism, which is now very popular among many collectors and investors.

In a moment of inspiration, Joel conceived the idea of painting doghouses in the photorealistic style. Moreover, he created a distinctive style, which eventually became his trademark, by mixing crushed walnut shells in with his acrylic paints. He took several of the new doghouse paintings and showed them to various galleries. One of these had sufficient vision to see the commercial possibilities in the fresh vision of life Joel managed to put down on marine-grade plywood. This gallery immediately added him to their stable and scheduled a one-man show.

Their more sophisticated customers could be counted on to buy the works of a promising new talent at bargain-basement prices. These ranged from $250 for a small doghouse to $750 for a large doghouse on fire. An expensive four-color brochure was printed and sold for one dollar to those curious art lovers who looked but did not buy. By the end of the first day, all of Joel's pictures had little red dots attached to them. Did this mean that all of the paintings were actually sold? No one but Joel and the gallery will ever know.

Whatever the answer, it did mean that when Joel's second show was held, his prices had almost doubled. Within two years, his doghouses were fetching as much as $3,500 apiece. His work was now mentioned in *ARTnews, Artforum,* and finally in *Time* magazine. A year or so later, one of Joel's paintings was first offered for sale at an auction house, where it made $5,000.

A few months later, another investor, who had tired of looking at a doghouse on fire, put up this particularly fine example of Joel's art for sale with the same auction house. This firm had the commendable policy of indicating in their advance catalog how much an art object might sell for. How much was this painting worth? The owner and the firm agreed on an estimated value of $10,000. After all, here was a rising star in the art firmament. It might also be pointed out that few people are inclined to underestimate the value of something they are about to sell. They further agreed on a "reserve" price of $9,000: Unless the bidding from authentic buyers reached that level, the picture would not be sold. Only the owner and the auctioneer knew about this advance arrangement.

On the afternoon of the auction, Joel's picture was finally placed on the easel and the auctioneer asked for opening bids. The first bid was for $4,000, and no one in the audience could tell where it originated—for a very good reason: it originated in the head of the auctioneer. Now that the ice was broken, a real bid of $4,500 was heard. The next bid of $4,750 was also an imaginary one designed to keep things moving and stimulate interest. Then a real bid of $5,000 was made. The final bona fide bid was for $8,000. However, the imaginary bids continued up to $8,750 in the hope that a real buyer would bid the $9,000 minimum. No one obliged, so the auction ended at $8,750.

The phony bids might have come from accomplices of the owner or of the auction firm, as well as from the auctioneer himself, to make the ritual seem more realistic to the uninitiated. In any case, the painting was finally and outwardly sold for $8,750 to the owner who, in effect, bought his own painting. I call this a wash sale if there ever was one. But all this camouflage has not been in vain. While the picture in question was not actually sold, the market for Joel's paintings now appears to be stronger than ever. Hasn't one just sold for a whopping 75% above the previous best price?

Dealers resort to a variety of other devices designed to artificially inflate the price of their merchandise. For example, the failure of *Dog House on Fire* to sell did not hurt Joel's sales at all; on the contrary, it helped. Soon Joel's pictures were routinely selling for $9,000 and more. With his usual excellent sense of timing, Joel now produced the largest and finest painting of his career. It was obviously a work of museum quality—at least in the eyes of his dealer.

To capitalize on this achievement, the dealer turned to one of his more ambitious customers who owned several of Joel's works and had visions of making a killing, as soon as the museums were willing to pay almost any price necessary to add the works of this innovative genius to their collections; after all, hadn't a Jackson Pollock recently sold to a museum for $2 million? The dealer proposed that his investor buy the new painting for $20,000, payable within two years, with the buyer having the option of returning the painting at any time without any strings attached.

What sort of a sale is this? It hardly qualifies as being even a wash sale. Yet the news that Joel's painting has sold for a new record high of $20,000 will spread like wildfire, and this will become the new standard by which his less valuable works are evaluated. Everyone benefits except prospective new buyers. The favored customer has a free two-year option to buy a potentially valuable painting, and during this interval he gains social prestige by being able to display it to his friends and lend it to exhibitions and shows with the ego-satisfying statement that it is on loan from the collection of Mr. and Mrs. So-and-So. While receiving no money, the dealer will presumably benefit many times over from the favorable publicity.

The same contrived transactions take place between dealers. The dealer who handles Joel may have a large inventory which isn't moving at the desired rate. He goes down the street to another dealer, who has a promising newcomer—Jones—under contract. He, too, has more paintings by Jones than his customers see fit to acquire at the moment. So the dealers negotiate a deal based on the fact that Joel's work is priced at about twice that of Jones. They will trade paintings at the rate of one Joel for two Joneses.

However, this turns out to be more than an ordinary swap, such as two less-imaginative businessmen might negotiate. Bills of sale are drawn up which reveal that Joel's painting was sold for $30,000 and the Joneses for $15,000 each. Actually, not one penny changed hands. Nonetheless, this now becomes a newsworthy transaction which is sure to be repeated endlessly by the fortunate owners of works by Joel and Jones, if by nobody else. It is newsworthy because these prices represent new record high prices for both artists.

Deceptions such as these are not only tolerated but applauded in the business because the art market is made up of equal quantities of snobbery, cupidity, venality, and stupidity. There is not much hope for reform because any measures designed to protect victims in the latter category are bitterly opposed in a realm where the greater-fool theory reigns supreme.

I have said some unkind things about stockbrokers, but in comparison with art dealers they are models of probity. Not that art dealers are more dishonest than the rest of the population; it's just the way the business they are in operates, and it operates the way it does because people buy art for the wrong reasons.

For several years I assiduously studied the behavior of people who buy art and concluded that, as in every area of human activity, the reason given for an action is seldom the real reason. The real reason collectors and investors buy art breaks down roughly as follows:

10%—Because they like it. They honestly don't care about the future price of what they buy, nor of the artist's reputation or lack of reputation.

30%—Because it's supposed to be a good investment or a

superior status symbol, which amounts to the same thing. They will pay $90,000 for a picture of soup or beer cans if they see a chance of eventually selling it for $125,000 to a greater fool (which may turn out to be a museum spending someone else's money).

60%—Because they are snobs, who hope the art they buy will endow them with social prestige. They think it will demonstrate their financial and cultural superiority over their friends and neighbors. If these ordinary mortals don't understand the art, so much the better. Actually, the buyer probably doesn't understand it either, and for a very good reason: more than likely, it has no meaning or merit whatsoever.

18

The Psychology of Speculation

You may have gathered by now that I am convinced that stocks offer the best possible hedge against inflation during the years ahead. Therefore I will discuss the psychology of speculation as it applies to the stock market, although the principles involved are valid in every area of human endeavor.

The heading of this chapter could have the word "investment" substituted for "speculation" without requiring a single word in what follows to be changed. In my opinion, there is no difference: every investment is really a speculation.

The wage earner who deposits a few dollars each week in his local savings bank is speculating on the severity of future inflation; although he may not be aware that he is speculating and would no doubt deny it vehemently.

And what about those "investors" seeking maximum safety, combined with liberal income—if there is such a combination—who recently bought General Public Utilities stock? They watched the value of their investment diminish by 50% within two months. U.S. Government bonds were once considered to be the safest haven of all for your nest egg. No longer. In fact, it's difficult to recall another investment that has produced larger inflation-adjusted losses in recent years.

No matter what you do with surplus funds or savings, you are gambling or speculating just as surely as the player in Las Vegas or Atlantic City. Therefore, during a period of runaway inflation, it becomes essential to adopt the psychology of the successful speculator, rather than that of the traditional investor. Hence this chapter heading.

Meanwhile, after all these pages about the inflation-hedge potential of natural-resource stocks, UPB companies, those with low labor costs and so on, in the final analysis, winning strategy can be summed up in one sentence: BUY STOCKS WHEN THEY ARE LOW, SELL WHEN THEY ARE HIGH!

After thirty-five years of speculating in the market, everything I have learned is summarized in those twelve words. All else is superfluous—including, most likely, the remainder of this chapter. Nonetheless, if these twelve words are to be meaningful, we must define two of them: "high" and "low."

A stock is low when there is little interest in it. A glance at any long-term stock chart will confirm the accuracy of this observation. This lack of interest can occur for many reasons; the usual one is lower earnings.

A stock is high when there is intense interest in it; i.e., when trading volume has soared to several times the normal rate when it was low. After you buy a stock that few others seem to want, the virtue most needed if you hope to arrive at this stage is patience, since you can do nothing further to influence the situation. All you can do is carefully avoid the common mistakes that thousands of investor-speculators commit every day of every year.

Winning psychology begins when you realize that success in the stock market is the result of what happens in your head, rather than what happens on Wall Street. So is failure. You are either dominated by *a will to succeed,* or a *will to fail.*

The *will to succeed* is activated psychologically by *positive* emotions and thoughts. The *will to fail* is activated by *negative* emotions and thoughts. The problem facing all of us is how to replace the subconscious *will to fail* with the conscious *will to succeed.*

If we permit ourselves to succumb to negative emotions 90% of the time, 90% of our market transactions will result in losses. If we are guided and motivated by positive emotions 90% of the time, 90% of our market transactions will result in profits. If our emotions are 50% positive–50% negative, we can expect our investment results to be the same.

In physics this relationship is known as the Law of Action and Reaction. For each action, there is an equal and opposite reaction. Even in the physical world this relationship is seldom obvious to us. Yet it is true, and while today's negative emotion may not produce its retribution until next month, next year, or even longer, the consequences cannot be escaped.

Unfortunately, the negative emotions are instinctive creature emotions, which we must constantly battle to overcome. This is why the stock market baffles so many people. It also explains my often-repeated observation that the stock market is irrational. The very instincts which have enabled the human race to evolve to its present material state assure failure when applied to the stock market. Action that appears to be most logical turns out to be folly. These instinctive negative emotions that must be replaced with their equal and opposite positive emotions can be summarized as follows:

Negative Emotion	Positive Emotion
Pride	Humility
Greed, Remorse	Gratitude
Fear	Courage
Laziness	Diligence
Impatience	Patience
Doubt	Faith, Confidence

Consider the first emotion listed. The person who hasn't the humility to admit his mistakes is headed for nothing but trouble in the stock market. And when that trouble arrives in the form of losses, the person who won't acknowledge them gracefully will not have the positive attitude needed to recover— and more than recover—from them.

Pride turns reality into illusion. The proud, self-centered person acts in a way that will bolster his ego without regard for the consequences. He is more concerned with outward appearance than with positive results—unconsciously, of course. Pride destroys the ability to choose the correct action. Humility unerringly leads us to the correct action.

To succeed, you must eliminate the possibility of failure from your mind. Confidence and faith in the future are necessary virtues. No skeptical, cynical person has ever made and kept a fortune in the stock market. All the famous bears died broke.

Before you can succeed, you must first know yourself and then master your emotions. Only character and courage can overcome the twin evils of greed and fear that lead to failure. Unlike most undertakings in a gregarious world, it's a lonely battle. Failure can be blamed only on yourself. Only the truly self-reliant individual will actually build a fortune. Collective decisions—like all collective action—result in mediocre results, at best.

Another reason for failure is lack of diligence, an inclination to take the easy way out. In the words of the great speculator Bernard Baruch, who lived in an era when there were no confiscatory taxes and hence "trading" was feasible, at least for the gifted few:

If you are willing and able to give up everything else, and will study the market and every stock listed there as carefully as a student studies anatomy, and will glue your nose to the ticker tape at the opening of every day of the year and never take it off till night; if you can do all that, and in addition have the cool nerves of a gambler, the sixth sense of a clairvoyant and the courage of a lion— you have a Chinaman's chance.

The same reasoning applies when investing for long-term capital gains, which is the only alternative today. Before buying a stock, investigate the company as thoroughly as though you were about to purchase 100% ownership of a small business. In the latter situation, you would probably spend many days investigating every aspect of the operation. The same should be done before buying a stock. Yet, unfortunately, all too often shortcuts are taken in an effort to find an easy path to wealth. Beware of such alluring shortcuts.

Greed combined with impatience leads to overtrading. The temptation to trade can also be blamed on the infallibility of hindsight. In the stock market, as in no other arena, everything you do is immediately subject to the test of hindsight. The issue is never in doubt: plainly the odds are heavily against buying a stock without having it sell still lower, or selling without watching it climb a point or ten points higher. Hindsight always implies that you have made a mistake and, worse still, that in the future you should profit by these "mistakes." Remorse clouds your ability to see the correct action to take *now*.

Consider the mental state of an investor who has held a stock for a year or so during which it fluctuated between 20 and 30. *After* each intermediate top, the natural tendency is to say: "I should have sold at 30 and bought back at or near 20." Only investors with great courage can hold a stock that declines from 30 to 20 more than once without resolving that the next time they will be among the fortunate few who sell at 30 and buy back at 20.

Yet, in the end, you can't do it. The real trouble is this: When your stock begins to rally the final time from 20 to 30, you say to yourself, "When it gets back to the old high of 30 I'll sell out and then buy it back lower down." Finally it does reach 30. You sell out only to watch it continue to rise with the usual reactions, which are always less severe than you anticipate—until it finally soars through the 100 level, which was your objective all along. The correct procedure in this case, as in all cases, is to hold on to the stock until the reasons you bought it in the first place are no longer valid. Never try to "scalp" a few points.

The instinctive reaction of some speculators is the precise opposite, due to fear. When a stock they buy at 30 declines to 20, they immediately visualize the worst: the company is going bankrupt, and the stock is about to sink to zero. This, of course, rarely happens. The antidote to this disease of acute negativism is patience, combined with faith and confidence. After all, if you thoroughly investigated the company, the chances of its going down the drain are probably a figment of your fear-inspired imagination. Perhaps you bought a forest-products stock at 30 because it had a tangible book value of $40 a share, steadily rising earnings and, furthermore, because after careful analysis, you concluded that the value of their timberlands alone exceeded $100 a share.

However, you have no control over the price at which other investors are willing to buy and sell the stock. If it sinks to 20 in a general market decline, what should you do? Sell or buy more? Obviously, you should hold your position and buy more if your resources permit. Psychologically, this is far more difficult to do than to talk about doing. The very atmosphere will radiate fear and pessimism to such a degree that you will need courage, plus a lot of faith and confidence in the soundness of your original decision, to buy more or even to hold on to your original commitment.

Success can prove even more destructive and upsetting to your normal equilibrium than failure because it leads to arrogance or overweening pride which, the ancient Greeks assured us, inevitably leads to our downfall. Long before the Greeks, the prophets of Israel repeatedly warned against the dire consequences that follow in the wake of pride and arrogance. Even the pagans concurred: the richest man in Babylon compiled Five Laws of Gold, which have been passed down to posterity.

The fifth law warned: "Fanciful propositions that thrill like adventure tales always come to the new owner of gold. These appear to endow his treasure with magic powers that will enable it to make impossible earnings. Yet heed ye the wise man, for verily they know the risks that lurk behind every plan to make great wealth suddenly."

DON'T SELL AMERICA SHORT

This was the sage advice of J. P. Morgan. It is also the policy of most of the nation's brokerage houses. They usually have two rules concerning how employees may invest their own personal funds. Rule 1: No short selling. Rule 2: No buying on margin.

These rules reflect the wisdom distilled from years of experience by some of the shrewdest brains on Wall Street. You may wonder: "If a broker who devotes his entire time to the stock market shouldn't sell short, who should?" The answer is simple: no one should—it disturbs psychological equilibrium. Brokerage house officers know that if their salesmen are short (or on margin), they will spend more time worrying about their own affairs than about those of their customers.

If you have ever been short in a stock which is soaring, you will know what I mean. If you buy a stock, the worst that can happen is for it to decline to zero. But, if you are short a stock, there is no limit to how high it might go—at least in your imagination. Looking at the positive side for the short seller, it is mathematically impossible for the short seller to realize a gain of more than 100% on his capital, and in practice the reality falls far short of this. In contrast, the owner of a stock may watch it climb 100%, 500%, or even 1,000%, and millions of investors have realized such gains over the years.

Second, there are practical as well as psychological arguments against selling short. All short sales are treated as short-term transactions for tax purposes, regardless of how long the position is actually held. Theoretically, it should be possible to rake in more rapid profits by selling short than by buying stocks for a rise because stocks often retrace in a few days a gain that required several months to achieve. This, however, is pure illusion. Theoretically, you can count every grain of sand in the Sahara Desert. In practice, it can't be done. The same is true of short selling. The very fact that timing must be much more precise when selling short than when buying, multiplies the already insurmountable psychological problems.

INVEST ONLY YOUR OWN MONEY

People who use borrowed money to buy stocks by buying on margin are prone to suffer the same psychological disturbances that cause the short seller to toss and turn at night. During the 1920's, the use of margin was viewed as the magic answer to getting rich quick. After 1929 the use of margin was generally viewed as a device invented by the devil. More recently, as installment financing became a way of life, the antipathy toward buying stocks on margin has mellowed.

Today there are a million or more active margin accounts, and we can assume that these individuals, at least, favor its use. And well they might in a period of double-digit inflation, which favors borrowers at the expense of lenders—at least over the long pull. But investors can get into all sorts of trouble within a matter of months or even weeks, during which the inroads of inflation are more theoretical than real.

The margin buyer thinks, "If 100 shares of Dynamic Electronic Lasers is a good investment for $2,000, 200 shares for the same $2,000 is twice as good." True enough—if it goes to 40. But the disconcerting thing about stocks is that they go down as well as up. What if DEL fools you and promptly falls to 10? At that point, if you bought using the current maximum 50% margin allowed, your equity has been reduced to zero—and on the way down, you would have received two or three calls for additional margin.

The stock market is made up of tangibles, but a telegram demanding more margin is not one of them. Fortunately, not so many of these are sent out today as there were before the Federal Reserve controls over margin requirements were introduced. When minimum margin requirements are set at 50%, as they are now, your stocks—if held on full margin—have to decline to a point where the broker's equity represents about 25% of the market value of the stock before you get a call to put up more money. However, the exact point at which margin calls are triggered varies from broker to broker.

Specifically, let's say you buy a stock at 30 on 50% margin. You put up $1,500 and your broker supplies the other $1,500.

Now suppose the stock declines to 20. If you sell, you realize $500 ($2,000 less the $1,500 you borrowed), so your equity is 25% of the market value of the stock. If you don't sell and it goes still lower (these things do happen), you must always put up sufficient money to restore the broker's required 25% equity. You can see by this pleasant little example, that when the stock goes down one-third, you not only lose two-thirds of your original investment, but you must also put up more money to protect the broker who lends you the money from suffering any loss at all. If you conclude from this example that where margin is involved, it is better to be a broker than a customer, I can only agree with you.

In general, the maxim "Never meet a margin call" is sound, but there are exceptions—especially toward the end of a severe market setback, when stocks will often open sharply lower on heavy volume. These sellers are the hapless buyers on margin who were unable to—or chose not to—meet the call for more margin and whose stock is being dumped by the broker "at the market." When this selling is out of the way prices rebound with great vigor, a reaction which adds insult to injury for investors who were sold out at the bottom.

Thus holding stocks on margin intensifies your feelings of greed when prices are rising. As a result, you will be encouraged to do what is clearly irrational: to hold stocks on full margin when prices are high rather than low. For a while, this leverage produces magic results—on paper. When the market starts down and keeps going, fear begins to replace greed. After a while, the profits disappear and losses begin to grow at twice the rate than if the stocks were not held on margin. You can now imagine all too vividly what your financial position will be if stocks sink much lower.

At last you can't stand the strain any longer and you say to yourself: "They can have them at any price." So you sell out— or are sold out by a margin call, which you can't meet. You then quietly retire from the market with the resolution that if you are ever again foolish enough to get back in the market, you will pay for your stocks in full. This resolution holds until the next big speculative spree, when your friends—to hear them tell it—are doubling and tripling their money in a matter of weeks.

All this leads to one conclusion: Remain fully invested (but not on margin) at all times. To succeed in the stock market, assets other than cash must be held. And this will more than ever be true during the inflationary 1980's. Probably 99% of those who attempt to take advantage of market fluctuations will fail in the end. And even if we assume that there is a 1% who succeed, they could achieve even better results by adopting the philosophy of being fully invested at all times. Failure to realize this truism accounts for the failure of mutual funds and other institutional investors to realize results as good as those turned in by an unmanaged market average. Their attempts to sell when the market is "high," then hold the cash until prices are "low," have been uniformly unsuccessful.

I repeat: Remain fully invested at all times to effectively eliminate the perplexing problem of timing transactions. You will, thereby, automatically eliminate 90% of the emotionally inspired mistakes that inevitably lead to losses rather than profits. The other 10% of the problem involves selection: selection of the stocks of several companies that will, over a period of years, advance more when the market advances and decline less when the market declines. Unlike timing, this is a problem that cannot be avoided. Therefore, the sensible policy is to devote 100% of your available time to solving it.

There is one time when margin can be utilized without suffering the usual disastrous results: when you already have achieved an impressively large backlog of paper profits—for example, when you have negotiated steps 4 or 5 of the Six-Step Plan. Modest borrowing at this point will not upset your psychological equilibrium because you feel secure knowing that losses merely reduce your tax liability, rather than threaten you with ruin.

YOUR DESTINY IS IN YOUR OWN HANDS

I have already warned against buying stocks for the wrong reason—such as tips, inside information, and rumors. You must live with the stocks you buy—perhaps for many years. Therefore it is of the utmost importance, from a psychological point of view, to own stocks which you have faith in, rather than stocks someone else has faith in.

Stocks represent part ownership of a business. If you understand and believe in the future of that business, your chances for success are immeasurably greater than if you don't understand it and don't believe in its future. Take action on the basis of your own analysis, rather than someone else's. That is the only way to survive the vicissitudes of the marketplace.

The stock market attempts to discount the future many years in advance. If you live in Peoria, Topeka, or some other area far removed from Wall Street, don't despair; your appraisal of the future has as much and probably more chance of being right than that of a member of the New York Stock Exchange.

The importance of specialized knowledge in the stock market is greatly overemphasized. Usually a little common sense is more helpful than a lot of specialized knowledge. This is one area of human endeavor where too many facts and too much knowledge can be positively harmful. In any event, we can never know all the facts anyway: we must look beyond them to the broader picture.

In addition, one of the most common errors everyone makes is to assign the wrong causes to a given effect. Usually a multitude of causes will contribute to the effect, only a few of which are known to the observer. In retrospect, the most familiar or the most logical causes will be chosen in an effort to explain why an event took place. More often than not, these explanations will be wrong.

This is especially true in the stock market, where the emotions of thousands of individuals may be influencing the price trend of a single stock. To try to anticipate what effect a known influence will have on stock prices is a matter of guesswork, pure and simple. True enough, *unexpected* news that is clearly bearish will usually cause a temporary price decline, and unexpected good news a temporary price rise. But there are a great many exceptions to this rule, and the exceptions can prove painfully costly to the investor who acts on the news.

The same piece of news may cause prices to rise one time and decline the next. The result depends on a multitude of factors, mostly unknown. Therefore, if the market declines on good news, the news is said to have already been discounted. Or, possibly, the explanation is that the technical condition of the market is weak and it's ripe for a decline anyway. Obviously, this is true, but as a cause it's meaningless.

Or again, if you buy a stock and it moves up, you will naturally conclude that the reason that caused you to buy was the reason it rose. More than likely, other completely different reasons that you were not even aware of were responsible. The next time you make a similar decision, based on similar reasoning, the stock may decline. The lesson to be learned from this is that stocks should be bought not on the strength of what seems likely to happen next week or next month, but rather what seems likely to happen next year or five years from now. In the meantime, you can be certain of only one thing in this uncertain world: At that time the dollar will buy much less than it does today. From this it follows that the time to buy and be fully invested in common stocks is *right now!*

ACKNOWLEDGMENTS

It will be evident that I am indebted for much of the material in Chapter 3 to that fascinating book, *Extraordinary Popular Delusions and the Madness of Crowds,* written by Charles Mackay and published a century and a half ago in London by Richard Bentley. No doubt, Mackay—like all writers—tended to exaggerate. However, I have checked the facts in standard histories and have concluded that the overall picture is reasonably true. I am also indebted to William Guttman and Patricia Meehan, authors of *The Great Inflation,* published by Saxon House, Westmead, England (1975) for background material and letters quoted in Chapter 4.

For background material used in Chapter 7, I referred to still another fascinating chronicle, Frederick Lewis Allen's *Only Yesterday,* published by Harper & Bros. in 1931. I can personally remember those long-gone days quite clearly.

SOURCES AND NOTES

1. Runaway inflation exists when prices rise at least 100% a year. Historically, prices usually rise much faster. In Germany, for example, prices doubled every two weeks. The same thing happened in Greece in 1944, in Poland in 1923, and in Russia in 1921–1923. In Hungary in 1946, prices doubled every two to three days.

2. From The Editors of *The Wall Street Journal*, *The New Millionaires*, p. 185. Copyright © 1961 by McGraw-Hill Book Company. Reprinted by permission of McGraw-Hill Book Company, New York, New York.

3. "Safely" is a relative term. On the rare occasions when too many depositors did turn up demanding gold for banknotes, bankers in 1720 were in trouble, just as bankers would be today.

4. From William Guttmann and Patricia Meehan, *The Great Inflation*, p. 130. Copyright © 1975 by William Guttmann and Patricia Meehan. Reprinted by permission of Saxon House, D. C. Heath Ltd., Hants, England.

5. From *The Great Inflation*, p. 144. Reprinted by permission of Saxon House, D. C. Heath Ltd., Hants, England.

6. From Stefan Zweig, *The World of Yesterday*, p. 289. Copyright © 1943 by Stefan Zweig. Published by Viking Press. Reprinted by permission of Williams Verlag AG, London, England.

7. From Stefan Zweig, *The World of Yesterday*, p. 300. Reprinted by permission of Williams Verlag AG, London, England.

8. From Stefan Zweig, *The World of Yesterday*, p. 312. Reprinted by permission of Williams Verlag AG, London, England.

9. From Stefan Zweig, *The World of Yesterday*, p. 312. Reprinted by permission of Williams Verlag AG, London, England.

10. From Alexander Paris, *The Coming Credit Collapse*, p. 189. Copyright © 1974 by Alexander Paris. Reprinted by permission of Arlington House, New Rochelle, New York.

11. From *The Value Line Investment Survey*, published by Arnold Bernhard & Co., Inc., New York, New York.

12. A gold bug is a person who overtly advocates a return to the gold standard on moral grounds, while covertly hoarding gold and loudly calling for an astronomically higher official price for it. *(Note:* A gold standard tends to keep a government from inflating its paper currency.)

13. From Rodger W. Bridwell, *Reality in the Stock Market.* Published in 1965 by Windfield Press, Vancouver, Canada.

14. From Charles Mackay, *Extraordinary Popular Delusions and the Madness of Crowds*, p. 95. Second edition published in 1852 by Richard Bently, London.

15. This figure is obtained by totaling the admitted holdings of central banks, official coinage, jewelry manufacturers, and the like, plus an estimate of private hoards. In other words, it is a guess. Who knows how much is held by individuals from Outer Mongolia to Peru, who make every effort to conceal their holdings? My own guess is that the total supply is closer to 5 billion ounces.

INDEX